Class of '47

Stephens Press
Las Vegas, Nevada

Class of '47

Annapolis—America's Best

Jack Sheehan

M.A. Duval, Editor
Sue Campbell, Art Director
Stacey Fott, Publishing Coordinator

ISBN 10: 1-932173-67-6
ISBN 13: 9781-932173-673

Cataloging in Publication

Sheehan, Jack.
Class of '47 : Annapolis—America's Best / Jack Sheehan.
280 p. : photos ; 23 cm.
Contents: Introduction – Chapter one. Jimmy Carter: the moral compass – Chapter two. Bill Crowe: an unconventional path – Chapter three. Jim Stockdale: as noble as they come – Chapter four. Stan Turner: the one they looked to – Chapter five. Jack Stephens: thinking big – Chapter six. Other alums – Graduates of the USNA Class of 1947
Summary: Chronicles the Annapolis graduating class of 1947, one of the most distinguished groups ever to give service to their country.
ISBN: 1-932173-67-6
ISBN-13: 978-1-932173-67-3
1. United States Naval Academy. Class of 1947. I. Title.
355.007   dc22   2007   2006907089

SD STEPHENS PRESS, LLC

Post Office Box 1600
Las Vegas, Nevada 89125-1600

www.stephenspress.com

Printed in Hong Kong

The Class *of '47 is dedicated to all the wonderful men and women of the United States Naval Academy at Annapolis, past and present, who represent the best our nation has to offer.*

Also, in memory of Dr. Norman Sheehan, a navy dentist during WWII, who would have had more interest in this book than any other I've written. I now fully appreciate why he got choked up every time he heard "The Star Spangled Banner."

CONTENTS

Acknowledgments

THIS BOOK WAS MADE POSSIBLE THROUGH THE DESIRE OF Ambassador Vernon Weaver to honor his classmates and friends from the Naval Academy. Whenever we needed a phone call made or a gentle nudge to gain someone's cooperation, Vernon provided it.

Warren Stephens was also greatly helpful in advancing the project by offering the full cooperation of the talented and generous employees of Stephens Inc.

Matt Jacob proved a valuable editorial assistant on the book, particularly in acquiring information from the Stockdale family and many other talented members of the Class of '47.

Class of '47 secretary, Chet Shaddeau, was always quick to answer questions and acquire information for me. The task of writing this book would have been far more daunting without his help.

I felt privileged to work with all of these fine people and to meet the many great men and their extended families from this gathering of American patriots.

— J. S.

Statue of the warrior Tecumseh, the Naval Academy landmark that greets all incoming midshipmen.

Introduction

*"I had never been away very much in my life, and so this was a major
excursion for me, away from my family. I went by train and my mind
just raced with the possibilities of the life that awaited me there. A lot
of young men had been away at prep schools and done a lot of traveling
before they entered the Naval Academy, but I had never been on a boat.
I was a land-lubber in every respect."*

—Jimmy Carter, 39th President of the United States and
recipient of the Nobel Peace Prize in 2002.

*"It took me a while to accept being bossed around, but I had wanted a
place at the Naval Academy so long and so badly that at first it never
occurred to me to do anything but what I was supposed to do. But by
the time I was a first classman, I was bridling under authority, going
over the wall on occasion, and accumulating a hefty share of demerits.
I knew even then that I was trying to protect my sanity by asserting
my independence. At the same time, I developed a talent for avoiding
detection—great training, as it turned out, for surviving in the Pentagon."*

—Admiral William Crowe Jr.
Former Chairman of the Joint Chiefs of Staff

*"One day on a New Year's weekend, Jack Stephens received a call from
Gabriel Lewis in Panama. Lewis was a friend of the United States who
had helped us harbor the Shah of Iran. Gabriel said, 'Jack, I am calling
you from the terrace of my house. There are three gunship helicopters
circling my house. Noriega's soldiers are coming after me, and they
are going to kill me. I know that you are friends with Admiral Crowe,
and I am imploring you to help me if you can. . . .' When Crowe was
informed of Gabriel Lewis's predicament, he asked Jack Stephens, 'Is
this something you really want me to do?' Jack said 'Yes.' And Crowe
said, "All right. I will do it, but I don't want to do it." One hour later,*

a car pulled up in front of Lewis's Panama estate, and eight soldiers
about six-foot-six inches tall, all blonde, not in uniform but obviously
military, piled out carrying machine guns. . . . Lewis lived nine more
years and died of natural causes."

—VERNON WEAVER, U.S. AMBASSADOR
TO THE EUROPEAN UNION UNDER PRESIDENT CLINTON.

"I thought plebe year turned out to be one of the most helpful nudges
I'd had in a lifetime of preparation for military challenges, particularly
those of prison. At the Naval Academy, the system had provided for
physical hazing of plebes, and I had profited from it in prison. I came
away from Hanoi believing that some people were so constituted as to
be poor prisoners in the absence of it."

—ADMIRAL JAMES STOCKDALE
(The highest-ranking naval officer held prisoner in Vietnam. He spent seven-and-a-half years in the "Hanoi Hilton," the first four in solitary confinement. For his leadership under great duress, he was awarded the Congressional Medal of Honor.)

"I have always been self-confident, but I also felt there were a lot of
others who would be very competitive at the Academy, and I didn't
know whether I was going to come out anywhere near the top. I do know
that my parents had instilled a great sense of ethics and the importance
of hard work in me, and that served me very well there. There was never
even a brief moment during my first year that I considered quitting. What
would I do if I quit? Go out as a sailor? No, that wasn't a possibility."

—STANSFIELD TURNER, RHODES SCHOLAR
FOUR-STAR ADMIRAL, AND FORMER DIRECTOR OF THE CIA.

"I was aware that I was not only associated with, but competing
academically with, a sample of the best this country had to offer. And
that was exhilarating. I could accommodate the possibility of failing,
but I was determined as hell that I wouldn't. And I learned that I
needed that straightening out during plebe year. I think I learned
something from it that helped me in the future, namely to take orders
without wincing, no matter what the damn orders were."

—FORMER U.S. SENATOR FROM ALABAMA AND FORMER PRISONER OF
WAR IN VIETNAM JEREMIAH (JERRY) DENTON

"In one sense, I knew that the guys in my class at Annapolis were rather special, because the requirements to get in there were pretty hard. On the other hand, these were just the guys around us, so for all I knew everybody was like that. The Naval Academy breeds integrity and love of country and a recognition of the value of the people around you. That manifests itself in the way you live out the rest of your life."

—ADMIRAL THOMAS HUDNER
FIRST RECIPIENT, AFTER WWII, OF THE MEDAL OF HONOR.

W HAT DO ALL OF THESE DISTINGUISHED MEN: former Joint Chiefs chairman 39th U.S. President Jimmy Carter, billionaire investment banker Jackson T. Stephens, Admiral William Crowe, former CIA Director Stansfield Turner, Medal of Honor winner Admiral James Stockdale, Medal of Honor winner Tom Hudner, former POW and U.S. Senator Jerry Denton, and Ambassador Vernon Weaver, have in common? They were all members of the United States Naval Academy Class of 1947.

Six of these men are in their early 80s, and Stockdale and Stephens each made it to their ninth decade. (Both died in July 2005 as this book was being written.) With the keen perspective of age, all of the men look back on their days at Annapolis as the most important years of their lives, essential for instilling in them the core values and discipline and sense of patriotism that guided them to such great achievements. The men don't put forth the proposition that they were the greatest-ever American military class, because humility is one of the values they hold dear. But it is a question they've thought about from time to time, because, by any measure, this group—a collection of men who finished a four-year course of study in an accelerated three-year curriculum in preparation for a global war that they thought might last a decade—was exceptional.

As Vernon Weaver said, "It's foolish to ponder whether our class was the best, but I can tell you that as a class, we did all right for ourselves."

-·⊲——·—⊳·-

On February 19, 2005, at Groton, Connecticut, the most heavily armed submarine ever built, the USS *Jimmy Carter,* entered the United States Navy's fleet. The $3.2 billion nuclear-powered fast-attack submarine was to be the last of the Seawolf class of attack subs that the Pentagon ordered during the Cold War's final years. It was also the first submarine named after a living ex-president.

Giving the keynote speech on that day was Admiral Stansfield Turner, Jimmy Carter's director of Central Intelligence from 1977–1981. Turner gave an inspired and emotional talk about his respect for President Carter and how the 130-person crew of the USS *Jimmy Carter* should appreciate that their boat would bear the name of a man who upheld the highest standards of integrity, decency, and moral courage during his time in the White House.

Turner told a story to illustrate the strength of Carter's character as president:

"During the 444 excruciating days where Americans were being held hostage in our own embassy in Iran . . . every day of that crisis you would just feel the president's chances for reelection ebbing away. But never once did I suspect that any decision President Carter made with respect to those hostages was colored by his electoral prospects. What he thought was most likely to rescue those hostages and get them back home safely, is exactly what he did."

Turner told how, at a meeting with his top advisors at Camp David, Carter explained that the Iranians had the day before put a proposal on the table. They would return the hostages if the U.S. would agree to have the United Nations make a thorough inspection of what the Iranians said was United States interference over many years in the internal affairs of Iran. Turner spoke up at that point and said, "Mr. President, I think we ought to agree to the proposal, get the hostages back, and then renege on the promise to let the United Nations conduct a review. After all, we're doing this under duress."

Shaking his head slightly as he recalled the moment, Turner said, "Well, I can't tell you the look I got across the table. I wish I could have slid under it. The president said to me, 'Stan, you know we can't do that.'"

"His presidential horizon was, of course, much broader than mine," Turner said. "He was thinking of the reputation of the United States in the world, and that we could not permit ourselves to be accused of duplicity."

Turner's self-deprecation takes on added dimension when you realize that Jimmy Carter has often said, as he did to me in an interview several months prior to the submarine dedication, that Stan Turner was easily the most outstanding member of the Naval Academy's Class of '47, and the one man that every other midshipman looked to as a model of intelligence and high moral character.

Near the end of his talk, Turner, 81, found his emotions getting the better of him. Perhaps he sensed that there would never be another chance for him to pay his respects publicly to a man he had known for over 60 years and for whom he had served at the highest level of government for four of those years. According to another of their Annapolis classmates, Vernon Weaver, who directed the Small Business Administration under Carter and who has remained personally and politically close to both Carter and Turner since their days at the Academy, it was only the second time he had seen Turner get that emotional. The other occasion was at the funeral of Turner's wife Karin, who was killed in a plane crash in Costa Rica in 2000.

In the audience the day that the USS *Jimmy Carter* was commissioned were no less than 50 other Class of '47 graduates who had come from around the country to pay their respects to their most celebrated and accomplished classmate. Jack Raftery, a father of nine who had flown from his home in Las Vegas to attend the ceremony, related how he was especially touched when the son of a deceased Class of '47 member circulated among his father's classmates, requesting their autographs on a photo of their class graduation mounted on wood. And later that morning, a middle-aged woman worked her way among the '47 grads, explaining that her father had hoped to attend but was unable to due to health reasons, but that he would appreciate his classmates signing a 25th anniversary log book from 1971.

As the years pass, and more and more of the distinguished United States Naval Academy Class of '47 members "graduate" beyond this life, moments like the dedication of this state-of-the-art submarine to their most distinguished classmate take on additional significance. It tells you volumes about their eternal devotion to their time in the navy and their years at the academy that so many would make the effort to be there on that day. And at the dedication ceremony, they were all moved when Jimmy Carter, a man who had served as governor of his state of Georgia and president of the United States, and had been awarded the Nobel Peace Prize, told them that, "This is the most deeply appreciated and emotional honor I've ever had, to have this ship bear my name."

Other members of the Class of '47 who didn't make it to the actual ceremony watched on C-SPAN, which provided uninterrupted coverage of the festivities. Among them were Jackson T. Stephens, one of the country's top investment bankers and philanthropists, who watched from his home in Little Rock, Arkansas. Stephens had left the navy following the commencement exercises in June of 1946 and joined his older brother Witt in building one of the nation's largest investment banks. But Stephens' warm feelings towards Annapolis had only grown deeper through the years and in 2002, he donated $10 million towards the construction of a new football field at the Academy, which is named in his honor.

Admiral William Crowe, who had served as Chairman of the Joint Chiefs of Staff under Republican presidents Ronald Reagan and George H. W. Bush, and then later surprised most of his classmates by endorsing Bill Clinton's run for the White House, was watching from his home in the Washington, D. C. area. In a casual interview the year before, he had jokingly told me that the two most important things he learned at the Naval Academy were "1) To get dressed quickly, and 2) To eat quickly."

Crowe also said in our conversation that the Naval Academy was "a pretty intense experience, and because when I was there they didn't have counselors available, your classmates were the only ones available for counseling, and thus you formed friendships that last a lifetime."

He remembers his battalion officer saying to him one day, "Crowe, you may make a good officer someday, but you're a damned poor midshipman." Little did that officer realize he was talking to a man who would years later become the top-ranking military official in the country.

And Admiral James Stockdale, who was awarded the Medal of Honor for his incredible bravery and leadership while a prisoner of war in Vietnam for nearly eight years, watched quietly from his home in Southern California. Admiral Stockdale's health had not been good of late, but he fought the Alzheimer's disease that would claim him five months later with the same determination and ferocity he exhibited in a prison hell-hole in North Vietnam.

One of the Stockdales' four sons, Sid, said this about his father in an interview a month earlier: "When you consider all the hardship and the loneliness and the struggle that my father endured in order to help protect the people he was in prison with, and whom he helped survive and with whom he helped thrive as a community in Vietnam, it's incredible. I am hoping that in the long run, history will bear out the truth. Perhaps it will happen when he dies. As so often happens, it takes someone's death before people finally come to put things into an appropriate perspective. But my father knows what he has accomplished. He knows exactly what the score is, and so I think that the family is satisfied that he is satisfied in knowing that."

Sid's younger brother Stan recently said, "Just this morning I was meeting with a client and he said, 'Your name is Stockdale? Stockdale, Stockdale . . . Oh, yeah, are you related to that guy who ran for vice president?' This happens a lot, and I said, 'Actually, I'm related to that guy who had his ass kicked for eight years in a prisoner-of-war camp so that we could live free lives over here in this country.'"

When Admiral Stockdale died, he received a memorial service with full military honors on the deck of the USS *Ronald Reagan*. Eight Medal of Honor winners served as pallbearers and more than a dozen former POWs were in attendance. It was clear that Stockdale's sacrifice would never be forgotten.

⚓ —— ⚓

The distinguished members of the Class of '47 have every reason to believe that theirs was as impressive a graduating class as ever tossed their hats in the air at Annapolis. And they have several points to bolster that argument. Among their ranks are a U.S. president and Nobel Peace Prize winner, two Medal of Honor winners, a United States senator, a self-made billionaire businessman and renowned philanthropist, a former chairman of the Joint Chiefs of Staff, a former director of the Central Intelligence Agency, a former U.S. ambassador to the European Union, five four-star admirals, and no less than 34 men who achieved the rank of admiral. And as Class of '47 secretary, Chet Shaddeau, reports, "In addition to these nationally recognized figures, there are also literally hundreds of physicians, financiers, engineers, scientists, teachers, businessmen and clerics, as well as Army and Air Force officers and civic and governmental leaders, many of whom commenced these efforts after a productive military career, who formed the core of this great class."

In an e-mail, Shaddeau modestly expressed to me the following assessment of his class, which would no doubt be supported by members of other USNA classes who might understandably feel that their own particular class was exceptional:

"I hope you haven't fallen into the trap, Jack, as so many have, of believing the unsupported and inaccurate belief of many in our class that we had some kind of record for quantity of stars. In fact, the numbers of our rank who achieved their status as admiral is about average for classes of the modern era."

So we'll leave the argument about which class was the greatest to be discussed at future reunions. The purpose of this book is, instead, to commemorate the singular achievements of a select group of individuals who happened to enter Annapolis during a hot summer day in 1943, when the world was engaged in its largest international conflict ever. What so many of them achieved, focused as they were on a war they expected to last beyond their commissioning as officers, was a form of true greatness.

Inspired partly by pure patriotism and partly by strong and nurturing families that instilled in them values that would render them unshakable in even the most torturous moments, and then polished to a gleam by the rigid training at "The Yard," the men we discuss in this book came to represent, with a nod to Tom Brokaw's chronicle, the best of "The Greatest Generation."

*James Earl Carter, Annapolis Class of '47
and 39th President of the United States of
America*

CHAPTER ONE
Jimmy Carter:

The Moral Compass

THE CARTER CENTER IS LOCATED JUST 10 MINUTES FROM DOWNTOWN ATLANTA IN AN IDYLLIC ARBORETUM OF SLOPING GRASSY SWALES THAT SURROUND FORMAL GARDENS, A CHERRY ORCHARD, SMALL LAKES, AND WATERFALLS. The site is as tranquil and heartwarming as the Center's mission: to create a world in which every man, woman, and child has the opportunity to enjoy good health and live in peace. The beautifully landscaped grounds have, since 1982, also served as a second home and major base of operations for former U.S. President Jimmy Carter.

The scope of the Carter Center's goals are no broader, however, than the vision of the man who is generally considered to be the most effective post-Oval Office president in American history. Whether it's helping discover cures for infectious diseases, confronting problems of hunger and diminishing food supplies in African nations, or serving as a peacemaker in places like Haiti and North Korea—on the brink of war prior to his intervention—Jimmy Carter has committed his time, energy, and influence to causes which make our world a better place to live.

On a warm July day in the summer of 2004, a father and his eight-year-old son tour the Jimmy Carter Library and Museum, stopping to watch television and film clips of Carter's career. Among the clips are his Camp David meetings with Egyptian President Anwar Sadat and Israeli President Menachem Begin, which led to both the first peace accord between these two at-odds nations and a shared Nobel Peace Prize for the two foreign leaders in 1978.

The eight-year-old boy, J.P., is intrigued by all the memorabilia about this former president, so his father purchases some mementos for him, including a placemat with the names and pictures of all 43 U.S. presidents. By the time the hour of their appointment with American president No. 39 arrives, J.P. has memorized more than half the names and their chronological order, and is quizzing his father about them. When the father rattles off the first eight presidents in correct order, the boy is impressed. But the admiration level drops considerably when his father botches the order of presidents in the middle nineteenth century.

"Dad, that's not too good," J.P. says. "You need to study this a lot more."

Shortly, the father and son are taken into Jimmy Carter's office in the main building of the Carter Center, where they are greeted warmly. When J.P. holds out his hand to shake, Carter feigns surprise. "A handshake?" he says. "Where's my hug?" and pulls the boy close and gives him a warm embrace. The boy's father is touched by this gesture and delays beginning the interview so that he can snap photos of the two.

"Now you be sure that when you get that picture developed, you mail it back here, and I'll autograph it for you," Carter says. And then he signs a children's book for J.P. titled *The Little Baby Snoogle-Fleejer*, a story that Carter made up for his sons while he was in service in the navy. This newer edition of the book contains illustrations by Carter's daughter Amy, the charming red-headed girl who grew up in the White House under the eyes of the world. It's a shock to learn that Amy is now 37 years old and has a six-year-old of her own, just one of the 11 grandchildren of Jimmy and Rosalyn Carter.

⚎ ——— ⚏

Just how much did James Earl Carter Jr., growing up in the tiny farming community of Plains, Georgia, want an appointment to the United States Naval Academy at Annapolis?

He actually rolled his feet over Coke bottles as a young boy to strengthen his arches. Young Jimmy learned in a book he'd sent away for that flat feet were one of the disqualifying factors for applicants to the USNA, and he wasn't about to let that keep him out. He also did push-ups every day and ran cross-country to prepare himself for the physical rigors that lay ahead. And fearing that he was too thin, the boy ate several bananas a day in an effort to bulk up.

No one in several generations of Jimmy Carter's family had ever gone off to college, and as a youngster Jimmy knew that an advanced education was unaffordable unless he managed to get an appointment to either West Point or Annapolis, where the government could pay his tuition. His uncle, Tom Gordy, youngest brother to his mother Lillian Carter, had been in the navy and told stories of his years abroad and on the high seas, and brought back to Jimmy souvenirs from his visits to exotic lands. Tom Gordy was later captured on Guam, a few days after the Japanese invaded Pearl Harbor. His wife Dorothy and their three children, living in San Francisco, moved to Georgia and were taken in by Tom's mother and other relatives. Two years later, the Red Cross informed Dorothy Gordy that her husband was dead. She moved back to San Francisco and remarried about a year later.

Shortly after the war ended, Tom Gordy was found alive in Japan, an isolated prisoner working on a railroad crew. He had been terribly ill and weighed less than one hundred pounds at the time he was found. He was never reconciled with Dorothy, partly because of the hard feelings Tom's other relatives felt towards her for remarrying so soon after his disappearance. In any event, Tom Gordy was a seminal and heroic figure in the life of Jimmy Carter.

"I grew up in the Depression," Carter says, "and nobody in my family had ever finished high school. The only possibility of my going away to college was to get an appointment. So my primary ambition from the time I was five years old was to do that. The mementos my uncle sent me and the reading I did about the navy convinced me I should do everything possible to prepare to go to Annapolis."

As Jimmy was nearing completion of high school, his father, called Earl by everyone in Plains, began to actively lobby Georgia Congressman Stephen Pace to give his son the appointment. Even though Jimmy had earned all A's in high school, had played on the basketball team, and was involved in several other school activities, the congressman was reluctant to appoint him. He postponed the decision for two years, during which time Jimmy attended community college for one year to study general requirements, and then spent a year at Georgia Tech, where he studied math and science courses that would apply directly to the Naval Academy curriculum.

"We were hoping that Congressman Pace would put the appointment on a competitive assignment commission, which is what some congressmen did at that time, but he didn't," Carter says. "However, my father put enough pressure on him that he finally gave me an appointment a year in advance, conditional on my completing the work at Georgia Tech."

Earl Carter was well respected in southwest Georgia, ran a good-sized peanut farm, and served in the state legislature. He was a strict parent of whom his son has said, "As a child, my greatest ambition was to be valuable around the farm and to please my father. He was the center of my life and the focus of my admiration. "

A staunch segregationist, as were nearly all of his neighbors and business associates, Earl Carter owned some 350 acres of land, where he planted corn, cotton, and peanuts, employing more than 200 workers at harvest time. Five sharecropper families, who depended on the farm for their survival, lived year round on the property.

Jimmy's mother Lillian—later known fondly to the country as "Miss Lillian," colorful and feisty defender of her son and late-life volunteer for the Peace Corps—not only filled the traditional Southern role of family caretaker but also extended her nurturing manner to the community at large. She worked long hours as a nurse at a nearby hospital and devoted much of her free time to helping sick neighbors, regardless of race. While most of her patients couldn't afford to pay her for her kindness, they would often give her chickens and vegetables or other practical tokens of their gratitude. The innate obligation Lillian Carter felt to help those less fortunate was passed down to all her children, as was her understanding that, despite the racist culture of the deep South, all men should be treated equal.

"She was the only person in Plains who would take up for Abraham Lincoln if he was ever brought up," Rosalynn Carter has said. "Today it's unbelievable to think about that, but back then it was just a way of life."

In his autobiographical book, *Why Not the Best*, published in 1974 as a way of introducing himself to the American voting public during his campaign for president, Jimmy Carter explained that, growing up outside Plains, nearly all of his childhood friends were black.

"We hunted, fished, explored, worked, and slept together," he wrote. "We ground sugar cane, plowed with mules, pruned watermelons, dug and bedded sweet potatoes, mopped cotton, stacked peanuts, cut stove wood, pumped water, fixed fences, fed chickens, picked velvet beans, and hauled cotton to the gin together. . . . But we never went to the same church or school. Our social life and our church life were strictly separate. We did not sit together on the two-car diesel train that could be flagged down in Archery. There was a scrupulous compliance with these unwritten and unspoken rules. I never heard them questioned. *Not then*."

Carter writes about how all his family's black neighbors came to visit Earl Carter on the night of the second Joe Louis-Max Schmeling heavyweight championship fight. They asked if they could listen to the fight on Earl Carter's radio, the only one within miles. He agreed, and with the radio propped in an open window, the neighbors gathered under a mulberry tree outside and listened carefully to the broadcast. Although Louis had lost the first bout against the German champion, he decisively won the title on this night, and Jimmy Carter recalled the quiet tension among the gathering as the bout unfolded. When it was over:

" . . . there was no sound from anyone in the yard, except a polite, 'Thank you, Mister Earl,' offered to my father.

"Then our several dozen visitors filed across the dirt road, across the railroad track, and quietly entered a house about a hundred yards away out in the field. At that point, pandemonium broke loose inside that house, as our black neighbors shouted and yelled in celebration of the Louis victory. But all the curious, accepted proprieties of a racially segregated society had been carefully observed."

While Earl Carter was by all accounts a good and honorable man and a devoted father, he was ingrained with the centuries-old traditions of a racist culture as much as the political philosophy of his son was later filled with a sense of outrage about the inequality of a segregated society.

Carter's entry in the Class of '47 yearbook testifies to his popularity with his classmates

When he enrolled in the Naval Academy in June of 1943, still just 18 years old, Jimmy Carter was the first in several generations of his family to leave Georgia to pursue a higher education.

But he had made an important connection before he left for the Academy. Through his sister Ruth, later a world-famous evangelist, Jimmy had met a girl named Rosalynn Smith.

"Ruth Carter was my best friend, and she had a picture of her brother on the wall of her bedroom," Rosalyn said in an interview in 2000. "I thought he was the most handsome young man I'd ever seen. One day I confessed to her that I wished she'd let me take that photograph home, because I just thought I had fallen in love with Jimmy Carter."

Some time later, Rosalynn went to a meeting at the local church, and she was standing outside when up drove Ruth and her boyfriend and Jimmy. "He got out of the car and came up and asked me to go to a movie," she says. "I was thrilled to death to go, and when he left he kissed me goodbye. And then we started corresponding. And by the time Christmas came, I was swept off my feet."

❧ —— ❧

Carter recalls his excitement when he left for Annapolis in June of 1943.

"I had never been away very much in my life," he says, "and so this was a major excursion for me, away from my family. I went by train and my mind just raced with the possibilities of the life that awaited me there. A lot of young men had been away at prep schools and done a lot of traveling before they entered the Naval Academy, but I had never been on a boat. I was a land-lubber in every respect."

His biggest concern, which was surely shared by the other thousand-some newly enrolled plebes, was whether he could cut the mustard at Annapolis. "It was more grueling than I had anticipated," he says. "The hazing back then was very rigorous, and part of the responsibility of a first classman was to put the plebes under tremendous psychological and physical pressure.

"I remember our standing up the first morning of seamanship class, and the chief petty officer said, 'Look to your right.' And then he said, 'Look to your left. At the end of this summer one of you will not be here.' There had to be a deep commitment to the Naval

Academy because there was a high attrition rate. They deliberately tried to get rid of a third of the midshipmen between admission and graduation."

Like all plebes, Carter was occasionally beaten with a broom or one of the long serving spoons used in the dining hall. "They were hard hacks," he says. "I mean they would leave a blister. And they piled it on pretty good, because I was from the Deep South. I remember they would have us do 47 push-ups and 94 deep knee bends, a multiple number, because we were the Class of '47. And sometimes we would be required to do these in a first sergeant's room, and then you'd go next door to another one and start all over again. And because I was a deeply committed Southerner, and my first officer soon found out how deep my commitment was, they would order me to sing 'Marching Through Georgia,' [a song that honored William Tecumseh Sherman's march through the state in the Civil War] and a Georgian just doesn't dishonor his home state by doing that. I declined that order and that led to more hazing."

Carter recalls a common punishment called "shoving out," which required a plebe to assume a normal sitting position at mealtime without actually touching the chair. Food deprivation was common, as was being ordered to eat under the table for violations of basic etiquette. And he can't forget a hazing activity called the Cruise Box Race that was created by the first classmen. He explains that a cruise box was a wooden trunk that each midshipman was issued to store all his private possessions. The plebes would be ordered to climb into the box, close the lid, change from a blue uniform into dress whites, then get out and run around one of the squares in Bancroft Hall. Then the plebes had to get back into the box and change back into the blue uniform. First one to finish won the race, and the others received further hazing.

There was no way to escape these daily punishments, and midshipmen who showed weakness in receiving the hazing were often forced out of the academy.

"The hazing and physical abuse taught me discipline," Carter says, "But in my opinion it was excessive. I'm glad that physical abuse at the Naval Academy has been done away with nowadays."

While Carter feels that there might have been secondary motives for many of the midshipmen to endure the rigors of Annapolis, such as getting a great education courtesy of the government, he says that the primary motive for all his classmates was to serve their country. "There was a great sense of patriotism that was infused in everything we did in our three years there," he says. "Our base at Pearl Harbor had been attacked just a year before most of us were accepted there, and we all felt honored to serve our country at that difficult time. I was determined when I went there to serve for the rest of my life. I was completely committed to a 30-year career in the navy, and my highest ambition was someday maybe to become the chief of naval operations. I'm sure many of my classmates had that same aspiration. One of them of course, Admiral Bill Crowe, became chairman of the Joint Chiefs of Staff. Never in my wildest dreams did the idea of becoming president ever occur to me at that time."

Physically slight, with disproportionately long legs, Carter ran cross-county at Annapolis, as he had in high school, and played on the under-140-pound football team in the intercompany league. He says he weighed only 121 pounds when he arrived in June of '43, and he had added just 14 pounds to his slight frame when he was commissioned three years later. There was no money to indulge his other interests in art and literature and music, although he would occasionally buy a classical phonograph record and share it with classmates. He became an expert at identifying the world's ships and planes during that time and was able to recognize hundreds of silhouettes of allied and enemy planes. During testing, images would be flashed on a screen for less than a second, and Carter was expected to name the make and model of the vessel or airplane. He eventually could identify every one of them.

He was in the North Atlantic in early August 1945, on a summer shipboard assignment with other midshipmen, when it was announced that President Truman had a military message of great importance to the nation. The pervasive thought among Carter's classmates at Annapolis was that an invasion of Japan would be the inevitable conclusion to the war, as the Japanese would never surrender. There was an expectation that he and his classmates might be involved in such an historic action. But all of the men onboard were shocked to hear Truman's flat voice informing them that a new atomic weapon had been dropped on Hiroshima, Japan. Three days later, a second bomb was dropped on Nagasaki. Within days, while Carter was still at sea, the word arrived that Japan had surrendered. The men onboard were envious of those who could celebrate the announcement of VJ Day in Times Square. Carter writes in *Why Not the Best?* that he had never even heard a rumor about this quantum leap in nuclear capability, nor did he suspect at the time that in the coming months he would devote a significant portion of his navy service to studying more peaceful uses of atomic power, such as propelling ships, generating electric power, and furthering scientific and medical research.

By the time the Class of '47 graduated in June of 1946 under an accelerated war-time program, Carter and his classmates knew that they would not be engaged in warfare after receiving their commissions but would instead be faced with other options. For Jimmy Carter, his intention was to use all he'd learned at Annapolis to build a career in the navy.

He says of the years following the end of World War II that the navy was in poor shape, that it was undermanned and that the country fell into a period of relaxation and fatigue after the longest and most expensive military conflict in our country's history. Jimmy Carter was disillusioned and says he would have resigned from the military had he not felt obligated, as an Annapolis graduate, to serve out his time "at the pleasure of the president."

His first assignment after graduation was to serve two years on a surface ship. In drawing lots to determine the assignments, Carter drew one of the highest numbers in the class. He was assigned to the oldest and most dilapidated ship in the navy, the USS *Wyoming*, which was scheduled for early decommissioning. It had so many oil leaks that when the ship was in the waters outside Norfolk, Virginia, it was not permitted to come into the pier area and was forced to anchor well out in the bay. But it so happened that the *Wyoming* was the only navy vessel doing experimental fire control, gunnery, and navigation work. With post-war spending tightly controlled, whenever the navy got ready to test a new radar system or navigational system of any kind, it would order just one model and try it out on the *Wyoming*.

VJ Day at Bancroft Hall, Annapolis, 1945.

There was a lot to be learned through these experiments and testing. Carter worked hard and was given the assignment of both electronic officer and photographic officer. By 1948, Carter was quickly learning about the latest technical developments and innovations in the navy and continued in his position when, after a year, the decrepit *Wyoming* was replaced by the *Mississippi*, as the navy's seagoing experiment station. He says of the two years on these vessels that the work was interesting, but the duty was terrible. For his next assignment, he had the option of putting in for naval intelligence, for the Air Force, or for submarines.

Carter put his request in for submarine school, because, like many others, he viewed submarines as the most elite, most advanced, and most challenging experience in the navy. He was chosen and spent the last half of 1948, learning everything he could about what would become his new home.

The next four years of Jimmy Carter's life were spent submerged, both in navy submarines and in the philosophy of Admiral Hyman Rickover. Regarded as the "Father of the Nuclear Submarine," Rickover has been called by Carter one of the most influential men in his life, second only to his father, and the person who instilled in him the belief that if a man was willing to push past his own limits, anything was possible.

Young Naval officer James Carter Jr. on command"

Before Carter received the plum assignment to join Rickover, he spent several months in the Pacific on a submarine, the USS *Pomfret*. When the Korean War began, the *Pomfret* was ordered to the Far East. It was during this trip that the course of American history was very nearly altered. A violent storm erupted while Carter was on nighttime duty charging batteries on the surfaced *Pomfret*. He was on the submarine bridge about 15 feet above the level of the ocean, holding on as tightly as he could to an iron pipe handrail inside the bridge shield, when a huge wave rose about six feet over Carter's head and tore him from the handrail. He was tossed about for what seemed like forever, but then fate intervened and dropped him on top of a five-inch gun barrel 30 feet toward the sub's stern. Had the currents been moving in any other direction, Carter would surely have been drowned.

Carter heard that the navy was in the planning stages of building its first new ship since the end of the war. It was to be a small anti-submarine sub whose only purpose was to remain extremely quiet, to go silent and go deep, and to intercept Soviet submarines and destroy them before they knew what hit them. It was called the USS *K-1*, or Killer 1, and Lt. JG Jimmy Carter was the only Naval officer assigned to it. It was a highly competitive assignment, sought by many submariners, but Carter's single-minded work ethic and intelligence won him the position. Just four years into his navy career, he was clearly tracking toward the loftier heights of the navy hierarchy.

Carter was assigned to Groton and the pre-commissioning detail. He wrote all of the detail requirements for the *K-1* and later put the submarine into commission. But then he heard about the navy's plans to build the first nuclear submarines.

"I guess almost every submarine officer wanted to go on that nuclear program," he says. "We all put in for it, I got it, and I was assigned to it and served under Admiral Rickover. That was a life-changing experience. Rickover had total dedication to this career. I thought then and I still feel that he was the greatest engineer who ever lived on earth. He was excruciatingly demanding. He expected the highest possible commitment from everyone who worked under him. He never smiled. He never gave a compliment, and he never said that you did a good job."

Rickover's methodology was all business, and his administrative policy was to demand more from all of his subordinates than they thought they could deliver.

Carter recalls how the men under Rickover strove to stay up with him and earn his respect: "I remember, I would get on an airplane with Rickover in Washington and we would fly out to the West Coast to visit the nuclear plant. And this was before the fast jets, so it would take us 11 hours of flying time. We had to land in Chicago on the way. And I would be determined that I was going to stay awake and at least pretend to be working as long as Rickover did. But eventually I would nod off. And I'd wake up and Rickover would still be working. When he came to the General Electric plant, they all knew he was coming, and they would all be uptight, as would the chief executive officer at GE. He was deliberately intimidating and very demanding. But he set a standard for us that we knew was genuine. I mean, he wasn't lazy in any situation. He was dedicated . . . more than the rest of us. He set the bar high, and he exceeded the bar that he set for others."

Carter says that the final appointment interview with Rickover was nerve-wracking. He was sweating as he answered questions. "I felt as it progressed that I was not answering his questions adequately. I had a sinking feeling. He knew more about every subject than I did. And he knew a method of asking questions, so that you were kind of led on about literature or art or music or current events until you proved to yourself that you didn't know as much as you expected.

"I had almost given up on the interview, and he finally asked me, 'How did you stand at the Naval Academy?'

"And I said, 'Sir, I stood fifty-ninth in a class of eight hundred and twenty.'

"And then he asked me one more question. He said, 'Did you do your best?'

"And I started to say, 'Yes, sir.' But I paused and remembered there were a lot of times when to get away from my studies I had read novels and listened to classical music and done other things. I swallowed a couple times, and I realized beyond a doubt that I was not going to get the appointment, but I told the truth. I said, 'No, sir. I didn't always do my best.'

"And he looked at me with cold steely eyes and never smiled and said, 'Why not?'

"Then he turned his chair around and ended the interview. He didn't even wait for my answer. I sat there for a minute or two. I didn't know what to do. And finally I got up and stumbled out of the room.

"Days later I got a call that said I had gotten the assignment. I couldn't believe it. What Rickover tried to do with all of the subordinates during the interviews was to induce or force them to make a misleading statement. To exaggerate what they had done. I have little doubt that had I said I did my best all the time at the Naval Academy, it would have cost me the appointment. I really believe that."

Carter was ordered to Schenectady, New York, where he served as a senior officer on the *Sea Wolf*, an atomic-powered submarine. He taught enlisted men sophisticated mathematics and participated in the building of the first nuclear propulsion components. With a high security clearance, he traveled frequently from New York to the Atomic Energy Commission headquarters in Washington, D.C., and to the Hanford nuclear works in Washington State, where plutonium was manufactured. He was even asked to assist in disassembling the core of a Canadian nuclear reactor that had melted down. For several months afterward, he and the men on his team were required to save their waste materials for monitoring, because they had absorbed a year's allowance of radiation in one minute and twenty-nine seconds. It was a period of time that Carter very much enjoyed, because his days were full, he was constantly challenged, and he felt that his education and service were highly valued.

⊰ ⸺ ⊱

Jimmy Carter's dreams of serving his entire career in the navy, hopefully ascending to the highest rank, were abruptly ended when he received the news in 1953 that his father was gravely ill with cancer. It had been 10 years since he'd enrolled at Annapolis and his visits home to Plains were rare. He and his father had grown somewhat distant. Carter returned home to his father's bedside, and over the next days, they shared long conversations, catching up and saying all the things that needed to be said. They were interrupted frequently by a steady stream of visitors. "There were as many black visitors as white," Carter says, "and a surprising number wanted to recount how my father's personal influence and many secret acts of generosity had affected their lives."

Carter told biographer Peter Bourne, "I wondered if I had died, how many people at that time would come to visit me, or would even care that I'd died."

His father's death made Jimmy assess what his life was truly all about. He saw the impact his father had made on his small community and the lives he had touched. And he also strongly sensed that it was his obligation to return to Georgia and run the family business. It was a huge decision for him, with immense repercussions.

"There were 637 people living in Plains then," he says. "It was this tiny little town, and yet my father had made an impact on nearly all of them. I saw for the first time the beneficial impact of my father's life and the diversity of his interest. I saw the breadth of his assistance to other people and the challenges that he faced. And almost without control over my decision, I decided to get out of the navy. And it was as much of a surprise to me as it was to my wife. Rosalynn absolutely resented it. She had grown up in Plains and left to see the world, and she did not want to return. She almost left me over that decision. She resented it for a long time. It was a very deep and personal hurt for a long time."

Presidential historian Douglas Brinkley put it this way in a documentary for *American Experience*. "Rosalynn had finally got out of the fly-speck village and had gotten to see the bright lights and big cities. Imagine being based in Hawaii, where you get a Pacific breeze and palm trees, and the smell of the Orient in the air. And now you're back in this suffocating, mosquito-plagued humidity of Plains, Georgia."

"I pouted for about a year," Rosalynn Carter says. "It was tough for a while."

Rosalynn was eventually reconciled to the new realities of their life, when she saw Jimmy's involvement with the community and his immersion in the peanut business, which he soon whipped back into shape. This, coupled with their children's happiness at being able to play in the woods and build forts and go hiking and fishing, enabled Rosalynn to find peace and solitude in rural Georgia.

Within a year of his return, Jimmy was fully engaged in finding new ways to improve production and efficiency in the peanut business. He soon realized that by getting Rosalynn involved in the business, all aspects of their relationship would improve. He asked her to keep the office and manage the books for the company. She took an accounting course in the local vocational school and soon knew more about the paper side of the business than her husband.

But political tides were changing, and a 1954 Supreme Court decision outlawing segregation in public schools was an affront to deeply ingrained ways of thinking in the Deep South. A prominent businessman approached Jimmy Carter and asked him to join the White Citizens' Council. The man even volunteered to pay the $5 initiation fee for him. Jimmy told the man that he could flush his money down the toilet, knowing full well that this decision would cost him customers in the peanut business. But as a man who had always followed his conscience and endeavored to do the right thing, Carter felt it was the only choice he could make.

Jimmy Carter had noticed, since his return to Plains, that the black youths he had grown up with as playmates had been stifled in their career development. He told *TIME* magazine, "We would play together as children, and then something would happen at about age 12 or 14. Suddenly, when you're playing, your playmate would step back and open a gate for you or you wouldn't do certain things together any more. Then in later years, you'd go off to college or a job, and he would stay. And everyone kind of expected that."

Over the next years, the Carters learned to balance hard work with recreation. The family went fishing, played golf, and took frequent vacations. They might work 50 hours straight, and days on end during peanut season, but they also knew how to have fun. And Jimmy emulated his father by becoming active in several roles in the Plains community. He served on the Sumter County Board of Education, taught Sunday school at the local Baptist Church, and was vice-president of the Lions Club, as well as a scoutmaster. But then, one night in 1962, he made a life-changing decision.

"I decided," he says, "that I was going to run for the state legislature. Georgia was more enlightened than Arkansas or Alabama or Mississippi about the race issue, in that we never defied the federal courts. And one of the major political leaders of our state was running for governor, and on his political posters he held up one finger with the slogan, 'No, not one.' By that he meant that if even one black kid came into a white Georgia school, he would shut down the whole public school. This was in defiance of the Supreme Court ruling. There was a special election in two weeks, and I just woke up one morning and said I was going to seek that office. I had never dreamed of pursuing a political career until that moment."

A power broker named Joe Hurst ran things in Quitman County, and he wanted another Democrat, Homer Moore, to be elected state senator. The ballot box for the election was a liquor box with a hole cut in the top of it, and as voters would mark their ballot and drop it in, Hurst and his people would monitor the activity. According to several sources, fraud was rampant, voters were threatened to vote a certain way, and ballots were destroyed. Joe Hurst even stuffed ballots of dead voters into the liquor box. Despite a sense by Carter's people that he had great support in his first run for office, when the votes were counted that evening, Jimmy Carter had lost. He immediately contested the election.

Carter appealed to newspapers, filed for injunctions, and took affidavits from voters. Threats were made against the Carters that if they contested the election, bad things would happen; one stranger even told Rosalynn that the last time anyone had opposed Joe Hurst, his business had burned down. It was the kind of corruption that one would expect to find on a remote island dictatorship, not in the United States in the 1960s, but the resistance only strengthened Jimmy's resolve to discover the truth.

Two weeks later, a local judge agreed to hear Carter's appeal. When the ballot box was opened in course, they found rolled up into a ball

all these ballots that had been stuffed. It became clear in the recount that Carter had been defeated by voters who were either dead, jailed, or never at the polls on Election Day. The results were overturned, and on January 14, 1963, Jimmy Carter was sworn in as a member of the Georgia Senate. There were 88 other new legislators sworn in that day, and many of them, like Carter, were determined to change the way politics was carried out in Georgia.

From the very beginning of his career in politics, Carter was not one to cater to special interests or sweetheart deals. He didn't like tit-for-tat politics or trading votes. He was a good and honest man, a great campaigner, but by most accounts not a good politician in the raw sense of the word. He contrasted sharply with a Lyndon Johnson-type politician, who would constantly work the phones, press the flesh, and finagle back room deals to forward his own causes. Carter fought for legislation that he felt would benefit the common citizen, and he closely studied the letter of the law and the wording of bills. Like his father before him, Jimmy treated his elected post in the legislature as an honor and a privilege, and he intended to make a difference in people's lives. It became clear to Rosalynn after her husband's two terms in the Georgia Senate that he had no intention of stopping there. He was just 39 years old when he took office and by his early 40s had learned many of the basic rules of political life. His great education in the navy and his lifelong habit of painstakingly studying issues that he didn't fully understand, gave him the confidence to tackle any challenges that lay ahead, so Jimmy decided to take on arch-segregationist, Lester Maddox, and other better-known candidates in the 1966 Georgia governor's race. Maddox had gained notoriety for wielding an ax handle to keep blacks from entering his chicken restaurant, and this gesture had found wide appeal among the white voters of his state. In the early polling, Carter ran well behind Maddox and the others, but he gradually caught up over the summer months by dispatching his family members throughout the state to meet with the voters. The Carters' oldest son Jack, then 18, recalls handing out pamphlets around the state and not being particularly well versed on the issues.

"Dad got into the race late, and we had only about three months to campaign in the summer before the September primary," Jack says, speaking in the fall of 2004 from his home in Las Vegas. "And my younger brothers weren't old enough to drive, so we just did the best we could under the circumstances."

The Carter team asked questions, shook hands, and blanketed every school hall and Piggly Wiggly in the state. Carter promised better roads and better schools and better hospitals. On weekends, the Carter campaign team would gather back in Atlanta to report on their progress and plan the next week's strategy. (The tactics they employed in this campaign would serve as a model for a much bigger campaign a decade later.) Jimmy closed the gap to a dead heat and went to bed the night before the primary thinking that he had won a place in the runoff. But it turned, out he fell half a percentage point short.

Maddox finished second in the primary, but an antiquated Georgia law authorized the state legislature to choose between the first- and second-place finishers, and the legislators chose Maddox to occupy the governor's mansion.

Jimmy Carter was devastated by the loss; he'd given the campaign his heart and soul, had lost 20 pounds walking the campaign trail, and was left with over $60,000 in personal debt. For a man who had won about every position he'd ever coveted, it was a crushing blow. He thought his career in politics had come to an end. Weeks later, still reeling from the defeat, he had a long talk with his sister Ruth, an evangelical Christian and a spiritual healer. He told her of his melancholy and how he felt his faith had been superficial. She responded that her happiness and contentment came from her total commitment to her faith.

"I belong to Jesus, everything that I am," she said.

"Ruth, that's what I want," he answered.

For the next couple of years, Jimmy Carter traveled to other cities and other states, talking to people about his faith and getting people to take Jesus into their lives.

As presidential historian Douglas Brinkley said, "Can you imagine that ten years later this man is president of the United States and here he was banging on doors, asking people, 'Do you want a Bible? Will you take God in your life?'"

Carter studied theologians and philosophers during these years, hoping to integrate their wisdom into his own personal beliefs and personality, and he tried to reconcile how these teachings could be implemented in his public service. His Christian faith gave him the resolve to believe that anything was possible, and he vowed to once again throw his hat in the ring and try to overcome the Georgia good-old-boy political machine.

His opponent in the 1970 Democratic nomination for governor (the Republican challenger would be merely token opposition) was Carl Sanders, who was backed by the Atlanta business establishment and had the support of African Americans, who were voting in bigger numbers since the Voting Rights Act of 1965.

Carter learned from the mistakes of his 1966 run for governor, and two of his bright young supporters, twenty-somethings Hamilton Jordan and Jody Powell, emerged as managers of his campaign.

Once again, the early polling showed Carter to be well behind his opponent—as much as 20 points in some polls. The Carter campaign strategy was to characterize Sanders as a pawn of the Atlanta business establishment and Carter as the embodiment of the hard-working middle class with a special understanding of the needs of the everyday Georgian. He softened his language on some of the racial issues like busing, having learned that every honest feeling did not need to be put forth in speeches; the important thing was to win the election and then implement all of those heartfelt programs that would, he felt, improve the quality of life in the state. For eight months, working 18 hours a day, Carter once again covered every base in Georgia, with a vow that he would not be outworked or outstrategized this time. He estimates that he gave 1,800 speeches during this time, from street corners to bowling alleys to car washes, and that he and Rosalynn shook hands with more than 600,000 people, more than half the total who vote in Georgia. This was an election that Jimmy Carter absolutely had to win to validate all the hard work in his life. And win he did.

His acceptance speech at his swearing in on January 12, 1971, surprised some people. "I say to you quite frankly that the time for racial discrimination is over," he said. "No poor, rural, weak, or black person should ever have to bear the additional burden of being deprived of the opportunity of an education, a job, or simple justice."

TIME magazine's cover story on May 31, 1971, featured a line-drawing of Carter on the cover with a story titled, "New Day A' Coming in the South." It profiled the new governor as a symbol of integration and the sudden erosion of hardened Southern principles. About his inauguration speech, *TIME* wrote: "[it] heralded the end of that final Southern extravagance, the class rhetoric of 'never.' The reality of 17 years of court decisions, demonstrations, black-voter registration and legislation was clearly seen across the South as Carter and other moderate governors took office this year, giving the region new political voices, new images, new goals."

Carter supporters and the black population of both Georgia and America were deeply moved by Carter's words. For perhaps the first time, a governor in the Deep South was speaking out forcefully against the inbred tradition of segregation and discrimination. But there was also a block of supporters that wondered openly why Carter had not revealed his intentions more clearly during the campaign. Some spoke out and said they would not have supported him if he had spoken so openly before the election. There was a sense that he'd hidden this "rabbit in a hat" so as not to alienate the segregationist voting block, and then pulled it out once the ballots were safely counted.

For the first time since 1953, when he'd made the difficult decision to leave the navy and return to his roots on the Carter farm, Jimmy and Rosalynn Carter would move their family, this time into the governor's mansion in Atlanta. The only furniture they brought was the children's favorite sofa.

If he was a studious legislator in the Georgia Senate, obsequious and not overly zealous, by all accounts Jimmy Carter was an aggressive governor, determined to invoke his political philosophy on the legislature. He proposed to slash a number of government agencies and often proclaimed in speeches that elected officials should never forget who pays the taxes and thereby their salaries. Historian Dan Carter (no relation) has said, "Carter had a tendency to take his case to the people and then try to force the legislature to follow him. He never, as governor, broke the unfortunate habit of seeing personal politics . . . as a kind of nuisance, something that had to be done. . . . He never developed the interest in or particularly good skills at working with individuals who may have disagreed with him."

"Jimmy reminds me of a south Georgia turtle who's been blocked by a log," said lawyer Warren Fortson, a friend of Carter's. "And he just keeps pushing, pushing, pushing straight ahead. He doesn't go around until he finally finds a soft spot in the log and then goes right on through. He is a man of great determination and steel."

One of Carter's duties in the role of governor was to serve as host to Democratic contenders during their run for the Presidency in 1972.

As he told this writer in July of 2004: "Candidates like Scoop Jackson and Ed Muskie and Hubert Humphrey and Ted Kennedy, all of them would come through the South campaigning, and because I was looked at as one of the up and coming Southern governors, I would invite them to stay in a beautiful suite in our mansion, which was called the Presidential Suite. I would stay up late at night talking to them about international affairs and domestic challenges. And I soon became convinced that I knew as much about these things as they did. They would pass a bill in Congress on welfare, health care, education, housing, or something of that kind, but they had no idea about the consequences of that legislation once it reached the delivery stage. And although I had nominated Scoop Jackson at the convention in Miami, and George McGovern got the nomination, I was mentioned as a possible vice-president selection. As soon as that convention was over and I wasn't chosen, I began to plan to run for president."

"When my father was on the cover of *TIME* magazine in the spring of 1971, in that story about the New South," Jack Carter recalls, "it really thrust him into a national spotlight for the first time. And this seemed pretty unreal to us at the time, that he could achieve such an honor. And you know growing up in a town as small and rural as Plains, you have to learn in sort of concentric circles where you fit into the universe. You start out pretty small. You are sort of a hick and you know it. You're living in an agricultural area and you don't know anybody who has ever been to Europe. And you're mesmerized by television. The TV seems to divide people. You are either on TV or you're not, and the thinking in a small town like Plains is that if you're on TV, you must be special because only a few people can be on TV. And then these guys who were on TV, like Hubert Humphrey and John Lindsey, they would come by the governor's mansion and we saw, and my dad saw, that they were no more special than he was. And Dad would ask them questions about political issues, and they would either not know the answer or they would fumble through it. So we all sensed at that time that Dad had everything it took to be a good candidate for president. He clearly held his own among those people."

Hamilton Jordan, who was Carter's executive secretary as governor of Georgia and would become the architect of his presidential campaign and later his Chief of Staff in the White House, concurs that the starting gate for the Carter presidential run was the Democratic convention of 1972. In November that year, Jordan, just 28 years old at the time, wrote an eighty-page memo to Carter that outlined everything he would need to do if he were to make a serious run for the White House.

"It turns out we had the correct strategy, and the memo makes me look smart after the fact because we were successful" Jordan says. "Of course, had we lost I would have been some young upstart. And

Carter, as he always did, executed everything he was supposed to do and did it better than you would have thought he could do it.

"We had some luck as well," he admits. "Our timing couldn't have been more perfect, in the aftermath of Watergate."

Carter had a clear advantage by making up his mind to run for the White House four years ahead of the election. His term as governor would end in 1974, and Georgia had a one-term limit in the statehouse. Thus he had two full years to campaign. Still, the odds against him were huge. No one in history had gone from being a virtual unknown on the national political radar to winning the most powerful position on earth in such a short time. And as a one-term governor of a small southern state, he was a distinct outsider. He was perceived to be so far outside the Washington political beltway that he would never be able to muster enough support within his own party to sway popular opinion. None of those facts deterred him for a minute.

Ham Jordan made several points in his memo that turned out to be prescient. He suggested that the Carter team look at politics from a different perspective and turn things that appeared to be liabilities into assets. One piece of prevailing conventional wisdom at the time was that the candidate had to be a U.S. senator and come forward and announce his candidacy with a clear platform outlined. Jordan pointed out that since he was out of office, Carter could campaign under the radar of the press for nearly two years full-time, gaining a foothold in several states while the other candidates weren't paying attention. Another widespread belief was that there would be a brokered Democratic convention in 1976, and that the prominent candidates would run in Iowa and New Hampshire and not in Florida, because George Wallace was seen as untouchable in Florida. Jordan's memo said that Carter should run everywhere, because he had the time to do it.

It wasn't until R. W. Apple reported in the *New York Times* in December 1975, that Jimmy Carter had a surprising lead in the January Iowa caucuses that the "cat was out of the bag."

But even three months later, wise old eagles in the Democratic party were skeptical. In March, long-time statesman and beltway insider Averill Harriman said, "Carter can't be elected president. I don't know him, and I don't even know anybody that knows him."

"We just snuck up on everybody," Jordan says. "And Carter and his family and his supporters . . . we just outworked them. It was a combination of all those things."

The Carter family used the same divide-and-conquer strategy that had worked so effectively in the Georgia governor's race. There was Jimmy and Rosalynn, their sons Jack and Chip and Jeff and their wives, Jimmy's mother Miss Lillian (a terrific campaigner with her diverse background as a nurse and teacher and integrationist), and Lillian's sister, Aunt Sissy. "So every day, we had seven campaigns going on in different parts of America," Jimmy Carter says. "We never went to the same state or part of the state. We blanketed the nation. We'd leave Plains after church on Sunday, go to Atlanta, go to a kind of pep rally, which at first had about 20 people and then later had 200 or 300 people. And then we would disperse all over the country. And we would come back to Plains on Saturday morning, and we would spend Saturday afternoon comparing notes, trying to ascertain what the different sections of people in America found to be of interest and also to make sure we were preaching the same sermon on abortion, and things like that. By the time, a year later, that the rest of the candidates woke up to the race, we had a huge lead."

Jack Carter says he visited 48 states campaigning for his father. "I think I missed only Oklahoma and Alaska," he says. "I was finishing up law school in May of 1975, and I started taking trips out to South Carolina on the weekends. I would stay with people on the campaign trail that were supportive of Dad, to save money. It was the first time that matching funds were available and we had to get $5,000 in donations in each of the 20 primary states, with nobody giving us more than $250. So we had to get some 20 people in each state. We all had issue papers with us so we could explain where Dad stood on the various issues, but we didn't engage in any really heavy debate."

Jack Carter recalls that year as challenging but very fun. "When I came out and started meeting people on the street," he says, "I was impressed with how much people really wanted to do the right thing. I discovered they wanted the same things I wanted, and to the extent that they needed to sacrifice to get those things, they were willing to do it. It was an amazing experience."

Jimmy and Rosalynn in the White House.

It is important to understand the historical context of the Carter run for the White House to appreciate just how appealing he was to the average American. In January of 1975, when Jimmy Carter made his formal announcement that he was running for president, the country had just emerged from two years of Watergate scandals, and the first-ever resignation of an American president; Vietnam was fresh in the public's mind; and the previous 11 years had seen Washington run by the ultimate political insiders, Lyndon Johnson and Richard Nixon. The voting public had an underlying distrust of the political establishment, and that included sitting president, Gerald Ford, the long-time Michigan congressman and Richard Nixon's vice president. Ford had put himself in political jeopardy by pardoning Nixon from his Watergate crimes just weeks after he took office.

Carter on the stump in his run for president.

The Carter strategy was to run early and run hard. His campaign team considered the fact that he was not currently holding office his biggest advantage.

"It enabled us to build a huge lead in awareness before the others got started, before they even announced their intentions to run," Carter says. His family delegations in those first several months got the word to every corner of the country. Carter himself, early on, had traveled more than 50,000 miles, visited 37 states, and delivered more than 200 speeches. But this grassroots effort, backed only by limited funds and Carter's down-home temperament and the mile-wide smile so loved by political cartoonists, was winning over voters one county at a time. The same discipline and work ethic that had served him so well in his navy career was achieving great results on the campaign trail. Clear goals were laid out from week to week, and the Carter cavalcade touched all the stepping stones along the path. At one point, the campaign had family members in 11 different states at the same time.

The first real test came in January 1976, a full year after Carter had started his campaign across America. It began with the Iowa caucuses. None of the better-known candidates like Mo Udall, Sargent Shriver, and Birch Bayh gave Iowa any attention. They were focused instead on the primary in New Hampshire, which had proven to be a bellwether so many times before. But Carter's brain trust, including Jody Powell, Hamilton Jordan, Bert Lance, and Gerald Rafshoon, later all key players in his administration, understood that Iowa could be pivotal for other reasons. If Carter won there, it would give him national recognition and increased press attention, clearly needed as the coming weeks and months would pit him against bigger names on a bigger stage.

"Nobody thought we had any chance in Iowa," Carter says.

And who could blame him? The first time he appeared for a campaign stop in Iowa in 1974, exactly one person showed up. But he ended up winning the Iowa caucus easily.

Hamilton Jordan says the often overlooked aspect of the Carter campaign that made the crucial difference, one that the former president does not talk about, was Carter's own multi-faceted personality and eminent charm.

"Jimmy Carter is very much a Renaissance man," Jordan says. "He had all these dimensions to his personality and his experience that allowed him to relate to nearly everyone. You know, if you walked in to talk to him and you were a small businessman, he could talk to you about how he started the peanut warehouse. If you walked in and you were an environmentalist, he could talk to you in a very sophisticated way about environmental issues. If you walked in and you were a retired military guy, he could talk to you about Annapolis. He had all of these dimensions to his personality and character that allowed him to appeal to rednecks in the South as a guy from a small town, to farmers in Iowa, and to big-city people, because he had seen the world in the navy."

There was about a month of heavy campaigning between Iowa and New Hampshire, and Carter built on the momentum. National articles came out profiling the long-shot peanut farmer with the elite navy training and the "apprenticeship" under Admiral Rickover on a nuclear submarine. The public increasingly liked what it saw. Also, the large-scale exposure helped the campaign to raise money to get through New Hampshire, with some left over for Florida and other primaries down the road. Campaign volunteers from Georgia flooded New Hampshire, knocking on more than 60,000 doors in the state. The goal was to talk to every registered Democrat in the state, and the corps of housewives and on-sabbatical professors in the Carter camp didn't miss many. Although few would have thought it possible six months earlier, Jimmy Carter won New Hampshire easily, and Walter Cronkite led the CBS Evening News with this proclamation: "Jimmy Carter took a long lead tonight in the race for the Democratic presidential nomination. . . ."

The next stop was Florida, where the leading Democratic contender was George Wallace, former governor of Alabama and an outspoken segregationist, who had become something of a liability for the party. While Wallace represented the views of many Southerners, he was thought to be too divisive in a national contest.

"All of the liberals that I had worked with got nervous in a room full of black people," said Andrew Young, who later would become mayor of Atlanta and U.S. Ambassador to the United Nations. "And Jimmy Carter didn't. He was very comfortable, very relaxed. When I talked with him I realized that he read more, he was more disciplined and organized, his personal life was more meaningful, and his religion was really way down deep in the marrow of his bones."

"Florida was very important to us," Carter says, "because we knew we could virtually lock up the nomination with a win there. Scoop Jackson had the Jewish vote locked up, and George Wallace the conservative vote. But Rosalynn had already spent 115 days in Florida by the time of the primary. We just covered that state from top to bottom. And I came in first there, and by the time the other campaigns woke up, it was too late. Our opponents' strategy in the weeks to come became what we called ABC, or Anybody But Carter. The campaign managers would go into a state like Pennsylvania or Maryland, and they would decide among them: Who in our group has the best chance of beating Carter in that particular state? The idea was that anything that would slow down our momentum would give all of them a chance. But they couldn't do it. I carried Maryland. I carried Pennsylvania, and by then there was no stopping us from getting the nomination."

The same qualities that had served Jimmy Carter so well in his navy career—honesty, integrity, tireless effort, and the discipline to study issues in detail and be prepared to tackle any question—won him his party's banner in the 1976 election. From the fall of 1975, when he registered below 5 percent in the national polls, he had knocked off one challenger after another, one state after another, and by the middle of summer had a huge lead over Gerald Ford in the polls. The press had nearly anointed him by this time, and many reporters found their way to Plains to learn more about this shining new face on the world scene. There wasn't as much discussion about issues as there was about core values and returning America to a more honest and open time, reminiscent of the 1950s, where skies were blue and father knew best and people were less cynical and more optimistic. And everything about the charming little Georgia community looked and felt wholesome. It was "Mayberry RFD," with Andy and Barney and Goober and Floyd, the barber.

Historian Douglas Brinkley recalled for *American Experience*, the wonderful story of Jimmy's mother Lillian welcoming a woman reporter down from New York to write an "atmosphere piece": "And Miss Lillian greeted her and said, 'Welcome to Plains. You know, it's so nice to see you. Would you like some lemonade? How was your journey? Your dress is beautiful.'

"And the reporter bypassed the hospitality and jumped right in and said, 'Now Miss Lillian, your son is running for president saying he'll never tell a lie. As a mother, are you telling me he's never told a lie?'

"And Miss Lillian goes, 'Oh well Jimmy tells me white lies all the time.'

"And the reporter says, 'Well tell me what . . . what do you mean? What is a white lie?'

"And Miss Lillian says, 'Well, remember when I said, welcome to Plains and how good it is to see you? That's a white lie.'"

Carter and his mother Miss Lillian, 1977

Despite having a fifteen-point lead over Gerald Ford in the polls early in the summer of '76, Carter's lead started to erode in the fall. He was criticized for not being more specific on issues like foreign policy and the economy. A *Playboy* magazine interview, designed to reduce fears about Carter's born-again Christianity, backfired when the candidate said—near the end of the interview when he feared he was being misunderstood—"I've looked on a lot of women with lust. I've committed adultery in my heart many times."

This comment, which could have been made by millions of American men without repercussion or even been applauded for its candor, caused the Carter campaign a collective headache. The line became fodder for late-night talk shows and cartoonists and nearly derailed the entire campaign. But Carter regained his momentum in two televised debates with Ford and was the beneficiary of his opponent's misstep, when Ford said in one of them, "There is no Soviet domination of Eastern Europe, and there never will be under a Ford administration."

The Carter people pounded away on this gaffe just before the election, and by polling day it was a dead heat. The networks didn't declare a winner until 3 a.m. the next morning. In what was one of the closest presidential elections in American history, Jimmy Carter had pulled off the impossible.

While history will be the ultimate judge of the Carter presidency, the former president characterized it to the writer this way: "If you go back and look at what we did as president, I am very proud of it. And I think increasingly it is recognized as being admirable. We normalized relations with China after 35 years. We had the only success in the Middle East that has ever been with the treaty. We kept our country at peace for four years, and we brought peace to others. We doubled the size of the national parks system. We tripled the wilderness area of our country. We were strong environmentally. We had a boom in business. Every oil drilling rig in America was hard at work when I left office. And we had dramatically increased opportunities with foreign oil. We deregulated banks and communications and transportation and airlines and everything else. And there are so many other things. You know, I look back on it as being very successful."

It is obvious that there is still residual pain and a touch of bitterness over Carter's loss to Ronald Reagan in his bid for a second term. When it is suggested that perhaps Reagan used the power of personality to win the election, in the same way Carter had done to defeat Ford in 1976, he eschews that notion.

"It was two things," he says. "One was that the hostages were being held. And that was an embarrassment to everyone and a horrible blight for me. And it happened that the exact one-year anniversary of the hostages being taken was Election Day in 1980. Another thing was that Ted Kennedy decided in late 1979 that he was going to run for president, so he did everything he could from the left wing of the Democratic Party to sabotage my reelection and to promote himself. Later, when I defeated him two to one, much of that support went to John Anderson, whose name has been forgotten, but he was a third-party guy. Remember, Reagan didn't get 51 percent of the vote. But the rest of the votes were divided between me and John Anderson, and a lot of the Democrats, who would have supported me from the left wing of our party, were discouraged by the Kennedy crowd from voting for me. They were a very liberal group, and they did everything they could to support Anderson and to discourage votes for me. And that made a lot of difference. But the hostages being held was obviously very bad timing for me."

Ham Jordan says that the double whammy of the energy crisis and the hostage situation were the main reasons Carter lost the election. "He always did what he perceived to be the right thing, rather than the politically expedient thing," he says. "He was the antithesis of the crafty politician, once he was in office. And I suppose we were naïve in thinking that if we got Carter elected president, then the Democratic Party would coalesce behind him, begin to fall into place, and redefine itself. That obviously was a mistaken notion. It's interesting because Jimmy Carter would have to be called a great politician when it came to campaigning and winning over voters, but it was a different mindset when he was in office. He just didn't weigh political consequences when making a decision.

"I've had a lot of time, obviously, to think about this, and I think the one thing you could say about Carter is that across the board, whether you looked at energy policy, environmental issues, or human rights, he was a president way ahead of his time. I also think about today if we had done some of the things in energy conservation and increased the gasoline tax and set our country on a course of building fuel-efficient cars, we wouldn't be in the mess we are in today in the Middle East. But Carter didn't play the Washington game. And you know, if he had to do it over again, he wouldn't do it much differently."

When the writer suggests that the public perception of Jimmy Carter is that he has been the most productive former president in American history and is thought of as being more effective out of office than in the White House, Carter smiles broadly and gives a slight shake of his head. Months later, President Carter's son Jack would tell the writer, "I have a Republican friend who says, 'You know, your daddy is by far, without qualification, the best ex-president we've ever had. It's a shame he had to be president first.'"

"Political analysts all think and state that I have changed my character," Jimmy Carter says. "You know, I've evolved. I don't think I have ever changed my character. Basically, I have learned. The same things that I tried to do while I was president, I have continued to do since I left the White House. But I have a different thrust, in that I don't have any authority now. I mean, this office [at the Carter Center] that we are sitting in is my total office. But I still have the influence of having been the president of the greatest and strongest nation on earth, and I have access to any foreign leader. And I have the knowledge that I accumulated as governor and president of things that go on in the world. And so we have now evolved the Carter Center into a viable force, not only in holding elections, of which we have held 50 very difficult and troubled elections, but we also negotiate peace agreements, we monitor every conflict in the world every day here. We alleviate suffering and fight major diseases in the world. We promote human life. We take an idealistic but very practical approach to some of the most serious problems that I see."

And it would seem, to his great delight, that Carter can go about his agenda without all the political baggage that accompanies every decision a president makes while in office.

"When I arrived in Venezuela recently, or when I arrive in any country that we serve as a mediator between two disputing factions in a troubled election environment, the first statement that I make is that I have absolutely no authority in that country," he says. "I don't represent the U.S. government. I just represent the small Carter

Center. And I inform them that I am here to offer my services under the constitution and laws, and the rules and regulations of applying workmanship."

Carter insists he is not a kinder or gentler person than he was in his White House years, it's just that he operates under a different set of rules.

With all the attention he has deservedly received for his humanitarian and peace efforts in the last quarter century, Carter once said that he hoped the day would come when nobody perceived that he had a hidden agenda with his charitable efforts. It had been suggested by some cynics that he was quietly campaigning for the Nobel Peace Prize before he actually received it in 2002. It's a topic that he clearly enjoys discussing, especially now that the suspense is over.

"There were two times previously when I thought I would get [the Nobel]," he says. "But I have never in my life asked anybody to recommend me. Other people do ask friends or contemporaries to recommend them. Some years back there was a book written by the Nobel Selection Committee, and it was revealed that in 1978 they voted to give the Prize to Begin, Sadat, *and* me. But when they submitted that list with my name on it to the central headquarters in Stockholm, they found out the rule was that only two people could get it. I didn't know anything about this at the time, and when Begin and Sadat got it I was very gratified, because I didn't make any great sacrifice at Camp David. You know, I did the negotiation, but Sadat later gave his life because of the agreement, and Begin faced horrible controversy when he went back home. So they deserved it."

In 1994, the buzz around Jimmy Carter receiving the Nobel Peace Prize reached such a fever pitch that on the day the recipient was to be announced, hordes of press converged on the Carter Center and set up television and newspaper interview stations in preparation for the announcement. Carter had been out jogging, and when he returned, he saw the gathering and logically made the assumption that he had been honored.

Carter joins hands with Anwar Sadat and Menachem Begin at the historic Camp David Peace talks.

"Earlier that year we had gone to North Korea and probably prevented a war," he says. "And later with Colin Powell, I went down to Haiti, and I don't think there's any doubt we prevented a war there. And a lot of us thought that I would probably get the Prize. Of course, we didn't tell anybody that or campaign for it. But I didn't get it. It went to the head of a relatively unknown little group in London who first started the efforts to control nuclear weapons. And he was very deserving." [The winner that year was Joseph Rotblat and the Pugwash Conferences on Science and World Affairs for their efforts to diminish the part played by nuclear arms in international politics.]

"When it didn't happen in 1994, I just wiped it off my list of expectations. I reasoned that if I didn't receive it that year, well that was it. . . ."

So when the call did arrive, early on a December morning in 2002, the news came as a complete shock.

"The morning the call came, the phone was answered by Rosalynn, because it's on her side of the bed," he recalls. "And it was a Secret Service agent who is from Nicaragua calling, and he was so excited he was speaking in Spanish. And she couldn't quite understand him. I speak Spanish a little better than she does, so I took the phone and he said there was a telephone call from Oslo, Norway, for me and it was the Nobel Prize committee. They wanted me to call them back within an hour, and I got the news. I wasn't even aware that it was the time of year for the selection, so the call caught me totally off guard. That night we celebrated with a glass of champagne. The thrill of that ranks very high on my list of wonderful moments."

As the interview ends, the writer looks around the room for his son J.P., who had been exploring bookshelves and peering out the window at some baby ducks. Not seeing the boy right away, he is concerned that he might have drifted into another part of the building, but then he notices President Carter smiling and nodding towards the back of the room. The boy has taken off his shoes and is sleeping soundly on a long couch. The writer wakes him and mildly scolds him for conking off in the middle of a presidential interview.

"No matter how hard you campaign, you just can't win every vote," says Jimmy Carter, with that unmistakable smile that lifted him all the way from Plains, Georgia, to the most powerful position on earth.

*Admiral William J. Crowe Jr., former
Chairman of the Joint Chiefs of Staff and
Annapolis Class of '47*

CHAPTER TWO
Bill Crowe:

An Unconventional Path

IT'S THE SPRING OF 2005, SOME 36 YEARS SINCE SHIRLEY CROWE AND HER HUSBAND SAT DOWN TO HAVE ONE OF THE MOST SERIOUS CONVERSATIONS OF THEIR LIFE TOGETHER, BUT SHE REMEMBERS IT AS THOUGH IT WERE YESTERDAY.

"Bill had spent his entire life preparing for warfare," she says. "In his heart, he was a warrior. But timing and circumstance had prevented him from ever going to war. When he told me he felt that he should go to Vietnam to be part of this war our country was engaged in, I had a sense that this was in his heart to do. He felt it was the right thing to do, at the right time. After thinking carefully about it for a few days, I had to agree with him."

At that time, late in 1969, their three children, Blake, Brent, and Bambi, were 14, 13, and 11; as Crowe writes in his autobiography, *The Line of Fire*, " they were a handful." But Shirley felt she had a good group of friends in the navy and their neighborhood, and another supportive circle of friends that belonged to their church. Still, it was no easy decision. Bill was 44 years old—beyond the age when most American men were heading off to Southeast Asia—and the body count was rising from week to week. Although not a lot of navy men had been killed in Vietnam, Crowe would be flying helicopters. Between chopper accidents and the Vietcong, there was a good chance he would not return.

"I needed her full support to go," Admiral Crowe says, as we visit at a reception at Annapolis to honor four distinguished graduates of the United States Naval Academy, a distinction also accorded to Crowe and Class of '47 classmates Jimmy Carter and Jim Stockdale. Being honored this day is, among others, industrialist Ross Perot, Class of '53 and a candidate for president in 1992, also a time when Crowe made a bold endorsement that alienated many of his navy brethren. But we'll get to that story later. At the moment, we're flashing back 35 years to one of many wrenching decisions he had to make in his long and glorious career.

"When I elected to go to Vietnam," he says, "Shirley's job, staying behind, was going to be as tough or tougher than mine in going. But she agreed that it was the right thing for me to do. I can't tell you how much respect and appreciation I have for her to make that sacrifice."

Several of Crowe's fellow naval officers who had watched his career with admiration told him he was crazy to go, that he was better off staying stateside operating in his valued role as a military/political analyst. He was, after all, one of the most highly educated men in the navy, with a master's degree in education from Stanford and a doctorate in politics from Princeton. Certainly, he was more valuable in that big-picture capacity than risking his life in a high-mortality zone in a war that had by that time become one of the most divisive conflicts in American history.

Sure enough, on New Year's Day 1970, just a few months after accepting an assignment as a commander in charge of the "brown-water navy," the riverine forces patrolling the Mekong Delta, and just one day shy of his 45th birthday, Crowe had a near brush with death. Whether it was from mechanical failure or being struck by ground fire—he's not sure to this day—Crowe's helicopter crashed into a swamp. As the chopper was going down, Crowe remembers thinking, "I'm not going to make my 45th birthday." But his number wasn't meant to be called that day, and Crowe was able to walk away from the wreckage without serious injury.

Thirty-five years later, Admiral Crowe says he says he still thinks about Vietnam every day—the death and destruction he witnessed and, worst of all, the Vietnamese children burned beyond recognition when entire villages were set ablaze. He frequently shares the perspective of his war experience with present-day midshipmen who are preparing for uncertain conflicts in a world on alert against terrorism.

One of Crowe's prize students, a Rhodes Scholar named Trevor Thompson who graduated number one in the Class of '05 and still found time to serve as captain and all-star first basemen for the USNA team in the Patriot League, says this about his studies with Crowe: "It's just been incredible having a class with Admiral Crowe and having a chance to discuss important issues with him. While most people know where he stands politically, he is so balanced and fair in the way he presents things that if you sat through his class from the first day to the last you would have no idea where his sympathies were politically. He insists that all his students carefully look at both sides of every issue before making the correct decision."

The methodology of analysis that Crowe drills into today's midshipmen sprung from his years as a champion debater, learning to argue the positive side of an issue one day and then make an equally convincing argument on the negative side the next.

In his book, Crowe assesses the many mistakes made in the Vietnam War:

"It took me a while to come to the conclusion that we really did not have ways to solve the problem in Southeast Asia. But once I arrived there, I found myself caught in a kind of moral ambiguity. We were killing and being killed, in support of a [South Vietnamese] government that did not deserve support, at the behest of our own government, which could not figure out how to win. While I did not start wringing my hands over the situation, I was not comfortable with it either. . . .

"For many military people, it was bitter to have fought for so long and at such cost in pursuit of a failed policy. It was even harder to discover that our efforts were not always appreciated and that blame for disastrous political judgments came to rest largely on the military's shoulders. I carried those scars out of Vietnam. I still carry them, as do so many others who fought there. But they also spurred some thought; some of the most important lessons of my life were learned in Vietnam and put to use later."

When Crowe returned to the United States one year after going to Vietnam, he was well aware that his good friend and navy classmate, Jim Stockdale was in his sixth year of confinement in a North Vietnamese prison camp, with no release date in sight. He was more determined than ever to bring his military/political skills into play and hasten the end of the war.

It was clear that Crowe had taken several unconventional turns in his navy life, and his career track toward the eventual rank of Admiral was considered idiosyncratic, but it was also obvious to those in a position to select flag officers that he was a man of exceptional intellect and political savvy, a man deserving of higher command. The next several years would see Bill Crowe assume higher levels of power and adapt smoothly to the responsibilities that such authority brought with it.

Like Jimmy Carter, his classmate at the United States Naval Academy, Bill Crowe was bitten by the navy bug as a child. A picture of the super-dreadnought USS *Pennsylvania* hung over his bed in Oklahoma City, and every night he would stare at it, with its imposing steel hump and two giant forward gun turrets. Bill's father, William Sr., had been a radioman on the *Pennsylvania* when the ship escorted Woodrow Wilson to France in 1918, and he had saved the ship's daily newspapers, which described each day of the voyage as the warship headed toward Brest. These clippings lit the spark of interest for young Crowe, and he read everything he could find about fleets and sea battles. He devoured the family's four-volume history of World War I, and was intimately familiar with the stories of Admiral Dewey and father of the modern navy John Paul Jones, who was interred under the chapel at the Naval Academy. Maybe because the largest body of water Crowe had ever seen was Lake Overholser in Oklahoma, a life at sea seemed incredibly romantic and exciting for a boy growing up in a landlocked state, and Bill dreamed from the age of seven that he would some day attend the Academy.

The leadership skills that would be so instrumental in his career emerged early in Crowe. He was elected president of the student body at Classen High School in Oklahoma City and was a member of the national champion debating team. His skill as an orator and ability to carefully analyze both sides of every issue before opening his mouth, would become one of his single greatest attributes in the decades to follow as he rose through the navy ranks.

After graduating from high school, Crowe enrolled at the University of Oklahoma, where he was elected president of the freshman class. Although his father was a lawyer and shared with his son valuable lessons in ethics and pragmatic thinking, Bill yearned for travel and adventure and knew that he would get plenty of both when he received an appointment to the Naval Academy in 1943.

Crowe calls his first day on campus, in June of 1943, "apprehensive." He felt like a fish out of water. He remembers listening to dark rumors in The Yard from other freshly shorn members during that plebe summer and wondering just how difficult the hazing would be and whether they would be able to keep up with the workload, which they were assured would be considerable. Crowe recalls a commander telling members of his class, "Remember, no matter how dumb you might be, someone dumber than you has already graduated from here." And, in what had become a navy tradition, they were told to look to their left and then to their right when they were in formation and to be assured that one of the three of them would not make it to graduation.

Bill quickly assimilated to the system at the Naval Academy and learned that his quick wit and the powers of persuasion he'd picked up on the debate team would serve him well. The open personality and easy smile that were characteristic of his Oklahoma upbringing would also help him fit in.

"I didn't know anyone in our class who didn't like Bill Crowe," says Vernon Weaver, who has been best of friends with Crowe for over 60 years. "The guys just liked being around him because they could sense his leadership, and yet he was a fun guy who would always make us laugh."

Crowe's 1947 Academy yearbook photo.

Crowe says it wasn't the hazing that bothered him so much in his first weeks and months at Annapolis, but the general lack of civility among the other plebes, especially when it came to women.

"Having attended a state university before I got there, and belonging to a fraternity, I was taught from the first day in college how to treat girls," he says. "But when I got to the Academy, I found that my classmates in general were very naïve about women. There was a lot in the literature that was presented to us about how to be an officer, but very little in our training that encouraged us to be gentlemen." He pauses as he weighs how times have changed. "I'd like to think that attitude has changed dramatically now that we have women in the student body."

Edward Scoles, a Kansas native and another member of the Class of '47, met Bill Crowe his first day on The Yard in 1943. He recalls a voice with an unmistakably Midwestern twang greeting him from the hallway.

"Howdy, welcome aboard," the voice said. "My name's Bill. I live right across the hall, but really I'm from Oklahoma."

Scoles sized up the lanky, half-slouching new plebe, and wondered whether he was a cowboy. Even with all the apprehension that went with his first day in this new world, the friendly greeting is one Scoles remembers vividly over 60 years later.

Edward was pleased to learn that he and Crowe had been assigned to the same cutter crew. It would make a strenuous challenge less so. "Some young men withered under the stress of physical demands and the discipline of plebe summer," Scoles wrote in a 2004 e-mail. "But for Bill, his own determination and the support of his peers insured his survival through the summer. He was thoroughly likable, and his droll sense of humor acted as a catalyst in forging the character of Cutter Crew 310. If we were having difficulty dipping our 12 oars simultaneously into the choppy waters of the Severn River, Bill would be the one to come up with a quip to break the tension and restore our rhythm."

While Scoles describes the young Bill Crowe as gangly and somewhat awkward, and "having a natural talent for looking casual even when standing at rigid attention in a perfectly pressed uniform," he offers praise for Crowe's keen intellect. "If Bill was found wanting in physical coordination, his mind was totally comfortable with facts and concepts. The guy was a brain, excelling in marine engineering, naval ordnance, naval history, math . . . anything requiring concentration and thought. A great talker, though at Oklahoma speeds, he led the debate team and organized round-table discussions on topics of interest. At graduation, Bill would rank in the top ten percent of the Class of '47. Still, when it came to purely military challenges, like attaining rank as a platoon or company commander, he seemed content to be just another midshipman."

"While it's true that Bill was an outstanding student and debater, it's also true that our group of friends liked to party," says Rear

Admiral Ken Sears, also an Oklahoma native. Every time we could legally party, we did, and many times when we weren't supposed to."

"The lights at the Academy went out at a certain hour," says classmate Andy Peacock, who would attend Mine Warfare School with Crowe and remains good friends with him today. "And when that happened, of course, you couldn't study any more, because you couldn't see. So whenever a particularly tough exam was coming up, Crowe would sneak out of his room and head over to Memorial Hall. You always knew when he did this bit, because he'd show up at formation the next day all blurry-eyed, like he'd really had it. Your thought was that he must have stayed awake all night."

Peacock also recalls that he and Crowe taught Sunday school to navy juniors in the chapel. "It was a way for us to get out of chapel," he admits. "I don't think the kids learned much. We were just babysitters, really."

One of the proudest moments in what Crowe describes as "an undistinguished career as a midshipman" was his captaincy of the navy debate team. Crowe led his navy debaters over archrival Army in the national finals, completing the rare double of winning national debating championships in both high school and college.

"The Army team was strongly supported by General Maxwell Taylor, who was superintendent of West Point and later a chairman of the Joint Chiefs of Staff," Crowe says. "The topic was compulsory military training, and he would allow Army to take only the positive side of the issue. Being on the debate team was the single most important educational experience I've had."

One of the moments that fall under the "undistinguished" category was a Sunday night gathering Crowe held in his room in Bancroft Hall. "This colonel I met in the Statler Hotel in D.C. was bragging to me that he'd acquired a taste for sake from being overseas," he says. "So he gave me a bottle but warned me to heat it before drinking or it would not be good. So on a Sunday night, I had a party in my room and put the bottle on a hot plate. It exploded with the cork in it. The guys were lapping it off the furniture, and I remember spraying

Aqua Velva in the air to try and kill the smell. Somehow, I got away with it."

Crowe says the two things he learned right away at the Naval Academy were, first, to get dressed quickly, and, second, to eat quickly. "It's a pretty intense experience to adapt to," he says. "You are actually over-programmed. There weren't counselors there back then, and I think they were needed. The only ones available to offer counseling were your classmates. It's a funny place. I don't know if you like [the Naval Academy] while you're there, but you sure appreciate it later in life."

Despite Crowe's insistence that his career as a midshipman was less than stellar, he graduated 81st in a class of 816, just 26 spots below his classmate Jimmy Carter, and 56 spots below Stansfield Turner, the unquestioned "golden boy" of the Class of '47. Crowe was slightly ahead of his close friend Jim Stockdale, who would serve seven-and-one-half years in a North Vietnam prison and be awarded the Medal of Honor for his heroic behavior, and also ahead of his other very close friend and debate teammate Vernon Weaver, who would go on to serve in the Carter administration and be named U.S. ambassador to the European Union by Bill Clinton.

Following graduation in June of 1946, Crowe was assigned to the USS *Carmick*, a destroyer-sweeper and one of the fastest ships in the navy fleet. He came to love submarines for the same reasons that others might detest them. He liked the tight quarters, the de-emphasis on bathing, and the looser attitudes and less authoritarian demeanors of those forced to live like sardines. He had learned in his latter years at the Naval Academy that he didn't particularly care for an overly rigid environment and in that sense was not a prototypical "military" person. To people who knew Crowe well, it was particularly surprising that he rose so consistently through the ranks in the navy. As Crowe himself says, "no one was more surprised than myself."

Crowe (right) with shipmates aboard the USS *Carmick.*

On July 1, 1948, Crowe entered submarine school at New Haven, Connecticut, beginning a ten-year period during which all of his seagoing was on diesel submarines, including the *Flying Fish*, the *Clamagore*, the *Wahoo*, and the *Trout*, which was his first command. These were small ships, about 2,000 tons, but still about twice the size of German U-boats of World War II. Crowe looks back on this period with great affection, as he loved the rolling seas and huge waves which splashed over the boats. Being a submariner was the fulfillment of all his boyhood dreams, but there was the academic and intellectual side of him that craved for more mental stimulation than he could find at sea.

After his first submarine tour, Crowe still yearned for further academic education. But navy protocol, in the years following WWII, held that post-graduate studies were a waste of time for a Naval officer. In 1950, while serving as an aide to Admiral George Crawford, Crowe expressed to the admiral a desire to apply for post-graduate training. Crawford carefully explained to Crowe that this would be a total waste of time for a forward-thinking officer and even pointed out to him—going page by page through the Naval

Academy register—how the men who had gone on to post-graduate studies had been unable to rise in the ranks in the navy.

But Crowe got Crawford to sign his application anyway, and shortly thereafter he was accepted to Yale University Law School. Unfortunately, just three weeks before the semester began, Congress deleted the funding for the post-graduate program, and Crowe found himself at sea again, this time aboard the diesel submarine USS *Clamagore.*

Fate would intervene again when, 15 months after his assignment to the *Clamagore*, Crowe got word that his father had suffered a heart attack. He flew back to Oklahoma to be with him. The trip turned out to have a doubly happy ending: his father survived the attack, and Crowe met his bride to be, Shirley Grennell, while in Oklahoma. They were married in February of 1954 and celebrated their golden wedding anniversary just two years ago.

Crowe's assignment on the *Clagamore* ended in 1954, at which time he was made an assistant to the naval aide to President Dwight D. Eisenhower. This was his first serious introduction to world of Capitol Hill politics and all the intrigue that accompanied it. He has written, "Even from my modest perch in the White House basement, it was apparent that the fundamental challenge in Washington was to get the various pieces of this huge machine to function together. The notion grew in me that doing that kind of work would be a challenge—utterly different from the world of the submarine officer, with its focus on engineering problems and handling crewmen."

With his administrative and political embers stoked, Crowe once again felt the siren's call of education—he was already taking night law school classes at George Washington University—and in 1956 enrolled at Stanford University, where he would earn a master's degree in education. His thinking was that higher education outside military parameters was the avenue to a more diverse set of horizons, and that the navy needed sailors with knowledge well beyond understanding the strategies of seagoing and war-fighting.

Nearly everything about Stanford appealed to him: the beautiful environment of Palo Alto, the outside-the-box thinking of the intellectuals who roamed the campus, and the freedom to study when and where he wanted. For Crowe, it was a year of stretching his intellectual muscles, and it not only served to broaden his thinking on the role of the military, it also increased his hunger for further study.

Several years later, he would again take a sabbatical to earn a PhD degree in politics as a Harold W. Dodds fellow at Princeton University. In his dissertation, "The Policy Roots of the Modern Royal Navy 1946–53," Crowe, who was by then a commander, stressed the need for the military to adapt to ever-changing conditions in civilian society. The decision to enroll at Princeton was one that was not easily made, but Crowe relied on some advice from a friend, Jay Beam, who was also a commanding officer of a submarine.

"Jay had a practical view on the matter," Crowe recounted in the spring of 2005. "He said, 'You know if you come out and have command of a submarine and you hit a rock, the navy will throw you away without even thinking about it. But if you go to Princeton and get your PhD they can never take it away from you.'

"I thought that was a pretty straightforward way of looking at it," Crowe says, "and it helped make up my mind, even though it meant I would have to pass up Admiral Rickover's offer to join the nuclear submarine program."

On two different occasions, when the iconic Rickover was prepared to select Crowe to join his prestigious submarine program, Crowe chose to go the academic route instead. Bill had applied for the program in 1952 and looked at it as the pinnacle of a sailor's career. He writes, "Nuclear submarines were the cutting edge. For a submariner who wanted to succeed there was no place else to be." But the timing of the admiral's offer to interview came just after Crowe had been accepted at Princeton, and his heart and mind at that point belonged to academia.

Crowe's squadron commander told him he'd have no choice but to accept Rickover's offer if it came. "You can't turn down this chance," the commander said. "Every submarine officer wants to be in that program. Everybody in there is going to make flag [admiral], and they're all going to heaven."

Even though he was aware of Crowe's academic inclinations, Rickover insisted that Crowe come down and see him and do a formal interview for the program, so he followed the order.

"Rickover put it to me directly during that interview," Crowe says. "He said, 'If I accept you for this program, are you ready to go right now?'

"And I replied, 'Well, I really want the program and if you accept me I would be honored to do it just as soon as I finish my studies at Princeton.'" Crowe had two years remaining to earn his doctorate.

Crowe said that wasn't what Rickover wanted to hear, and Rickover threw him out of his office, but not until he had browbeat him further.

"Goddamit!" Rickover snarled at him. "A PhD isn't worth anything. Who gives a damn about a PhD? You just want something to secure your civilian existence. You're just looking to get out of the navy, that's what you're doing."

When Crowe is reminded of how his classmate Jimmy Carter idolized Rickover and considered him the great role model of his life, Crowe just nods his head and smiles. "There were two distinctly different Admiral Rickovers," he says. "Carter is very romantic about the whole thing. Rickover was a celebrity, but he was considered by many to be a mean man, very hard driving and narrow-minded. What he did by making inroads in Congress was an achievement. The nuclear submarine program would have come anyway, but it was quicker because of Rickover. But there's no doubt that many questioned my decision to pass up his offer and finish at Princeton. They thought it would definitely stall my advancement in the military. As difficult as it was to make at the time, I have always looked back on it as the right decision."

At Princeton, Crowe was exposed to great instructors like George Kennan, the American diplomat whose writings had in great part shaped the American political policy of containment after World War II; sociologist Marion Levy; and James Billington, who was an expert on the Soviet Union and would go on to become the librarian of Congress. As Crowe writes, "These were people with superb intellects and the ability to conceptualize in a nuanced fashion, which I had never before encountered."

The navy had always operated by the book and according to rigid standards, and here Crowe was meeting fellow students and professors who had a far broader worldview; he loved the challenge of problem solving with new and inventive methodologies.

"From an intellectual standpoint, Princeton was a world-shaking experience," Crowe says. "It fundamentally changed my approach to life and made me appreciate the complexities of political systems and issues."

It is this broader worldview that Crowe endeavors to share with his students at the Naval Academy today. He has invited, as guest lecturers to his class, journalists like Eleanor Clift, a regular on *The McLaughlin Group*, and Bob Woodward, the prolific author and investigative reporter who, with his partner Carl Bernstein, broke the Watergate scandal story that brought down Richard Nixon's presidency.

Crowe relished the moment in 2003 when Woodward, after speaking for much of the hour about his frustration with the amount of privacy and secrecy there is in politics, faced the following question from a female student: "Since you dislike secrecy so much, Mr. Woodward, why don't you tell us who your sources are?"

"That really stumped him," Crowe says, laughing. "That was a moment in our class that I'll never forget."

The Princeton experience opened Crowe to new ways of viewing the world and America's role in it. Once again, he learned the value of applying deep thinking to situations, rather than just reacting in the traditional navy mode. As he wrote in his book, "Clearly the navy is more than a job; it is a way of life (as all the services are). And the culture captures its members, and it encapsulates them . . . Princeton forced me to become more analytical and more tolerant than I had previously been. It challenged me to reassess some of my more conventional and ingrained navy views. It was one of the things that set me somewhat apart from many of my colleagues, that at times made my career so tenuous, but that also lifted it up. I became more willing to question, to reexamine, to argue for alternatives."

Just as he had as a debating champion, Crowe learned to argue convincingly on both sides of an issue. He says that when he would meet with navy classmates during his years at Princeton, some would come away thinking he had become a raving liberal and others would align him with Genghis Khan. That ability to keep people off balance with his arguments and to offer totally convincing yet unpredictable viewpoints is one that he still has to this day.

Naturally, when Crowe had completed his doctorate, he took a lot of good-natured ribbing back in the navy. Some accused him of being educated well beyond his intelligence level. A squadron commander gave him this introduction one day: "This is Dr. Crowe, but I wouldn't trust him to put a damn Band-Aid on me."

The inherent conflict between Crowe's time in academia and the culture of the navy came to a head when he returned to the office of naval operations in the late '60s. His office was in the Pentagon, in an area called OP 61, the navy's political-military branch. He was assigned the job of heading the East Asian desk, which dealt with the entire Pacific region. Crowe had not been in the post long when he submitted a paper suggesting that the navy take a particular course of action that diverged from the standard approach. His boss, a four-stripe deputy director of the office, called Crowe into his office after reading it and unloaded on him. He told Crowe that the navy hadn't sent him to Princeton so he could come back and instruct his superiors on how to run the navy. As Crowe writes in his book, the directive went something like this: "We sent you up there to learn how to argue for the things we want done back here [at the Pentagon], not to listen to what you think are original ideas. We're not going to do a single one of the things you've got in this report."

Crowe recalled in a 2005 interview for this book, how he got another reminder that he could take his advanced education only so far in the navy. It came in 1968 when the head of plans and policy for the navy, Vice Admiral Francis Blouin, called Crowe down one day and said, "All these people who work for me, they don't understand Vietnam. I was out there when [South Vietnam's President Ngo Dinh] was assassinated, and our people here don't understand the good guys from the bad guys. Anyway, I want you to go back and dig out the Geneva Accord and write a paper that I can distribute which makes it clear why we're the good guys and why they [the North Vietnamese] are the bad guys."

Crowe assigned the research for the paper to a staffer named Dick Knott, who would later marry Colin Powell's daughter. Crowe and Knott discovered that, although North Vietnam was clearly in violation of the Geneva Accord, the United States was also a culprit. Not only had the U.S. not actually signed the accord, it had pledged to not use force to disturb its provisions.

"The truth was, we were violating the hell out of the accords," Crowe says, "so I wrote a balanced paper, but I didn't disguise anything, and I said that the U.S. had done this and this and that, and that's not what we should have done.

"Well, Blouin wasn't happy when he read that paper, to say the least. Gosh, he was mad. It got so bad that he called a meeting with all the people on the plans and policy staff. He was afraid that the opinions I expressed in the paper might be prevalent among the entire staff, so he made certain that everyone knew just who was in the right and who was in the wrong."

Understandably, Crowe was conflicted by this turn of events. He had been given an assignment and he had followed the facts judiciously, but the navy wasn't as interested in the facts as it was in presenting the American side of things. Crowe went to his superior, Rear Admiral Blackie Weinel, and told him that he could not in good conscience rewrite the paper that the navy wanted—it would go against everything he had learned at Princeton about presenting the facts in a well researched and balanced way.

Weinel told him, "I understand your problem, but I can tell you that I'm not part of your solution." Weinel advised Crowe to put the paper in his desk and never mention it again. He was certain that Blouin wouldn't bring it up again either. And he didn't.

Another crash course in the delicate balance of navy politics occurred in January of 1968, when the USS *Pueblo*, a light cargo ship that had been converted into an intelligence-gathering vessel, was captured and surrendered to North Korean patrol boats. It was not certain whether the ship's captain, Commander Lloyd Bucher, had penetrated territorial waters, but when he ignored North Korean demands and headed out to open waters, the *Pueblo* was fired upon. One American crewman was killed and several others seriously injured.

With the entire American crew held captive by the North Koreans, there was confusion on several points, including whether Bucher had violated the essential navy credo of "Never give up the ship," whether the intelligence manuals had been completely destroyed before the ship was captured, and a host of other issues. The incident became a huge public relations disaster for the navy, and congressmen and senators, nearly all of whom had constituents directly involved in the crisis, wanted quick answers. Crowe was assigned the task of answering nearly 1,000 congressional letters, and he had to do so with flimsy evidence about what had actually occurred.

President Johnson, consumed by the raging war in Vietnam, had to determine what economic penalties to invoke on North Korea, and he even contemplated a military strike against the country. Of course, such action might further alienate a nation already divided over the ever-rising death toll in Southeast Asia.

"I've always thought that the political ramifications over the *Pueblo* event would make a great political science course for a semester," Crowe says. "We had the *Pueblo* repatriation plan [which Crowe himself wrote], that virtually everyone disagreed with. The intelligence community was upset at Bucher for not doing a better job destroying intelligence before the ship was captured, we had the navy legal community that wanted to know everything that had occurred but didn't want to jeopardize a legal case against the commander, and we had a state department that wanted the public to think that everything Bucher had done was totally above board and that the Commander and his crewmen were heroes."

Even as Crowe spent nearly the entire year of 1968 studying and strategizing the best way to handle all of the delicate issues surrounding the capture of the *Pueblo*, his thoughts were never far from his close friend and classmate Jim Stockdale, who was in his third year of solitary confinement in a North Vietnamese prison. Little had been said or written about *these* clearly heroic American POWs, and yet the men of the *Pueblo* were being treated as heroes even before they returned home.

Stockdale's wife, Sybil, was particularly incensed by the government's handling of the affair, as she conveys in the book she co-wrote with her husband, *In Love and War:*

"Publicity about the welfare of these [*Pueblo*] men ran rampant through all the media," Sybil wrote. "The tremendous amount of attention the incident received in the press doubled my frustration and agony over [POW and MIA wives'] guidelines for silence about our men in North Vietnam. The wife of the *Pueblo*'s captain was extremely critical of the U.S. government in the press. There was a bitter feeling of resentment about her among the POW wives in San Diego. We felt her public criticism of her own government demeaned her service and her country in the eyes of the world. It was also terribly frustrating to have all the hullabaloo about the *Pueblo* prisoners going on in the press while nothing was being said by our own government about our men in North Vietnam."

Soon after the capture of the *Pueblo*, U.S. Secretary of State Dean Rusk declared that the ship had not violated territorial waters, even though the navy was decidedly unclear on that matter. This made the situation even dicier, because the capture of the ship had been so heavily publicized—and the matter so contentious—that whatever response the navy gave would prove divisive.

When the crew was returned to the U.S. 11 months after they were taken captive, Crowe was given the assignment of interviewing all the sailors to find out what had actually happened and to determine the culpability of the U.S.

Crowe assured the men that nothing they told him would be used outside of his own investigation, not even in any future court proceedings.

Although there was strong sentiment in military ranks that Commander Bucher should face court-martial proceedings for giving up his ship so readily, public opinion was clearly on his side. Even if Bucher was to blame, he had spent 11 months as a prisoner, and the general feeling was that he had suffered punishment enough. Although a court of inquiry came out with a recommendation of a court-martial for Bucher, a trial would not happen.

Crowe underscored the eventual result of the *Pueblo* crisis in his book: "This was not justice, perhaps, but justice was not the pole around which this event flowed. There was the public consensus; there were the needs of the navy as a living organization. The conflict was between those two, and political necessity ordained the outcome."

⚓ —— ⚓

After his year in Vietnam, and despite doing everything in his power to extend his stay there, Crowe was called back to Washington to become a military representative in negotiations to end the U.N. Trusteeship of Micronesia. He had misgivings about this unusual assignment. Crowe felt that his best shot at making admiral was to be given a significant sea command. Yet, here he was, not technically working for the navy, but employed as a civilian with an office in the Department of Interior.

So it came as a great surprise to Crowe when, in early 1973, he was elevated to the rank of rear admiral. His unconventional career as a part-time academic and an advisor in sensitive political military issues had not gone unnoticed by the secretive navy selection board. And as usual, even the way he was selected was highly unusual. He learned later that when the cut-down was made from 1,400 captains to the 30 admiral openings, his name had not made the final list. But someone on the board, as per the rules, had requested additional discussion on his candidacy. When Crowe's eclectic résumé was examined more closely, he was deemed worthy of admiral rank.

Once that honor was accorded, Crowe's career took on added luster, and high command started to see what an exceptional navy man he had become. Although he had fewer sea commands than many of his peers, he had experience in a number of prestigious areas, including international affairs, strategic planning, and political/military affairs.

When the Vietnam War ended and political interests shifted to other parts of the world, Crowe became a viable candidate for a number of positions. He was named commander of a Middle East task force headquartered in Bahrain in 1976–1977. From there, he was promoted to vice-admiral and appointed deputy chief of naval operations, a position he held for three years.

Then, in May of 1980, he accepted an extremely challenging position as the NATO Commander-in-Chief for Southern Europe. By then he was a four-star admiral, and this position put forces from five countries under his command. It was a prestigious assignment with a glamorous base in Naples, Italy, at the foot of Mt. Vesuvius, but it was also full of new challenges. Crowe's staff included army, navy, and air force officers from all the NATO countries with forces in the Mediterranean: Greece, Turkey, Italy, the U.S., and Great Britain. His command also cooperated with France and maintained friendly contacts with Portugal and Spain, which was in the early stages of NATO entry. By far the biggest challenge he faced in his leadership role was mediating the rivalries between Greece and Turkey.

As NATO Commander, Crowe was in charge of three or four military exercises every year, and getting Turkey and Greece to agree to the ground rules was next to impossible. In almost every instance, each side would lay down conditions for the exercises that they knew the other side would never accept. When Crowe would meet with the country's leaders to iron out the differences, they would invariably agree to his proposals and then change their minds and issue press releases announcing their opposition to the plans. The job required the highest degree of diplomacy and patience. But the NATO command proved to be ideal training for the next level in Crowe's career.

Crowe during a NATO exercise, 1982.

In 1983, Admiral Bill Crowe was appointed CINCPAC—commander-in-chief of the Pacific forces. It was a huge assignment, but one he felt more prepared for than any of his previous posts. The year before, it had been rumored that he was going to be named CINCLANT—commander-in-chief of the Atlantic forces, but that position went to another member of the Class of '47, Admiral Wesley McDonald. It was one of the few times that two members of the same military class had been named to such high positions of responsibility.

Crowe's responsibilities as CINCPAC extended from the West Coast of the U.S. to the Far East and from the Aleutians to Antarctica, an expanse covering 100 million square miles, or about half the globe, which meant he was in charge of the largest unified command in the U.S. military structure.

Historically, Crowe says the role of CINCPAC was to be the "Paul Revere of the Pacific," ever ready to holler "The Russians are coming! The Russians are coming!" But after Crowe and his staff had spent months assessing the situation, they determined that the Soviet Union in the mid-1980s was not a viable economic or military threat to the Pacific region. Despite that assessment, he felt there was no good reason to back off military posturing or force.

In his book, Crowe said, "Developments of vast moment have a habit of materializing unexpectedly. . . . Our policy of being forward deployed in order to deal with unforeseen events and uncertainties and to express interest in our friends' welfare has been consistently successful in the past and should not be lightly cast aside."

Japan was the most significant nation on Crowe's beat as CINCPAC, and his assessment was that the Japanese didn't spend an appropriate amount of money or manpower on their own security, relying too heavily on the American defense umbrella. But during this time, even North Korea was surprisingly quiet and had backed off some of its more contentious statements against the U.S. Crowe's overall assessment was that the United States was generally better off in his vast area of command than any place else in the world. So rather than maintaining a reactionary posture against aggression, Crowe and his staff were able to rework plans to take maximum advantage of America air and sea superiority to bolster U.S. confidence that it could ward off Soviet forces if the need arose.

By the spring of 1985, chairman of the Joint Chiefs of Staff General John Vessey was preparing to step down, despite the urgings of President Ronald Reagan to finish out a second term. A year earlier, Crowe and other top-ranking officers had accompanied Vessey on an historic trip to China, the first visit by a high-ranking American military delegation since the Communist takeover of the mainland in 1949. Later, President Regan visited China and came through Hawaii, Crowe gave a ninety-minute status report on the Pacific region to Reagan and the other officials, and had done so with his usual insightfulness and humor. By all accounts, his extemporaneous speaking skills were at a high polish, and he never once referred to a note. It was reported by several media outlets that when Reagan returned home, he mentioned to Defense Secretary Caspar Weinberger and said, "If we ever need a new chairman, I have found the guy."

By the next year, according to the Washington rumor mill, the field of potential candidates for chairman had been reduced to two, Crowe and Chief of Naval Operations Jim Watkins.

Crowe felt that, in his words, he was "too far from the flagpole" to be named chairman of the Joint Chiefs. When Watkins asked to see Crowe in his Washington office, the two contemporaries laughed about all the rumors, but Crowe saw that Watkins was every bit as in the dark as he was about the imminent selection. The silence prevailed for another month, until Colin Powell, who was then the military assistant to Weinberger, told Crowe that the secretary of defense wanted to meet with him. In early June of 1985, the champion debater from Oklahoma, the rumpled young man who by his own admission didn't make a very good midshipman and who had finished lower than 80 of his classmates at the Naval Academy, assumed the position of the highest ranking military officer in the country.

But when the honor came, Crowe accepted it with as much ambivalence as enthusiasm. He well knew the pressures and demands the job would have on him, and once again it would cause his family to make sacrifices. Still, as always, Shirley was fully supportive of her husband's promotion and all the responsibilities that came with it, and she concurred with the decision to accept the offer.

At his swearing-in ceremony on October 1, Admiral Crowe made it clear that his top priority was to eliminate inter-service rivalry, which he said was to blame for wasteful expenditures on both missions and weapons systems, and that had also caused loss of life. He felt that lack of coordination among the services had been responsible for the failure of the hostage rescue mission in Iran in 1980, an event that had directly affected two of his classmates, Admiral Stansfield Turner, at the time director of the CIA, and President Jimmy Carter, who would later cite the Iranian hostage crisis as the single most important reason for his defeat to Ronald Reagan in the presidential election later that year.

Crowe felt that inter-service rivalries also led to confusion on the ground during the invasion of Grenada in 1983. In his speech Crowe said that "there has never been a greater need for joint operations, joint thinking, and joint leadership as we meet the global challenges, and in order to get the most out of our finite resources."

Eventually, a bill calling for an entire realignment of the armed services was passed in Congress. The Goldwater-Nichols Act gave Crowe considerably more power and allowed him to report to the president by giving his own opinions on geopolitical matters, untainted by the composite views of the service chiefs. Another provision of the bill transferred some of the civilian staffs of the secretaries of the army, navy, and air force to the Joint Chiefs of Staff. The realignment brought the number of personnel under Crowe to more than 1,600.

"The pressure was building in Congress," Crowe says in 2005, "and we finally got that bill through. I certainly supported it, and the air force and army supported it, but the navy and marine corp had reservations, which led to people believing that I had not supported the navy and marines sufficiently. That was a difficult period . . . very contentious."

⊰———⊱

Certainly a low point of Crowe's time as chairman of the Joint Chiefs occurred in July of 1988, when the USS *Vincennes*, having every reason to believe that it was about to be attacked by an Iranian Air Force F-14 fighter jet, shot down an aircraft that turned out to be an Iranian airbus carrying 230 passengers. After careful examination of all the facts of the situation, no charges were filed against the captain of the *Vincennes*, Captain Will Rogers, but the political ramifications on the U.S. military were unfortunate. Crowe drafted, and gave the media the news.

Crowe publicly expressed the government's deep regret for the loss of life, but he also placed the incident in its total context: he explained the action the *Vincennes* was engaged in at the time, the recent background of attacks on American ships in the region, how the approaching aircraft had been heading directly at the cruiser and had ignored repeated warnings to turn away, and how the ship's captain had an ultimate responsibility to protect his vessel. He explained how the Iranians had shown a callous indifference to life by flying a civilian airliner directly above an area that they themselves had turned into a battle zone.

The press briefing was a decidedly unpleasant task, but Crowe was careful to say more than a dozen times that first reports are inherently sketchy and often contain factual errors. Sure enough, two years after his retirement from chairman of the Joint Chiefs, Crowe was taken to task by a joint report from *Newsweek* magazine and ABC's *Nightline*, which claimed that the *Vincennes* incident constituted a "cover-up" and a "conspiracy" against the American people. Crowe would later testify for three hours about the affair to the House Armed Services Committee and refute the allegations of a cover-up. The committee apparently agreed with Crowe's assessment and the matter was dropped. As Crowe writes in his book, "Of course, it was not possible to correct all the damage the article had caused, as it rarely is when the media badly misstep."

All in all, Crowe enjoyed an excellent reputation with the media during his time as chairman of the Joint Chiefs of Staff, although he admits that he probably received more attention from a seven-minute acting stint playing himself on the hit television show *Cheers* than he ever did in his years of military and political power. For years afterward people would come up to Crowe, tell him they had seen him on the show, and congratulate him on doing a great job, even though, he says, "they probably didn't have the foggiest notion what it was that I actually did."

Crowe appeared twice on the news magazine show *60 Minutes*, often a dicey proposition for someone in high office. But Crowe's overall feeling was that Mike Wallace and the show treated him fairly. It all came about, as Crowe told his Naval Academy class in 2005, when Crowe's public affairs officer, Jay Coupe, told him that he could get him on *60 Minutes*. This was far down on Crowe's list of things he wanted to do, especially after the infamous lawsuit five years earlier between General William Westmoreland and CBS News over a story Wallace had done claiming Westmoreland had falsified enemy troop strength in Vietnam.

Crowe at media press conference, 1989.

Nevertheless, Coupe argued that this could be a good thing for Crowe and the military, so Crowe decided to take the gamble. He started to review stories Wallace had done for *60 Minutes* and found that his reporting, while at times aggressive and hard-edged, was on balance fair and informative. Crowe approached the impending interview with the same level of preparation he had used to get ready for debates in high school and at the Academy. He even employed a group called the Air Force Media Training Team to conduct formal mock interviews with him and ask controversial and even embarrassing questions. The training team was even allowed to ambush him in the hallways when his mind might have been elsewhere.

By the time the multi-session interview was conducted, Crowe was more than prepared, and even those in the Pentagon, who were most skeptical about giving Mike Wallace entrée to their world, found that the resulting piece on *60 Minutes* was positive and beneficial to their cause.

In June 1989, Crowe convinced Pentagon officials and the Russian government to allow him to bring Mike Wallace and *60 Minutes* to Russia, the first time a Chairman of the Joint Chiefs had been invited to visit the Soviet Union since World War II. This was a real breakthrough for Wallace, who never expected to receive the invitation, and it showed to the American people a human side of Russia that they'd never seen before. It reinforced in Crowe that the relationship between the press and the military, often filled with suspicion, can be mutually beneficial as long as honesty prevails and there is a fair exchange of give and take.

To his Naval Academy class in April 2005, he had this to say: "Whether you like or dislike the press, it is not going to go away. It is here for all time. It is part of our culture, part of our system, and no matter how you come out on the issue of how much influence or power the press has, it is a very important institution and it does influence the outcome of many security subjects and is a constant source of discussion and decision-making in the military."

Crowe added this historical perspective: "In the ongoing posturing between the media and the military, Vietnam was really the biggest factor. In WWII, the world was different in that the press considered itself very much a part of the war effort against Hitler. There was less criticism, and the press subjected itself to censorship without much screaming and hollering. But by the time Vietnam came around, we had this tremendous development called "television" which brought some of the dark sides of the war right into living rooms. The political environment had changed a great deal. It was no longer considered unpatriotic to criticize, as it had been in World War II. If Vietnam didn't do anything else, it truly split asunder a working relationship between the press and the military—particularly the Army—which bore the brunt of the news. The Army literally came out of Vietnam very, very disillusioned with the media. And many career officers were more than prepared to do direct battle with the press and to take issue with not only the accuracy of their reporting, but with the basic fundamental rationale of the media. From a military perspective, many wondered whether the free press was worth it. The schism has slowly moderated," Crowe says, "but it hasn't gone away completely."

Crowe freely shares insights about the delicate dance between the media and the military with his students, and few are more qualified to talk on this subject. He says that one of the alarming lessons he learned upon becoming chairman of the Joint Chiefs was that leaking information to the press was not the sole purview of politicians. There were an alarming number of leaks coming from military personnel at even the highest levels, and the reasons were many and varied. Sometimes the leak occurs to discredit specific policies or operations that the leaker opposes. Other times it might be because the leaker enjoys seeing something he said appear in the newspaper, or it might be to gain favor with a reporter who might be useful to him or her some time in the future.

Crowe recalls a time as chairman of the Joint Chiefs when he walked out of his office in the Pentagon and encountered David Martin, who was the defense correspondent for one of the major networks.

"David was clearly upset," Crowe says, "so I asked him what the matter was. He said, 'That gawd-dang leaker lied to me.'

"I had to think about that one awhile," he says. "Here was a reporter doing business with a leaker, and leaking is against the law or at least the code of conduct of the person passing on the information, and David was upset because the man wasn't totally honest. It's an interesting dilemma. So I said to David, 'Well, if you'll give me his name, I'll fix his clock.' But he wouldn't give me his name."

Crowe's advice to his Naval Academy students was that first of all you have to be truthful in dealing with the media. He says if you are going to be embarrassed by the answer to a question, you should never fabricate an answer just to satisfy the press, because if you get caught doing that, your credibility is totally shot. If the information being sought will be embarrassing to you, or the information is classified, or if you feel it is not the press's right to know something, then his advice is simply not to answer the question.

Because of his congenial personality and gift with language, Crowe always enjoyed a good relationship with the media. "I feel that if you can convince the press that you are giving them everything that is within your capability to give them, that meets your own standards and doesn't jeopardize national security, they will play ball with you. And they will appreciate your efforts, and you will in return get some good and fair treatment. But sometimes I think of something told me by a fellow board member at Merrill Lynch. He said, 'If you can fake sincerity, you've got it made.' And I would say that I've applied that once or twice with the press, and it has worked.

"I think the military sometimes think we have a corner on patriotism," he adds, "but the members of the media think that what they are doing by practicing our First Amendment right of free speech and disseminating information to the public is just as much in the American tradition as what we are doing, and you always have to keep that in mind. We may not like the way they do it, and we may not like what they say, but they have a solid rationale for their business."

Earlier that day, in a private interview, Crowe had shared his opinion about the problems with the military's culture of regimentation. He talked about how it bothers him that the lockstep behavior encouraged and taught by the military in peacetime does not adequately prepare our men and women to be leaders who can adjust to the unique elements of war, which necessitate flexibility and the ability to weigh complex issues and react appropriately, often against limited time constraints.

"Too much management makes everything predictable," he says.

In his book Crowe wrote, "During World War II, Eisenhower had to discard a series of commanders before he found some who had the necessary qualities. In the Pacific during that war, the navy sometimes turned rigidity into an art form—in the way we initially used our submarine force, for example, or in the early refusal to acknowledge that our torpedoes simply did not work. Struggling with this problem during the Gulf crisis convinced me that flexibility of thought was our single most crucial need."

Crowe likes to use a line at commencement exercises to illustrate this point: "Your mind," he'll tell graduates, "is a lot like a parachute—it won't help you much if it doesn't open when you need it."

And Crowe's own unconventional path to military leadership certainly underscores his argument. At several junctures in his career—the academic detours to Stanford and Princeton, turning down Admiral Rickover's offer of a prestigious position in the nuclear submarine program, the unlikely tour of duty in Vietnam in his mid-40s—Crowe went against conventional wisdom and pursued the course that felt right to him. And in each of those situations, the decision broadened his worldview and prepared him better for the responsibilities that came his way.

⊰ — ⊱

In the fall of 1987, as the Intermediate Nuclear Forces (INF) Treaty began to accelerate to a conclusion and relations with the Soviet Union were improving dramatically, Crowe entertained the idea of having personal meetings with the Chief of Staff of the Soviet armed forces, Marshal Sergei Akhromeyev, who had made a favorable impression on several American diplomats, including Secretary of State George Shultz. Most American observers felt that Akhromeyev was a strong and intelligent leader with a flexible mind and an engaging manner, and that, most importantly, he had the ear of Soviet President Mikhail Gorbachev. From all Crowe heard, his Russian counterpart was very much like himself, so he felt that personal meetings with him could lead to further harmony with our long-time enemy as the Cold War continued to rapidly defrost.

When Crowe met Akhromeyev during the INF Treaty signing, he extended a personal invitation to him to come back to the United States for an extended visit the following year to see our country beyond the confines of Washington, D.C. He even invited the Soviet

leader to visit his home state of Oklahoma, where the Russian could
see "the real United States."

Crowe shaking hands with Marshall Akhromeyev.

When the time for the visit arrived, Akhromeyev brought with him
a full contingent of Russian generals from the various armed forces.
To take full advantage of the political opportunities this presented,
Crowe set an agenda that would show them the full strength of
the American military. This included a visit to the USS *Theodore
Roosevelt*, the navy's newest nuclear carrier. There the Russians
witnessed some target bombing drills and wire-arrested landings.
They were more than impressed with seeing U.S. aircraft come
aboard the ship at 140 knots, then hit the wire and stop dead within
200 feet. While some in the American military hierarchy felt that
Crowe was giving away important secrets, the display accomplished
what the chairman of the Joint Chiefs had set out to do: show the
Russians the felt extent of American technology and give them a full
appreciation for our military capabilities.

In long discussions with Akhromeyev over the next couple days, Admiral Crowe saw that his counterpart's mission for the trip was twofold: to convince Crowe that the Soviet military machine was not the threat the U.S. perceived it to be, and to make it known that the Soviet security establishment firmly believed that the United States represented a major threat to his country.

On plane flights to military bases, Crowe took the opportunity to educate Akhromeyev on historical and cultural aspects of the United States: how the fledgling nation expanded west from the original colonies, the integral role of the railroad in connecting American communities, how entrepreneurship and a "can do" attitude was at the heart of America's growth and success.

Akhromeyev was a good listener and promised to take all he was learning back to General Secretary Gorbachev. The talks provided an ideal opportunity for Crowe to use his vast education and people skills to further dissolve cultural barriers between the U.S. and the Soviet Union.

On subsequent visits to Texas and then Oklahoma, Akhromeyev quickly picked up on the rivalry between the two states. When he made his final toast at a Chamber of Commerce dinner in San Antonio, the Russian ingratiated himself to the Texans by announcing through his interpreter that when he arrived in Oklahoma, he would tell the waiting crowd that he had left his heart in Texas. Crowe relates in his book that "when I repeated this story in Oklahoma, everybody had a good laugh. To them, it just proved that Texans will believe anything."

Akhromeyev also got a kick out of meeting two female military leaders, one of them the crew chief of an F-16, the other a first lieutenant at a missile training installation. Seeing women in positions of governmental authority was foreign to this old-guard Russian leader.

When they parted company after Akhromeyev's one-week stay, he startled Crowe by telling him. "Admiral, you know you and I have become very friendly. I think you and I can talk to each other. But I must tell you, I still believe the prospects for your country attacking mine are very high."

Akhromeyev had invited Crowe to reciprocate and visit Russia the following year, and Crowe promised he would. By the time Crowe scheduled his visit in June of 1989, Akhromeyev had stepped down as Russia's chief military official and was then in the position of Gorbachev's special assistant. Crowe was hoping to find that the friendship he had forged with the Russian the year before in the U.S. hadn't cooled off, and he was assured when Akhromeyev greeted him with a bear hug and kisses on both cheeks.

Their conversations picked up as naturally as they had left off, but Akhromeyev was still unwavering in his position that the Russians were simply preparing a "defensive" military complex, one that was readying for the inevitable attack by the U.S. But there had been progress towards neutrality made on both sides. An agreement had been reached the previous year to form a joint military group between the two countries with the purpose of averting incidents that might escalate to crisis proportions. And it was determined that future, direct talks would be held between Soviet and American military leaders to resolve any technical problems that stood in the way of agreement on reductions in conventional forces.

Gorbachev had told Akhromeyev, upon his return from the U.S., that he had made a fundamental decision to change the direction of Soviet foreign policy, and Crowe was told that to demonstrate their good intentions, the USSR. would be making unilateral reductions in land forces on both their southern and eastern borders.

Skepticism ran high back in the U.S. after Crowe conveyed Akhromeyev's promises. Colin Powell's reaction, according to Crowe's book, was to say, "I don't believe it. You can't take a guy like that at his word. It's just not Russian."

Crowe fully understood after his visit why the Russians still harbored hatred for the Germans, and why the ruling Communist Party continued to promote the victorious war effort as proof that communism worked. Crowe learned that of all the males born the same year as Sergei Akhromeyev—1923—fully 80 percent of them had lost their lives in World War II. Akhromeyev told Crowe that of the 32 boys in his high school class, only two had survived the war, himself and one other. It was estimated that 25 to 30 million Russians died during WWII.

Despite all the devastation and poverty the war brought to the country, communist leaders still pointed proudly to their leadership during the conflict, even though many military historians regard the outcome as something of a Pyrrhic victory for the country.

Before they parted, Akhromeyev amended his comment from the previous year and told Crowe that he felt the likelihood of a major war between the two countries was at its lowest point in years.

The two leaders kept in touch after retirement, and Crowe accepted another invitation to visit Russia in early 1990, after he'd retired as chairman of the Joint Chiefs. He and Akhromeyev went into the Russian countryside and met with common people to gauge their feelings about the political and economic climate of the Soviet Union, clearly in a major downturn. Crowe spoke with the manager of a collective farm, who told him that if he had John Deere tractors and other modern equipment—the kind that didn't break down constantly—his farm could be 10 times more productive. And he said that if his group could own the land privately, they would be far more productive than they currently were. Of course, this went dead against the grain of communism, and Crowe was taken aback when Akhromeyev objected strenuously to the man's claims, even getting into a loud argument with him.

Crowe also met with a woman political official who complained that of all those voted into office in the recent elections, less than two percent were women. Women were simply not interested in running, even though the political system was digressing in every direction away from communism.

Akhromeyev was depressed and bitter during the trip, and far more argumentative than he had been on previous meetings with Crowe. He hated the fact that communist rule in Russia was dissipating and that America was growing stronger in direct proportion to the weakening of his homeland. The Russian military leader had also become disillusioned with course of events.

A few months after his trip to Russia, Crowe received a letter from Akhromeyev, reporting that things were looking increasingly bleak in his country. Crowe heard from a Russian officer that he had complained that his own daughter didn't understand him, that she thought his ideas were outdated, and that she was urging him to keep his views silent and stay out of the way. Shortly afterwards, Akhromeyev was walking down the street in his marshal's uniform and people spit on him and threw things at him. The day after that happened, Akhromeyev committed suicide.

Crowe wrote, "I did not really think he would commit suicide . . . but when I began to think about it, I was not too surprised. The basic problem was that Akhromeyev could never bring himself to the conclusion that most of the bad things that were happening so quickly in his last year were the fault of the system, the fault of communism itself. This required one intellectual leap too many."

⊰ — ⊱

Crowe stepped down as chairman of the Joint Chiefs in 1989, despite the fact that the Goldwater-Nichols Act of 1986 had given him more authority. President Bush asked him to extend his service, but health was an issue.

After nearly 50 years in the navy, Bill Crowe was also eager to enjoy life as a civilian. Over the next several years, he would get a first-hand look at the corporate world, since he was asked to serve on several prestigious boards of directors, including Pfizer, Merrill Lynch, General Dynamics, Norfolk and Southern, and Texaco.

Crowe came to understand and appreciate the symbiotic relationship between government and business, and how industry can be sustained—or deterred—by governmental policy. He feels there would be great benefit in finding ways for people who are moving into senior leadership positions in the military to experience the practical challenges that face the private sector daily.

He has written, "Once you have laid down your tools, it is easier to become detached from specific interests, more relaxed about the ongoing debate, and more tolerant of opposing views."

Crowe greets his wife, attended by the first President Bush, 1989.

In his retirement, even as he was taking life a little easier, Admiral Bill Crowe continued to follow the unconventional path and keep observers on their toes. Even though he had served as the top military officer in the country under two Republican presidents, he had never exactly toed the company line. And as he had with Sergei Akhromeyev, his preference was to look at the man and evaluate him on his own merits rather than the labels or institutions that surrounded him. And so it was with Democratic nominee Bill Clinton, whom Crowe came to support in his 1992 presidential campaign against George H. W. Bush, a man Crowe had served under.

As always with Crowe, careful thought and research were behind his decision. In the three years since his retirement, he had become involved in the corporate world and was able to reflect objectively, without any military constraints, on the political philosophies of the two parties. While he generally was pleased with the direction of the Bush administration, Crowe had become disenchanted with the Republican Party's tendency, as he writes, "to exclude certain groups from the mainstream of American life and exploit antagonisms within the society. It seemed to me that our economic and industrial deterioration had replaced superpower confrontation as the greatest threat to our national security."

Crowe also disliked the way the Republican advisors were succeeding in shifting attention away from serious economic and social problems in the country to more peripheral matters, such as Clinton's stance on the Vietnam War a quarter century earlier.

Along with three other retired high-level military officers, Crowe agreed to meet with candidate Clinton to brief him on military affairs. He found the Arkansas governor highly intelligent and a quick study. Over the next several weeks, Crowe spent several more sessions with Clinton and came to feel that he was extremely qualified to be president and therefore deserving of in-depth military advice. He found the candidate in no sense to be "anti-military" or "anti-defense," the labels that the Republican brain trust were trying to hang on Clinton. And Crowe agreed with fellow Naval Academy alum Ross Perot (who was running for president on an independent ticket and was thought by many post-game analysts to be instrumental in Clinton's eventual victory) that a man should be judged by his actions as a mature adult, not on what he said or did as a twenty-three-year-old. Thinking back to some of his pranks and transgressions in his last year at Annapolis, Crowe said he was glad people didn't judge him on his actions at that age.

On September 19, just six weeks before the election, Crowe publicly endorsed Bill Clinton for president. In a speech in Little Rock, Crowe said that a man didn't need a military background to be an effective commander-in-chief. He immediately faced criticism from those who felt it was inappropriate for a former chairman of the Joint Chiefs of Staff to involve himself so deeply in the political process.

Crowe explains himself this way in his book: "I was trained to believe that a professional military officer expresses his opinion, then carries out the orders of his political leaders, regardless of whether he agrees with them. If he feels he cannot do so in good conscience, he resigns his commission. But once he leaves active service, he is then completely free to express his opinion in any legitimate fashion and to participate fully in the country's political life. I wasn't surprised that some of my diehard Republican friends were unhappy or that a few truly had reservations about military people mixing in politics, but I never doubted my right to do it."

"I lost some friends with that speech," Crowe said in a 2005 interview for this book. "And I also made some new friends. Ninety-five percent of the Naval Academy guys are Republican, and they bugged the hell out of me for that speech."

A few weeks before the election, Crowe explained his position further to a combined meeting of the Naval Academy Association and the West Point Alumni Association. His endorsement of Clinton had been a hot topic in recent days, and he knew that many in his audience were suspicious of his position. He explained himself by saying that career military people were obligated to defend the country's ideals and institutions, and that includes defending the rights of people who disagree with the government or the military. Once someone retires from the military, he or she cannot then call someone who disagrees with their position unpatriotic or claim that person doesn't have the right to dissent. Crowe went on to say that he was practicing his freedom of opinion in retirement and that he hoped people would accord him that same privilege. As usual, Crowe's public-speaking ability served him well. His speech that day earned him a standing ovation.

Crowe hosting President Clinton in London, 1995.

Although no one would call it a tit-for-tat arrangement, it came as little surprise when, in 1994, President Clinton appointed Crowe to be the ambassador to the Court of St. James, with headquarters in a beautiful wooded area of London. Crowe calls the assignment "one of the greatest periods of my life. Shirley and I met so many wonderful people during that time. When my term was up in 1997, it was difficult to leave England."

⚜ — ⚜

The final resting place for two classmates from the distinguished United States Naval Academy Class of '47, one a Medal of Honor winner, the other a man who became the highest ranking military officer in the country, will be on the grounds of the school that shaped them 60 years ago.

Reminiscing with Academy classmates, 1993, (left to right) Rear Admiral Ken Sears, Captain Dan Bailey, Vice Admiral Jim Doyle, Admiral Bill Crowe, Ambassador Vernon Weaver.

"We went down the road and picked out four plots," Crowe says, a smile forming at the corners of his mouth. "For the Stockdales and the Crowes. Sybil gave us instructions. She said, 'Make sure the drainage is good.' That wasn't what I was really concerned about."

He gives a big laugh, then grows serious. "You know when Jim was captured," he says, "he wrote Sybil a long letter, which wasn't delivered to her for many months. A line in the letter said, "You know how we've always saved for the rainy day? Well . . . the rainy day is here."

"That's what you call classic understatement," Crowe says, as he slowly rises from his chair and heads to his classroom.

Crowe with Arizona Memorial in background, 1984.

Admiral Stansfield Turner, the "Golden Boy," in his Annapolis 40th anniversary yearbook photo.

CHAPTER THREE

Stan Turner:

The One They Looked To

I N EVERY SCHOOL CLASS THERE'S A GOLDEN BOY. He's the one that all the others look to with admiration and a touch of envy. He's the natural leader, the one who commands respect without campaigning for it. It's all in the way he carries himself, the way he comports himself in his studies and extracurricular activities, and the way he treats others. Typically he's handsome, smart, athletic, more eloquent than average, equally good with women and men, respected as much by his instructors as his peers. He seems to walk in perpetual sunshine even when others are shadowed by clouds.

In the United States Naval Academy Class of 1947, the clear-cut Golden Boy was Stansfield Turner. Without exception, when the extraordinary members of his class were asked to name the one classmate who stood out in their elite company, their answer was the same.

Here's a sampling—

Former U.S. President Jimmy Carter: "Stansfield was an outstanding football player and person. We didn't even consider him to be one of our peers; he was that far ahead of us. He was good looking, very eloquent, and everyone at the Naval Academy knew that he was going to be the outstanding man to graduate from our class. When I appointed him to be the director of Central Intelligence, I think what he really wanted was to be chairman of the Joint Chiefs of Staff, but I talked him into it, and he did an excellent job. There was never any question who was in charge there."

Jack Raftery, close friend, and in the same company at Annapolis all three years:

"We became friends right away, because he was such a nice, down-to-earth person, but I quickly saw his leadership qualities and how he stood out from the rest in everything he did. Nothing Stan accomplished in his career surprised me or any of our other classmates, because we could see right away that he had it all. And to top it off, he was a humble person, not one to remind you of his accomplishments or his status."

Ambassador Vernon Weaver: "If you ask anyone from our class to pick the guy who stood out above the rest, they'd all tell you it was Stan Turner. It wasn't even close."

Admiral William Crowe: "He was *the* guy at the Naval Academy. Everyone in our class knew who he was, and everyone admired him."

Stansfield Turner was born on December 1, 1923, in Chicago, one of two children of Oliver Stansfield Turner and Wilhelmina (Wagner) Turner. His father had come to the United States in 1909 at the age of 10, entered the real estate business six years later, and by 1929 had risen to the vice-presidency of a Chicago real estate firm. The family lived in the well-to-do Chicago suburb of Highland Park, where Stansfield attended high school and excelled in both academics and athletics. He had one brother, Twain, six years younger.

In an interview in late 2004, Turner remembered his upbringing as being very happy, and he recalled only one or two incidents where he was disciplined by his parents as he was growing up. His parents had a strong sense of ethics, and perhaps because Oliver Turner had never completed high school, he wanted to make certain his sons had the best education possible. "My father was always seeking out role models for me, and he would solicit advice from his friends about the best schools and activities for me," Turner says. "If a friend or co-worker of my father's had sons who were excelling at some activity, he would inquire about it and use that as a model. He just wanted the very best for me in every situation."

The Boy Scouts offered Stan Turner his first opportunity to demonstrate leadership, and he recalls "chomping at the bit" to join, which he did at age 12. He says his troop didn't have strong adult leadership—"there was a Scoutmaster who showed up once in a while, but he wasn't a regular presence"—so young Stan took it upon himself to direct the 20–30 kids in his troop. He organized hikes and outings and delegated responsibilities to the others, relishing the fact that he was given more authority at that age than Scouts were normally allowed.

While Turner said his father pushed him to take on several extracurricular activities and participate in student government (he was elected president of the student council in high school), it was never in a way that drew the boy's resentment. "It was more like my father expressing that he never had the opportunities that I was being given, and that I should take advantage of all of them," he says.

When it came time to select a college for Stansfield, Oliver Turner looked to his boss for advice. "His employer, Mr. Beard, had two sons who attended Williams College, so my father suggested we consider a small New England college," Turner says, "and I chose Amherst."

Turner was comfortable with Amherst instead of a larger and more prestigious college like Princeton because, he says, "I liked the idea of being a big fish in a small pond rather than a small fish in a big pond. But without trying to sound conceited, I would learn later that I could have been a big fish in a big pond. I remember avoiding Princeton, because I didn't think I could be the top guy at Princeton, and I did want to be the top guy."

Turner took part in student politics at Amherst, and served as president of the Sphinx Society, the highest honor he could achieve in his second year. He also starred on the football team and became a member of the Naval Reserve. After two full-years and a summer session at the small college, Turner accepted an appointment to the United States Naval Academy. Unlike his soon-to-be-classmate Jimmy Carter, attending Annapolis had not been one of Turner's lifelong goals.

"I had never thought of joining the navy or staying in the navy as a career," he says. "I went to Annapolis because our country was at war, and it was the patriotic thing to do. I thought the war was going to last a very long time, and my thinking was that by going to the Naval Academy, I could come out a very good naval officer, as opposed to a 90-day wonder," referring to college graduates who went to the 90-day officer candidate school, were commissioned as reserve officers, and then sent into combat. The phrase "90-day wonder" was sometimes used as a derogatory term by GIs who served under these officers, reflecting a lack of confidence in the combat leadership ability of men with such limited training. Very few 90-day wonders remained on active duty after the war because as reserve officers they were involuntarily discharged from active duty as part of post-war reductions in force.

Naval Cadet Stansfield Turner

"I also recall being personally disappointed when we won the war so quickly," Turner says. "I had a sense of disappointment that I had let the side down by not being out there fighting. Who would have imagined that we'd end the war with an atomic bomb?

"Now understand," he explains, "I wasn't sorry for the war to end. I'm not that selfish. But when it did come to an end, I was a midshipman out at sea, and they shot off flares and had a celebration, and I remember watching those rockets go up and everyone shouting. And I was feeling a profound sense of disappointment that I hadn't been directly involved in the war and contributed in a more significant way."

Although others saw him from his first days on campus as potentially the most outstanding member of their plebe class in 1943, Stan Turner didn't consciously dwell on his leadership skills. "I have always been self-confident," he says, "but I also felt there were a lot of others who would be very competitive at the Academy, and I didn't know whether I was going to come out anywhere near the top. I do know that my parents had instilled a great sense of ethics and the importance of hard work in me, and that served me very well there. Having nearly graduated from Amherst by the time I enrolled at Annapolis was certainly helpful. I was on average a little older than the other guys at nineteen and a half, but a lot of midshipmen had also attended college before they started there."

While Turner falls short of saying that the curriculum at the Naval Academy was easy, when questioned about his first year there, he doesn't have vivid memories of stern hazing or an especially rigorous regimen. "I know that paddling with an oar was fairly common," he says, "but I recall being paddled only once my plebe year. I think maybe those of us who came in from college being a little older and wiser were perhaps more deft at staying out of trouble. Oh, there were times when I might be asked to stand at attention in a first classman's room and be asked a bunch of silly questions, or memorize things. And at meals we might be asked to shove off, which meant to grab your chair and sling it under the table and continue eating as though you were still sitting, but I don't recall the hazing as being excessive.

I had been through fraternity hazing at Amherst, so I thought of it mostly as being silly, but not all that bad."

Was there ever a moment during his first year when he considered quitting? "Oh, no, never," he says. "I mean that wasn't even an option. What would you do if you quit? Go out as a sailor? No, that wasn't a possibility."

Class of '47 vice-president Stan Turner

⟨—⟩

Opinions vary from Stan Turner's classmates about his talents as a football player at Annapolis. One classmate recalls him being "the star of the team," another as "the toughest lineman you ever saw considering how much smaller he was than the others," but Turner's self-evaluation is far more modest.

"I understood the mechanics of blocking and tackling from an early age," he says. "Again, it was the influence of my father, who saw that many of his successful friends had sons that played football, so he started me playing Pop Warner and sandlot football as a little boy. I remember going to football camp and playing in Stagg Stadium at the University of Chicago, when I was just seven years old."

Turner excelled in football in high school and at Amherst, but when he got to Annapolis, he found himself the fifth-string blocking black. In those days, the navy varsity played a single-wing formation where one back did nothing but block for the others. When the final cuts were made to four 11-man units, Turner was the odd man out as the 45th player, but the line coach liked him so much he approached Turner and asked if he would like to play guard. At just five-foot-nine and 165 pounds, he would be about the smallest member of the offensive line, but it was a chance to stay on the team, so he readily accepted. Turner spent a week of practice learning the position and adapted quickly because he understood the principles of balance, and he could carry out his assignments flawlessly. The night before the opening game the second-string guard was injured, and Turner saw some playing time in the opener and performed well.

One play in particular made the highlight reel. Turner recalls it as though it were yesterday.

"We were punting, and the rule for a guard then was that when we punted we were to hold our ground. They didn't want you to charge downfield because that could leave an opening where a defender could break through and get the punter. But I was all excited and when no one came at me I charged downfield and I found myself alone down there with the Penn State punt returner, a guy named Elwood Petchell—I can still remember his name—and he was a big-name player. I recalled being taught way back when I was seven years old to watch someone's belly button when you tackled him. And so I looked at Elwood Petchell's belly and I creamed him. No one else was within 10 yards of us. And the play got a huge ovation, and it gave me such confidence. The coach was all excited, and within a couple weeks, I was the first-string guard."

While Turner got a lot of playing time during his second year at Annapolis, he was relegated to second-string his final year and functioned primarily as a backup at both left and right guard. The seasons of 1944 and 1945 saw Navy lose to Army in the "Big Game," and Turner readily cites two primary reasons for Army's superiority. "Their names were Blanchard and Davis," he says with a laugh, referring to Felix "Doc" Blanchard and Glenn Davis, considered in football folklore as the best tandem of running backs ever in college football. Blanchard won the Heisman Trophy in 1945 and Davis in 1946.

During Turner's final year, he was named commander of the brigade of midshipmen, the highest honor that could be bestowed on a final-year student. He graduated 25th in a class of 820, exactly 34 places above Jimmy Carter.

Stan Turner says he took many valuable lessons with him upon being commissioned from Annapolis in 1946. "Most important was to look after your people," he says. "I think my instructors instilled that leadership principle in us very well, and I got some practice with that at Annapolis. There was a great emphasis on showing a genuine interest in subordinates, always looking after them. I was also taught that you always have to set the example. That you can't expect other people to perform the way you want them to unless you are consistent in performing the way that you should.

"I learned that you motivate people in two ways," he adds. "First, by gaining their respect, and second, by getting those you lead to believe in what they're doing. To earn respect, you as a leader must be professional, be honest, and care for your people. It is my experience that those who get ahead in life are those who act as leaders, whether in positions of authority at the top, or positions of no authority at the bottom of the ladder. . . whether a junior sailor in the navy, a rookie cop on the beat, the newest mechanic in the shop, a professor in the classroom, or a businessman in an office. If you use the principles of leadership to encourage others to do their jobs well, whether they are above or below you, your job will be easier and the mission will be accomplished better."

He gives the example of helping his classmate Jack Raftery, who repeated his first year at Annapolis after struggling academically. "Jack did pretty well after that," Turner says, "but in our last year he found himself in academic trouble again. Here we were in the spring semester and it looked like he was going to flunk and not graduate. I was down there in his room beating him over the head with some of our lessons, and we went over it time and again, whether it was physics or whatever the subject was, and we just pounded it into him until we helped him get through. There were several of us willing and anxious to help him because he is such a fine person. We didn't consider it a sacrifice; it was just natural to us to give our friend that help."

After a year aboard a navy cruiser, Turner was awarded a Rhodes Scholarship to Oxford University, where he studied philosophy, politics, and economics, obtaining his master's degree in 1950. Returning to sea, he served on destroyers in both the Atlantic and Pacific and earned a Bronze Star and other service decorations in the Korean War. His résumé was becoming increasingly impressive with each passing year.

During this time, Stan's only brother, Twain, was killed in a car crash at the age of 18. Turner says that event made him realize he needed something more to anchor his life, and he turned to religion and the Christian Science principles he'd been raised with. "I had been quite dedicated as a young person to the precepts of Christian Science but had gotten away from it," he says. "Christian Scientists try not to go to doctors. It is not against our religion to do so, but we hope we can solve our physical problems through prayer. I had deviated from Christian Science in that I went quite willingly to doctors rather than waiting until the last resort, and I had also taken up alcohol, but not smoking. So when my brother was killed, and I felt I really needed more support and more deep-seated religious principles to guide me, I turned to Christian Science and gave up alcohol and gave up doctors to the extent that I could handle it otherwise. And I'm still very active in it today."

In December 1953, Stan Turner married Patricia Busby Whitney of Chicago and adopted her two children, Laurel and Geoffrey, ages seven and five. Their natural father had died the previous year of a heart ailment. Lieutenant Geoffrey Turner, who (in 2005) works as chief of staff on the counter-terrorism program for Bechtel Nevada, a government defense contractor in Las Vegas, has great memories of growing up the son of a high-ranking naval officer.

"Oh, every time we had a family cruise day, I would get to go out on a ship," Geoff Turner said in an interview in 2005. "I went out to sea with my father a number of times on his different ships, starting with his first command, which was the USS *Conquest*. That was a mine-sweeper. And I always knew that he was highly regarded in the navy and that I was being awarded special privileges because of that."

As his father was moved around the country with each promotion or new assignment, Geoff Turner attended five different grade schools, but he didn't consider being the perpetual outsider a disadvantage.

"There was something like a community of navy juniors/military brats, and what I found is that it did change your outlook on interacting with your environment, because you are never one of the 'insiders.' You are always coming in from the outside, so you have to be a lot more perceptive about the nuances of the environment. I was always observant in my classes of who was doing what to whom and why, and what was popular, so I could figure out how to fit in. If I wasn't able to do that, I knew I would remain an outsider the whole time I was there. So those experiences developed into social skills that I have found particularly useful. I looked at all the moving around and discovering new environments as a benefit rather than a penalty."

A particularly vivid memory from Geoffrey's youth was going out with his father for a week on Stan Turner's major command, the USS *Horne*. "They did their first operational tests and launched missiles while I was onboard," he recalls. "I got a real sense of the power of these missiles when they launched from 50 feet away on the other side of a pane of glass from where I was standing."

Geoffrey says the adjustment to becoming the child of Stansfield Turner was more difficult for his sister Laurel. "She remembered our natural father more than I did," he says, "because she was six when he died. And being the daughter, she was not heavily vested in the navy mystique, so for her the experience was pretty much that of a girl being dragged around the country, and the social adjustment was more difficult for her."

Stan Turner's assignments at sea during this time included his command of the USS *Conquest* from 1956 to 1958 and the USS *Rowan* in 1962. He alternated time at sea with tours of duty in the politico-military division of the office of the chief of naval operations and in the office of the assistant secretary of defense for systems analysis. He was also assigned by the navy to a period of study in the advanced management program at Harvard Business School.

Turner gradually advanced through the naval grades, acquiring a reputation as an effective and open-minded officer and administrator, and his assignments grew more sensitive and important. Geoffrey Turner recalls that his father was always promoted ahead of the anticipated schedule from his class rank at Annapolis.

"Dad graduated well up in his class," he says, "and there was an expectation that he would be promoted at a specific point in time, but at every single promotion from lieutenant on up, he was selected early for the next rank. When he was in Hawaii, he made lieutenant commander early. When he got to Coronado, he was promoted to commander early and immediately got his destroyer command. And so it went through his entire career."

In 1967, with the rank of commander, Stansfield Turner captained the USS *Horne*, a guided missile frigate, off the coast of Vietnam. Moving up to the rank of captain, he served for the next two years as executive assistant and military aide to Secretary of the Navy Paul Ignatius, advising on budget, manpower, and other matters. He was awarded his two stars as rear admiral, assisted Admiral Elmo R. Zumwalt Jr., chief of naval operations, on a navy modernization project, and assumed command of a carrier task group of the Sixth Fleet in the Mediterranean in 1970.

During the early 1970s, as Turner's responsibilities increased and his credentials became even more impressive, he was mentioned often as a possible chief of naval operations, an assignment he greatly desired. In 1971, he was named to head the systems analysis division in the office of the chief of naval operations, and the following year, shortly after receiving the third star of a vice-admiral, he was appointed president of the Naval War College in Newport, Rhode Island. In that post, he broke with tradition by dispensing of the requirement to wear uniforms at the college, and he expanded the curriculum to increase reading requirements, assigning, for instance, Thucydides' *History of the Peloponnesian War*. He also stipulated that examinations be given in military tactics, analysis, and management. His goal was to get the students "to do their thinking for themselves, lest the think tanks do our thinking for us." It was a clear case of the Rhodes Scholar applying some of his worldly knowledge to the more staid and traditional military curriculum.

Geoffrey Turner recalls his father's War College assignment as being the result of the navy's decision to "shake up the College. . . . It had evolved into sort of a country club where commanders and captains, 05's and 06's, would go on field trips and have parties and then go back to their careers," he says. "Admiral Elmo Zumwalt, who gave Dad the assignment, wanted these men to be instilled with some academic rigor, where they would actually learn something and come out with greater capabilities than when they entered."

Turner also invited a variety of independent and provocative speakers to the lecture podium at the War College. Among them were Herman Wouk, the author of *The Caine Mutiny*, and Jimmy Carter, his Annapolis classmate, who had recently been elected governor of Georgia. This invitation started a correspondence between Turner and Carter that continued over the next couple of years.

After he finished the War College assignment, Turner was contacted by H. R. Haldeman, President Nixon's chief of staff, and told that Nixon was interested in naming Turner chief of naval operations or even chairman of the Joint Chiefs of Staff, two positions that would represent for Turner the culmination of all his goals and dreams in the navy. As a three-star admiral, Geoff Turner equated that consideration as "sort of like being a quarterback sitting on the bench, being told that he could be the next Joe Montana."

Haldeman's most pointed question to Stan Turner was simple and direct: He asked Turner whether he was a good Republican. But Turner refused to answer the question. His reply was "I'm a military officer on active duty. I don't have a political affiliation. I serve the country." And he refused to budge from that position. As Geoff Turner says, "That reluctance to give Haldeman the answer he wanted cost him the nomination to one of those two posts, and that was the consequence of his sticking to his beliefs. That was a pretty heavy penalty to pay on principle." Geoff says, "That is a story that I don't believe has ever been in print, but it tells you a lot about my father."

Geoff shares another story about the privilege or, as he calls it, the "hazards" of being the son of a navy superstar.

"About the same time my father became commander of the Second Fleet in Norfolk, Virginia, around 1973, I arrived to be a junior officer on a ship in the Second Fleet," he says. "Dad was based on the USS *Albany*, which is a big cruiser. [There are about 200 ships in a fleet, everything from carriers to cruisers to submarines to destroyers and amphibians.] Pretty much everything on the East Coast was under the Second Fleet. I was an ensign at the time and functioning as a communications officer. Anyway, we were coming into port, and the flagship of the fleet was coming out. So that was a big deal. Everyone on our ship was going, 'Wow, there is the flagship!' Then all of a sudden comes a light from the flagship flashing at us. I ran up to the signal bridge, and my captain came running up there, and I was writing down the message in Morse code. The captain asked me to hand it to him, and he read it and said, 'Oh, it's for you.' It said, 'See you at dinner tonight.' It was a personal message from my father. I was mortified, but it was just a case of how being Stansfield Turner's son could put the spotlight on you, whether you liked it or not."

◁ —— ▷

In 1974, during Jimmy Carter's last year as Georgia governor, Stansfield Turner was in Atlanta for a joint exercise with the Army at Fort McPherson. While there, he called Carter's office and asked for an appointment. He was given 30 minutes, and was called into Carter's office at the exact minute the appointment was to begin. Three decades later, he remembers the meeting vividly.

"After a few minutes of pleasantries about old times, Governor Carter drained me of every bit of information I had about how the U.S. military was operating," Turner says. "And he asked me a lot of questions I didn't have answers for. At precisely 29 minutes, 30 seconds, he stood up and ushered me to the door. He said, 'By the way, Stan, the day after tomorrow, I am announcing that I am running for the presidency.'

"I said, 'Good luck, Jimmy,' walked out the door, and laughed at myself, and that was the last time I ever called him Jimmy."

Turner had the foresight to write Carter a long memo a few days later and provide answers to the intricate questions he could not answer in their meeting. He recalls how thorough and analytical Carter was in his questioning.

"I mean, here's a governor, and he is asking me detailed questions about how the U.S. military operates," Turner says. "And I am a vice admiral and I think a pretty broad-based one. I didn't just have a knowledge of submarines or destroyers. I felt I had a broad perspective on the military. I was just stumped by this governor with some of his intricate questions, and so I was compelled to write him and provide all the information I could about his requests. So when he was elected president in 1976, I naturally wondered to myself if anything would happen. But nothing happened . . . and nothing happened . . . as the weeks went by."

Finally, on the third of February 1977, two weeks after Jimmy Carter had been inaugurated, Turner got a phone call in Naples, Italy, where he was serving as the commander in chief of the Southern Flank of NATO, from Harold Brown, Carter's secretary of defense, saying the president wanted to see him in Washington the next day. Turner asked Brown if he could tell him what it was about, and Brown replied that he would have to get that information from President Carter.

Turner called in his chief of staff and two navy commanders, who were his personal advisors and asked them for their opinions about why he was being called to Washington. They all had different answers. One thought certainly that Turner would be named chairman of the Joint Chiefs of Staff. Another said he thought he would be appointed chief of the navy. And the third said, "Maybe he just wants your advice on an important military matter."

Turner told them he had read in the newspaper that the man Carter had originally nominated to run the CIA, Theodore Sorensen, had not found approval in Congress and that his nomination had been withdrawn. And Turner's chief of staff said, "President Carter is your classmate and friend. He wouldn't do that to you, sir."

"Of course," Turner adds, "what my chief of staff meant was that Carter wouldn't give me the dirty job of running the Central Intelligence Agency."

Geoff Turner recalls that when his father left for Washington, Admiral Turner told Geoff's mother that he wouldn't be able to tell her in plain language on the phone which position he'd been offered, so he would use a code. If he was going to be named chairman of the Joint Chiefs of Staff, he would refer to the appointment as the "major leagues." If he was offered the chief of naval operations, he would call it the "minor leagues." And if was going to become CIA director, he would call it the "Bush leagues," after the previous director and eventual President George Herbert Walker Bush.

"I think that tells you something about his thinking on those three positions," Geoff says.

Stan Turner's aide got him on a navy plane to Paris that day, where he then took the Concorde to Washington. He arrived in Washington, D.C. by sunset.

Hamilton Jordan, the architect of Jimmy Carter's masterful 1976 presidential campaign and later his chief of staff, gave the White

House perspective on Turner's call to Washington in an interview for this book:

"In the transition and right after the inauguration, I was basically in charge of the talent hunt, and I remember at some point in that process Carter calling me in and saying that he had this unbelievable classmate at Annapolis and that he just *had* to find a role for him in government. The president was just in awe of this guy, and I do use the word 'awe' carefully here. I believe he held Turner in the same esteem as he held Admiral Hyman Rickover. President Carter remarked on how as a student, as a soldier, and as a leader, Turner was just head and shoulders above everyone else in his class at the Naval Academy. He said, 'If we leave Stan Turner where he is, he is going to be chairman of the Joint Chiefs of Staff some day, but I would like to find a way to use him in an important role in my administration.'

"It was certainly not me that came up with the idea of him going to the CIA," Jordan says. "That was Carter's idea."

All the night before the meeting with President Carter, Turner worried over which job he might be offered. The one that by far he felt the least prepared for was director of Central Intelligence.

"When President Carter offered me the CIA job, I actually suggested to him that I would prefer to stay in the military and serve the country that way," he says. "I said that I would like to be the vice-chief of the navy because the chief would change in about 18 months, and I didn't want to ask for the chief's job, because that would mean firing the chief.

"And Carter replied that becoming chief of intelligence would be better preparation for being chief of the navy in two years anyway, and he said we could look at the situation then."

"I think Jimmy Carter's respect for Stan Turner was so great," says Hamilton Jordan, "that when he had Turner working for him as the director of the CIA, he was probably pinching himself and saying, 'I can't believe Stan is working for me.' I suspect that he always felt that Stan was the guy that was going to make it to the top. And remember that when Carter's father died and he went back to run the family business in Georgia, he had to forfeit his goal of ever becoming head of the navy. And if I can be allowed to think out loud, it wouldn't surprise me if while he was pursuing that goal, Carter didn't wonder if the one person who would always be in front of him would be Stan Turner."

⊰⊱ —·— ⊰⊱

So that was that. Stansfield Turner would take over the biggest intelligence and spying organization in the world, and he would be given more authority to run that agency than any director before or since. It was to be a daunting task.

When he's asked how long it took for him to get up to speed in understanding the agency and what was required of him, Turner says, with a laugh, "It took me about eight years to learn how the CIA operates, and the problem was that I was there only four years."

It helped that the CIA was run much like a military organization, with one exception. "In the military we have a great sense of loyalty to command," says Turner. "When you are on a ship and they change commanding officers, your loyalty shifts to that new man. You may not like the new son-of-a-bitch, but he's the captain. But that's not how it works in the CIA. They don't have that ethic. If they don't like you in the CIA, they will cut your throat from behind."

President Carter had not only named Stan Turner the director of the CIA, but he had also made him his primary adviser on foreign intelligence. The nomination of Turner came during a period in which the CIA had been pilloried in the media and had been investigated by Congress for illegal activities. In the previous four years, the agency had undergone two major reorganizations and had operated under three directors, James Schlesinger, William Colby, and George Bush. When Turner testified before the Senate Intelligence Committee, he said he would conduct intelligence operations "strictly in accordance with the law and American values," and that he would keep the members informed about covert operations. He said his goals would be to provide unbiased intelligence estimates and to restore the reputation of the United States intelligence community.

The committee recommended his confirmation 17-0 on February 23, 1977, and a day later the Senate unanimously confirmed his appointment. Turner was permitted to retain his navy commission and remain on the active duty list. He also agreed not to seek the position of chief of naval operations or chairman of the Joint Chiefs of Staff during his time at the CIA, but the agreement would not prevent President Carter from naming him to either post.

One of Turner's first duties as CIA director was to finish some of the mandates set forth by his predecessor Schlesinger. As he was getting ready to leave his directorship, Schlesinger had said that the U.S. had too many spies for the current national security environment. He felt that what was needed was a reduction in force of the people who had run agents in the jungle in Vietnam and who had run Operation Phoenix, which was the assassination program. Schlesinger laid out a plan for reduction of personnel over six to eight years with an increased reliance on technical and satellite surveillance, but he didn't have time to act on it before he left. So that was one of the matters that Stan Turner had to address when he came in. It was unfinished business awaiting a new directive.

When Turner saw that the plan made sense, he accelerated the trimming of staff to a two-year timetable. In the fall of 1977, he began the paring by having termination notices sent to 212 agents in the directorate of operations, the agency's clandestine branch. Many press accounts at the time called the cutbacks unnecessarily abrupt, and some reported that the action further damaged morale at an agency that had recently experienced a string of scandals.

Geoffrey Turner recalls the outcry from dismissed agents and political opponents:

"My father took a lot of unfair flack for the trimming of staff. Although he reduced the number of billets to which people could be assigned, he didn't greatly reduce the number of employees. A lot of those people were assigned somewhere else, and some of them retired. I don't know the exact number, but I believe only about 15 or 20 were actually forced out, yet this was seen by critics of my father or the Carter administration as a huge betrayal of the ground forces for the CIA. Some in the press labeled the reduction in staff as 'The Halloween Massacre,' even though my father was really just carrying out the wishes of the previous director and doing it as efficiently as possible."

"Stan was pretty shrewd the way he handled the criticism," says Hamilton Jordan. "He had so much experience from dealing with difficult situations in the military. He had a very broad view of all kinds of issues having been in the service, having been all over the world and assigned to different places, I think that he was able to handle all the controversy pretty well. I mean he had to push a very controversial agenda, because he and Carter were trying to change the way the CIA operated with the over-reliance on human intelligence and the implementation of new technology. And there actually was a lot of deadwood in the CIA from the Cold War."

Stan Turner faced another big challenge less than a year into office when a low-ranking CIA employee stole a top-secret satellite manual and turned it over to the Russians for $3,000. Twenty-three-year-old William Kampiles, who dreamed of becoming a spy, was convicted in 1978 on four espionage counts for selling a manual explaining the intricacies of the KH-11 photographic satellite, a multi-billion dollar program that the Russians had been unaware of. The KH11 had been misclassified by the Soviets as a non-photographic satellite, so that they did not try to hide sensitive weapons or operations from it when it passed overhead. Prior to Kampiles' act of espionage, the KH11 had been able to look down on Russia from space for more than a year without interference.

Geoff Turner feels that one of the big challenges his father faced at the CIA was how to get the intelligence community to operate effectively in support of national security when he didn't have control in terms of budget. "My father didn't come from the secretive 'old boys' school,'" Turner says. "He was coming from the perspective that the agency needed to establish a collaboration with both the media and the military like he had experienced at the War College. He knew it was imperative that he establish a trust between the CIA and congressional oversight committees and this was in a period where there wasn't much trust between these two factions. And he did. He probably testified more before congressional committees than any CIA director before or since."

President Carter was impressed with Stan Turner's performance and the enhanced level of respect he brought to Central Intelligence, so, just one year after appointing him director, Carter signed an executive order to give Turner "full and exclusive authority" over the budgets (estimated at $7 billion) of all the country's intelligence agencies, direct control over the CIA, and the responsibility of working through the new National Intelligence Tasking Center to assign projects to the agencies and coordinate their activities. These agencies included the FBI, the National Security Agency, State Department Intelligence, Defense Intelligence Agency, Military Intelligence, Treasury Department Intelligence, Energy Department Intelligence, and Drug Enforcement Administration.

Carter's order also put restrictions on certain kinds of covert actions that had discredited the CIA. Assassinations and medical experiments on unwitting or vulnerable human subjects were prohibited. And a special coordinating committee under the chairmanship of National Security Council director Zbigniew Brzezinski was given the responsibility of supervising all sensitive clandestine intelligence activities. Defense Secretary Harold Brown retained control over the electronic signal interception and the satellite surveillance programs. Although Turner's power increased substantially from that held by CIA directors under other administrations, he did not have the total authority that could have given him the title of intelligence czar, an idea that has been revived in the twenty-first century amidst the increased threat of international terrorism in the wake of September 11, 2001.

In a speech given at George Washington University in December 1997, Turner said, "Intelligence professionals are never satisfied that the policy makers use their intelligence adequately or properly. But that's part of the game and that's part of the profession. It's not that the policy-makers are necessarily wrong; sometimes they have better information than you do. Whenever I briefed President Carter, I always had to keep in the back of my mind that 'He met with Brezhnev last week.' I'd never met with Brezhnev, so if he interpreted what Brezhnev was going to do tomorrow differently than we interpreted what Brezhnev might do tomorrow, I had to give him some credit that maybe he understood Brezhnev better than we did. That's just a hypothetical example, but that's all you can do in intelligence, is produce the best analysis you can, send it out there, but try to make it as responsive as possible to the policy maker's needs."

Admiral Turner looks back with gratitude at the opportunity that his former classmate Jimmy Carter gave him. "We really had very little contact with each other at the Naval Academy," he says. "And I'm just eternally grateful for the faith he put in me. My life, of course, would be totally different today if I had stayed in the navy and become chief of the navy. I would be just another retired admiral."

Turner says one of the nicest aspects of working under Jimmy Carter as his chief of intelligence was Carter's ethical behavior, and that, as president, Carter never tried to take advantage of the secretive activities of the CIA. "Under Carter, I had no pressure to do anything unethical. I feel that George W. Bush obviously pressured George Tenet to twist the intelligence when it came to Iraq, and of course, Nixon tried to take advantage of the secretive activities of the CIA, but I never had that kind of concern."

Turner says that it is impossible to be totally ethical and a spy, but there are ethical limits to what can be done and what a person would be willing to justify as something the United States should do.

"I would go to Jimmy Carter with a tough one sometimes and ask, 'What should I do, sir?'" he says. "And the answer he gave me was always in terms of principle and what was the right thing to do under the circumstances. At one time, I was lied to by a staff person of a U.S. senator, and I wasn't certain whether the lie came directly from the senator. So I said to the president, 'I want to confront this senator, because there are some important things at stake here, besides just the lying.' And I said that I couldn't just do that without his permission because the senator was one of Carter's own people.

"And President Carter said, 'You do what is right, Stan.' So off I went to the senator. It worked out all right, but the point is there wasn't any question of 'Well, my political interests are such that I think you ought to skip this and not raise that issue.' It was just really wonderful, because when you have secret authority, you have got to worry about people trying to get you to abuse it, and that never happened in the Carter administration."

The CIA directorship thrust Turner into the national spotlight as a voice on many issues, from national security to the spy business to how to deal with life in the nuclear age. And it's not uncommon to see him interviewed on national television today about any of these issues.

When President Carter's term ended with his 1980 defeat by Ronald Reagan, Admiral Turner volunteered to stay on, but William Casey, who had managed Reagan's campaign for the White House, got the nod. Casey was an old hand at the spy game and had been close to many of the CIA employees let go when Turner resumed Schlesinger's cutbacks. Casey would go on to serve as CIA chief under Reagan for eight years, the longest stretch in that office in modern history, and was also considered a key figure in the Iran-Contra scandal, which centered around allegations that guns had been traded for hostages early in the Reagan administration.

Geoff Turner says that when his father left the CIA, he was looking for opportunities outside government, much like a Don Rumsfeld found in the business sector, where he could become chairman of a company, serve on boards of directors, and earn income commensurate with his talents and abilities.

"The problem for him," Geoff explains, "and I don't think he recognized it at the time, was that because the Reagan administration was a proponent of big business as opposed to times past, those big companies were not interested in bringing in as their top executive someone who was considered anathema to the new powers in Washington. So Dad wasn't really a hot commodity, in spite of his capability to manage and lead."

So Stansfield Turner focused on writing his first book, titled *Secrecy and Democracy*. The book addresses the inherent tension between secrecy for national security purposes and the health of a democracy.

"The book's subject matter goes back to when my father first became CIA director and we had long discussions about what to do with the intelligence community for the next four years," Geoff says. "And one of the options was to break away from the traditional model of official secrets. The U.S. is a country that depends upon openness and exchange of information, and the more you restrict it, the weaker you make the country. And Stansfield's position was that we had all this great intelligence, but we were not using it properly. So let's see how we can use this intelligence to help more sectors of the country, not just the White House or the Pentagon."

In a 1990 book, *Terrorism and Democracy*, Turner tackles the delicate issue of how American presidents have—and should—deal with terrorism. In it, he discusses his key role in planning the failed effort in April of 1980, to free the American hostages, who had been held captive for over five months, from Iran. He is critical in the book of National Security Advisor Zbigniew Brzezinski and is unsparing in his indictment of the operation's entire chain of command including the head of the operation, Colonel Charlie Beckwith, whom he calls "the wrong man to head the operation."

The plan, which was called Desert 1, had been to fly helicopters into Tehran, free the hostages from the embassy and bring everybody out. It was a very ambitious, risky mission, and one that was taken on against the wishes of Secretary of State Cyrus Vance, who was away from Washington when the orders were issued and who later resigned in displeasure at what he felt was the subordination of his authority.

Geoff Turner describes it as a pivotal moment in American history, and one that clearly changed the political tides against Jimmy Carter. "The failure of the mission was because they didn't have enough helicopters at Desert I to continue the mission to be able to carry all the people," he says, "and that was a failure based upon the pilots and the mechanics. It really boiled down to the intestinal fortitude of the pilots of the aircraft. They weren't the pilots that had been trained to do that kind of mission. It was a case of expecting a lot from the wrong guys."

Both President Carter and Hamilton Jordan believe that the Iran hostage crisis was the single biggest reason that Carter was defeated in his 1980 re-election bid.

The high-powered military and political career of Stan Turner took its toll on his marriage, especially when his stint as CIA director came to an end. Geoff Turner describes the breakup with a bi-partisan view, sympathetic to both parties.

"When Stansfield left the CIA, he wanted to stay involved in national security, and the center of the universe, of course, for national security is Washington, D.C.," Geoff says. "He wanted to stay there so he could be one of the talking heads, so he could testify before Congress and subcommittees and be one of the wise old men, which was appropriate. But my mother had been the beautiful navy wife for 30-some odd years and was beginning to get some arthritis, and the damp winters in Washington were not helpful. Dad had promised her that if she helped him get through his political career, he would then retire and they would go to a better climate. So they got a home in red rock country, near Sedona, Arizona, and they were splitting time between the two areas. But Stansfield would get extremely bored in Sedona and found he was having a tough time down there. Mother's idea was that any time spent in Washington was just part of a gradual transition, which would lead to permanently settling in Sedona. But that permanent retreat was like death to him. Being engaged with national security was what kept him going his entire life, and he felt totally disconnected and discontent down there. Basically, at one point Mother said, "Okay, I'm moving to Sedona, and she refused to go back to Washington, and they divorced.""

Stan Turner's second wife, Eli Karin, was tragically killed in the crash of a sightseeing plane in Costa Rica on January 15, 2000. Turner was with her on the flight and was hospitalized with serious injuries, but his lifelong penchant for staying fit and active helped him survive, and within three months he was nearly fully recovered.

A few years later Turner married again, and he and his wife, the former Marion Weiss, live near Washington. He remains active on the lecture circuit and continues to work on books and share his vast knowledge of the military and intelligence communities with the country.

In February 2005, Stan Turner became a great-grandfather when grandson Grant Stansfield Turner and his wife Kay welcomed a son, Benjamin von Turner, into the world.

ᚵ — ᚦ

On February 19, 2005, the navy commissioned its newest nuclear-powered attack submarine, the USS *Jimmy Carter*, in a ceremony at Naval Submarine Base New London, in Groton, Connecticut.

Retired Admiral Stansfield Turner, Carter's classmate at Annapolis, director of Central Intelligence, and good friend, gave the ceremony's principal address. In it he said, "This is a great day for the navy; this is a great day for the nation; and it's a great day for a great president. . . . As a nation I suggest when we look back at the years 1977 to 1981, when Jimmy Carter was our president, we should thank him for the moral light that he brought and which has never shone brighter. . . . So as you sail this ship around the world, never forget that the name of your ship tells the world that the United States does care for others, that the United States does do what it deems to be right, that the United States lives up to its word, that the United States' role in the world is based on morality and a quest for peace."

Once again, Jimmy Carter had called on his old classmate and his old hero to come through under pressure. And, once again, Turner delivered.

ᚵ — ᚦ

Vice Admiral James B. Stockdale,
Congressional Medal of Honor winner and
Naval Academy Class of '47

CHAPTER FOUR
Jim Stockdale:

As Noble as They Come

Because this account of Admiral Stockdale's incredible life could not include any recent interviews with him, we relied in part on the book In Love and War, *co-authored by Jim and Sybil Stockdale in 1984, and on personal interviews with Sybil and the four Stockdale sons conducted in 2004 and 2005, as well as several interviews with members of the Class of '47.*

EARLY IN THE MORNING ON SEPTEMBER 9, 1965, NAVY FIGHTER PILOT CAPTAIN JIM STOCKDALE ROSE SOONER THAN USUAL TO PREPARE FOR THE DAY'S COMBAT MISSION OVER NORTH VIETNAM. As he was dressing, he realized his laundry was a day late being returned, so he put on a pair of red polka-dot boxer shorts. He had bought the shorts at the Navy Exchange men's shop a few weeks before on a shopping trip with his wife Sybil in Yokosuka, Japan. He hoped the gaudy underwear the couple had laughed about would bring him luck on the day's mission. Stockdale had ably flown over 200 missions since his first bombing raid 13 months before to destroy Vinh City oil tanks, and he had no reason to believe that this assignment would be any more dramatic than all the others.

That bombing of the oil tanks, ordered after what Stockdale describes as "a Chinese fire drill" on the night of August 4, 1964, turned out ultimately to be very significant, because it led to the Tonkin Gulf Resolution, passed by both the U.S. House of Representatives and Senate on August 7. The raid effectively started the Vietnam War, and it's one that never should have been ordered.

It had erroneously been reported that the USS *Maddox* had been attacked by Russian PT boats on August 4. Even though it quickly became apparent to Stockdale and others on the scene that no such attack had in fact occurred, the piece of critical misinformation had been carried on all the major wire services and in news magazines like *TIME* and *Newsweek*. It soon became clear that the "non-battle" would provide President Lyndon Johnson just the excuse he needed to wage an attack on North Vietnam. When the bombing of Vinh City was carried out by Stockdale and other ace fighter pilots, Johnson's poll numbers instantly surged 14 points, exactly what he was hoping for with the presidential election just three months away.

Besides swaying public opinion in the U.S. for aggressive action in Southeast Asia, the Tonkin Gulf Resolution also signaled the end of battle commanders in Vietnam having the authority to carry out orders on-site, requiring them instead to yield to directives from Washington. From August 7, 1964, on, Stockdale and other top American fighter pilots were instructed to precisely carry out orders from the nation's capitol, even though they privately questioned the strategies and intelligence information that dictated their assignments.

As was his custom, on that morning of September 9, Stockdale put his United States Naval Academy Class of '47 ring in his safe, knowing that if he didn't return from his mission it could be passed on as an heirloom to his four sons, who were back home with their mother in Coronado, California, waiting and praying for his safe return.

Jim kept his most prized possession strapped to his wrist. It was an Abercrombie & Fitch "Shipmate" wristwatch that his father Vernon had given him 23 years earlier upon receiving word that Jim had been awarded an appointment to the Naval Academy from their local congressman in Illinois. The watch was inscribed "JBS, 1942, Love Dad," and as he checked the time on the watch, James Bond Stockdale's thoughts went back to exactly one year before, when he had been at his father's deathbed in their hometown of Abingdon. Vernon Stockdale had been brave at the end, a character trait he'd instilled in abundant measure to his son, who was regarded as one of America's ace combat pilots in the early months of this imposing new conflict in Southeast Asia.

After a quick breakfast, Stockdale went up to the flight deck on the USS *Oriskany*, and from the 37 planes lined up there he chose the one he would pilot this day, a lead Skyhawk in the flak-suppression group. The plane had been loaded with snake-eye configured bombs for flat, low-level runs, and Jim was relieved to hear that a new switch had been installed on the control panel. This would allow him to employ either the dive-bomb mode of delivering the bombs or the snake-eye mode, in which the fins of the plane pop out to ensure that the rapidly dropping plane is far enough ahead to avoid blast damage when the low-drop bombs hit the earth.

Stockdale's mission on that day was to once and for all take out the Ham Rong (Dragon's Jaw) Bridge, which had proven to be a formidable target in previous bombing runs. The bridge was used by the Vietcong to receive truckloads of munitions from the seaport of Haiphong, and although 500-pound and 1,000-pound bombs had damaged portions of it in the weeks prior, the bridge somehow still held together. The mission didn't seem much more complicated than the dozens that had preceded it, so Stockdale was confident he would get the job done and safely return to the *Oriskany* early in the afternoon.

At precisely 12:12 p.m., as he began a gentle pull-up and admired in his rearview mirror the perfection of his bomb drop on a string of boxcars making their way for the bridge, Stockdale heard a sound he didn't expect. He knew instinctively that it was coming from a 57mm anti-aircraft gun. He felt the initial impact on the plane, then within a second an even greater impact. He knew immediately that he had taken a direct hit. A glance at the instrument panel showed the fire-warning light on, then the hydraulic-system light, then all red lights on. Although he was only three miles from the Gulf of Tonkin, where American rescue ships could pull him to safety if he landed in the water, Stockdale knew his aircraft was fatally damaged and that he wouldn't make it as far as the Gulf. His Skyhawk weaved and pitched toward the ground. At the last second he found the alternate seat-firing handle located between his legs. The cockpit canopy flew off with a huge noise, and Stockdale watched his parachute begin to deploy as he tumbled end over end through the air. He then heard the shouts of people running on the ground, as gunfire ripped slits in the parachute above him.

Within two minutes, Stockdale's chute snagged on the branches of a scrub tree and, as he writes in *In Love and War*, the autobiography he co-authored with his wife Sybil in 1984, "I bobbed down onto the main street like a puppet on a string."

Jim was immediately gang-rushed and beaten with sticks and clubs by a mob he describes as "town roughnecks." It seemed the whole village had rushed to the scene, among them dozens of children and teenagers. Immediately, he was stripped of his clothes, even the red polka-dot boxers he'd worn for good luck. His treasured watch from his father was ripped from his wrist. He would never see it again.

Stockdale's left knee was shredded and his shoulder dislocated, but he wouldn't realize the full intensity of pain from those injuries until the shock and terror of the moment subsided. It occurred to him amidst the chaos and screaming as he looked down at the bloody mess that used to be his knee that he would never run again. Stockdale had been a good athlete. He had played football in high school and college and ran hurdles, and the realization that he was seriously wounded and might never be able to run and roughhouse with his four sons, if God allowed him ever to return home, put him on the edge of shock. Even at a moment like this, his family, 11,000 miles away, was foremost in his mind.

But, just then, he was surprised by a man in civilian clothes who made his way through the mob and asked in perfectly clear English, "Are you James Bond Stockdale?"

Jim yelled "Yes," hoping against hope that he had discovered one ally among the enemy, but the man just nodded knowingly and ran away as though he were confirming that a prize capture had descended into their midst.

Those five minutes, from the time he felt the first impact on his aircraft until he was lugged away, naked and seriously wounded, by the Vietnamese, represented the worst shock and horror a combat pilot could experience. But if ever there was a man physically and mentally prepared for the seven years of torture, isolation, and physical deprivation that was about to befall him, it was James Bond Stockdale, U.S. Naval Academy Class of 1947.

⊰ —— ⊱

Flash forward to January, 2005: For the most part, the exterior of the classic A-frame home on "A" Avenue in Coronado, California, looks the same as it did more than 40 years ago when navy fighter pilot James Stockdale walked out the front door on his way to the Gulf of Tonkin. Visitors approaching from the sidewalk pass under an archway that's connected to a white picket fence surrounding the lush front yard. A concrete pathway cuts through the yard's center and leads to a porch that's covered by a second story, which is held up by four tall white columns.

From the outside, this charming abode is not unlike many others lining the street on this tony little island off the San Diego coast. From the inside, well, that's a different story entirely—a riveting story, in fact, of love and pain, of heroism and struggle, of separation and the wedge it creates, of life and near death.

The uplifting parts of the story—the love and heroism and life at its loudest pitch—is on display throughout the house. There's the bronzed bust of Stockdale that sits on a pedestal in the living room and a portrait that stares at you as you make your way down the staircase from the second story. The citation for the Medal of Honor is on display, and the medal itself is kept nearby. It is the highest distinction a soldier or sailor or pilot can be given. There's also the Distinguished Graduate Award from the Naval Academy, which Stockdale received in 2001 at the same time as his close friend Admiral William Crowe, who served as chairman of the Joint Chiefs of Staff under Ronald Reagan and George H. W. Bush. Another classmate, former President Jimmy Carter, would receive the award in 2002. (As of spring 2005, only one other USNA class, the wartime class of 1942, had as many as three graduates receive this honor.)

And there are the pictures—dozens and dozens of pictures—that cover nearly every inch of every wall and flat surface in the house, pictures that show Jim Stockdale and sometimes family members posing with old navy pals, as well as various military and political dignitaries, including the last six U.S. presidents.

But what of the pain and struggle and evidence of mortality? That's all on display, too. Downstairs in the kitchen, Stockdale, the fighter pilot turned American hero, portrayed by the early 90s media as an object of humor following his ill-fated agreement to serve as Ross Perot's vice-presidential running mate, struggles to lift himself from his wheelchair. At 81, Jim Stockdale has been stripped of his memory and much of his ability to communicate. The man who spent more than seven grueling and torturous years in a Vietnam prison, including four in complete isolation, is now reaching for a Lincoln log as part of a manual dexterity exercise being overseen by a live-in caregiver. It seems that only the ravages of age have been strong enough to weaken this fiercely proud and heroic man. It is obvious that his time on earth has been reduced to days and weeks, but still he pushes on. The indomitable will that was fueled by stoic philosophy and the works of great thinkers like Epictetus and then molded into steel by torture and deprivation in the jungles of North Vietnam will not allow him to give in to the ravages of age and the Alzheimer's disease that has crept up on him in recent years.

Upstairs, Sybil Stockdale, Jim's adoring wife of nearly 60 years—a woman who became the public face of all wives waiting at home for their POW or MIA husbands in Vietnam—is confined to her own wheelchair. Parkinson's disease has taken control of much of her body but not, thankfully, her mind. Speaking can be difficult, and on some days even impossible, but she at least remembers who she is and what it was that attracted her to her now-frail husband. She, too, has a wall of honors, including the navy's Distinguished Public Service Award, the only such award given to the wife of an active duty naval officer.

Indeed, life has been anything but easy for the Stockdale clan, which includes four sons—James Jr., Sid, Stanford, and Taylor—as well as eight grandchildren. But when you consider the rough waters that have been navigated, it's somewhat of a miracle that they've come this far and that the family core, occasionally fractured and disjointed by the violent waves of fortune that have washed over them, has remained whole.

⊹⊱ —— ⊰⊹

The dream of Jim Stockdale attending Annapolis had been planted years before it actually happened. Jim's father, Vernon, wanted far more for his son than circumstances allowed. After working full-time from his teens into his late 20s to help support a family with an invalid father, Vernon Stockdale was able to "escape" his home of Abingdon, Illinois, and join the navy at a time when the United States was mobilizing for World War I. The navy provided freedom for Vernon and removed him from the pressures of being the family's main breadwinner. Jim would later describe his father's two-year navy stint as his "college." Vernon Stockdale didn't have the education required for Officer Candidate School, but he went up through the enlisted ranks and within a year made chief petty officer. He spent his entire enlistment near Chicago, at the Great Lakes Naval Training Station, where he worked in parts procurement for the airplanes in the newly formed Naval Aviation division.

Vernon married his longtime girlfriend, Mabel Bond, in 1919, shortly after he got out of the navy, and four years later, two days before Christmas, she gave birth to their only child, James Bond Stockdale. Later in Stockdale's life, after the fictional British spy James Bond became popular, his friends gave him an apt nickname: "Double-O-Seven."

While Jim would later write that his father insisted on having his way on very few issues in Jim's life, on the biggest one—having his son attend the Naval Academy—he was unwavering. When Jim was just seven years old, the family visited Annapolis, and the boy stood by the Tecumseh figurehead in front of Bancroft Hall and watched the midshipmen march back into the dormitory for their evening meal to the rhythm of drums and bugles.

"From the time of my first memories, there had been no question about it," Jim wrote in *In Love and War*. "I would be going to Annapolis to make a career in the navy my dad loved so much."

Four years after the Annapolis visit, Vernon took his son to a commencement speech at little Iowa Wesleyan College, not to see a friend or relative graduate but to hear the commencement speaker, Admiral Richard Byrd, talk about his recent expedition to the South Pole. Jim would vividly recall how splendid Admiral Byrd looked in his white service uniform with gold shoulder boards.

Even with little education and a limited naval experience, Vernon Stockdale was much admired in his small community for his work ethic and willingness to help others, and he had gained enough respect in Abingdon that by the time Jim was a freshman in high school there was an implicit promise from their Illinois congressman that if the boy met the rigid academic and physical requirements of the Naval Academy, he would receive an appointment to Annapolis.

On a night in June of 1943—the night before he was to be sworn into the navy—Jim stood with his father by the Tecumseh statue that he'd first seen 12 years before, and once again they watched the evening parade into Bancroft Hall. "I want you to try your best to be the best man in that hall," Vernon said. Those were words Jim lived by until the day he was commissioned in June of 1946.

In an early 2005 interview, Sybil would say of Jim's first years there, "Jim loved being at Annapolis, but it was hard for him. The work was very difficult, and he was younger than many of the plebes. (A good portion of the entering class in the fall of 1943 had already attended college for one or two years.) You know, they post the grades every week, and the first year he was very worried. And his mother wrote to him and said, 'You must not humiliate us. You must do well.' There had been one other boy from Abingdon who had been appointed to the Naval Academy. He had come from the most prominent family in town, and he had flunked out. So you see it was very important for Jim to succeed, especially as far as his parents were concerned."

One of the activities Stockdale tried was the debate team, and as part of his "initiation" the more experienced champion debaters in the class, like Bill Crowe and Vernon Weaver, instructed him on the importance of being a team player.

"We had a debate against Army early in the season, and Crowe told Jim that he could be the time-keeper," Weaver recalls. "The one stipulation was that Jim had to give all the navy guys an extra 10 seconds for our openings and our rebuttals. Of course, he did as he was told. We won the debate, and no one was the wiser for it."

Stockdale's 1947 yearbook entry.

Weaver also recalled how Stockdale always had a great sense of humor and a keen sense of play as well. "In our last year at Annapolis, we used to go down to the Statler Hotel in Washington on weekend leave, and of course we were interested in having a cocktail and meeting some girls, but we didn't have any money to speak of. It was always Crowe and Stockdale and myself and a couple other classmates in the group. Now because we figured Jim was the most dignified and honest-looking guy among us, we would have him go to the front of the checkout line at the registration desk and introduce himself to businessmen checking out of the hotel. He would salute and say, 'Excuse me, sir, I'm Midshipman Stockdale, and my friends and I are here for just a few hours before we go back to the Naval Academy this afternoon. We'd like to have a room to clean up a little before we return to the Academy, and I notice you're checking out a couple hours ahead of the checkout time. Is there any chance you could check out and then give us your room key so we'd have a room to do that?'

"The amazing thing," Weaver says, "is that more often than not the man would let us use the room. I would never have had the guts to do that, but Stockdale was a master at it. We'd then send our classmate Santozi, who was the best-looking guy in our group, out to find some girls and invite them to a party in the room with his fellow midshipmen. He never failed to deliver. Just imagine the guts it took for Stockdale to do that. I tell the story because Jim is so often portrayed as this stoic person, and that's another side to him."

Jim had been a starter on the varsity football team for three years in high school, and he greatly desired to play on the varsity team at the Naval Academy, but his small stature prevented him from realizing that dream. So he settled for playing on the junior varsity squad, and years later he said that the all-work, no-glory aspect of being on that team prepared him well for some of the hardships he would face in his confinement in Vietnam. (It is an interesting coincidence that the one other member of the Class of '47 to receive the Medal of Honor, Admiral Tom Hudner, also played jayvee football with Jim Stockdale.) Jim told himself that to fulfill his aspiration to be the "best man in that hall," he would play hard no matter what the rewards, and so he pushed himself to the limits in his practice sessions against the varsity. He would show up for practice early on those cold autumn afternoons, and during warm-up drills would dive on his belly through icy puddles to keep himself mentally tough. He expressed to Sybil that the jayvee squad did all the work, and the varsity team got all the glory.

On the football field, Stockdale was tenacious end-to-end player.

"I passed Jim Stockdale on the practice field during plebe year," recalls Admiral Jerry Denton, a classmate who was later imprisoned with Stockdale in Vietnam and then became the first Republican elected to the U.S. Senate from Alabama. "Jim was acting as fodder for two All-Americans, Don Whitmeyer from Alabama and Bobby Jenkins. They and the center were practicing plays and they wanted a lineman in there to try and tackle them. On this hot and humid afternoon, as small as he was, Jim was giving them hell and tackling them on nearly every down. And I thought, 'Golly, this guy is really something. I would never do that!' Watching him repeatedly bring those guys down was the most impressive thing I'd ever seen in sports. So I knew the stuff that Jim had in him before he went over to Vietnam."

One of those who reaped a portion of that varsity glory was Stansfield Turner, who became close friends with Jim at the Naval Academy and remained so for decades to come.

In a 2004 interview for this book, Admiral Turner recalled how he became friends with Jim Stockdale at Annapolis. "We were both from Illinois, and we both played football," Turner says. "So we had that in common, and although I was small for football, Jim was even smaller than I was, and I admired his tenacity. We struck up a friendship, and we just became closer through the years, even to the point where I got to know Sybil through Jim while we were midshipmen. And on my first duty station, which was Norfolk, Sybil was teaching in Richmond, and I started dating her. This was before she started seriously dating Jim, before he he'd made up his mind to marry her.

"I wasn't cutting into his time or anything," Turner is quick to add.

Jim's first date with Sybil occurred during his senior year at the Academy, in 1946. She had graduated early from Mount Holyoke College and was teaching at a high school in Richmond, Virginia. It was a blind date and Jim was apprehensive, having just had a dismal blind date a week before. He and a classmate, Marvin Scoggins, were to be paired off with Sybil Bailey and Bebe Woolfolk, but it hadn't been predetermined who would go with whom. Similar heights dictated that Jim choose Sybil, as Bebe was much was taller than Jim, and Jim and Sybil had a splendid time.

"I wanted to make a good impression, because I was attracted to him," Sybil says, "but he had a Midwestern accent and spoke rapidly, and I couldn't really understand every word he said. So I had to listen carefully, but I was impressed immediately with his sense of humor and his natural leadership. He laid out the plans for all of us, and I really liked the way he took charge of everything."

Before the weekend was through, they had made plans to meet again in three weeks, and Jim even offered an invitation for her to come back for June Week, when he would graduate and be commissioned. "I knew very well that a midshipman invited only a special girl for those festivities," she says. She later told her friend Bebe about the invitation, and said, "I think I've found the man I want to marry."

Jim was stationed in the Pacific off the coast of San Francisco in the fall of 1946, and as he was heading back to Philadelphia for the Army-Navy football game, he called Sybil and invited her to join him for the weekend. She agreed.

"The next morning, we had breakfast together," Sybil recounted in 2005, "and Jim said, 'Would you be interested in driving down to the Naval Academy today to look at miniatures?' And I said, 'Do you mean by that what I think you mean?' because a miniature, of course, was an engagement ring. And he said, 'Yes, I think I do.'

"And I said, 'I would love to.' That was the only proposal I ever had. We went down to the Naval Academy and I picked out an aquamarine, which was the stone of the sea, and it cost fifty-four dollars. My wedding ring cost another eleven dollars."

Jim and Sybil Stockdale were married on June 28, 1947. They had their first child, a son, James Jr., in December of 1950, and he was followed by three brothers: Sidney in 1954, Stanford in 1959, and Taylor in 1962.

The first 18 years of their marriage followed a relatively traditional pattern, with all of the military and social obligations that attended a couple where the husband was quickly being considered a navy superstar. But then came the life-changing knock on the door, just before 10 p.m. on the evening of Sept. 9, 1965.

Since school was starting, Sybil had recently returned with the boys from a summer stay at her parents' home in Connecticut. That day, September 9, she had been to San Diego to see a matinee performance of *Hello Dolly*, starring Carol Channing.

Sybil had put five-year-old Stan and three-year-old Taylor to bed and then dozed off, only to awaken to the sound of her 14-year-old son Jimmy talking to someone downstairs.

Four decades later, Jim Stockdale Jr. recalls the conversation:

"It was about 9:30 at night, and the doorbell rang. I answered it, and there was a chaplain standing at the door, visibly shaken, and our neighbor Doyen Salsig was with him. She just said, 'Hi, Jimmy, I have to see your mom,' and she ran upstairs. I knew right away what was happening. So I sat down with this young lieutenant and said, 'Can you tell me what's happening?' And he said, 'Well, your dad's missing.'

"I said, 'Has he been shot down?'

"'Well, yeah,' he said. 'They're searching for him.'"

Upstairs, when Mrs. Salsig broke the news, Sybil had difficulty grasping it. But later, the chaplain, Lieutenant Parker, told her what little he knew, that Jim's parachute had been sighted, but that there were no signs of life after the chute hit the ground. There had been no sound from the radio beeper that was supposed to activate automatically when the parachute opened, nor had there been any sign of gathering up the chute after Jim descended. He could be dead, or he could be alive. Until more was known, he would be listed as "missing."

As the days and weeks crawled forward, Sybil felt she had three choices in how to handle her situation: one was to drink heavily and remove herself from reality, another was to rant and rave and wring her hands, and the third was to cope as rationally as possible with her circumstances and become stronger than ever as the sole caretaker of her four sons. She, of course, chose the last one and determined to do everything she could to make her husband proud in the event that she ever saw him again.

A heart-tugging moment occurred in the days following the news of Jim's disappearance. One morning, Sybil was approached by Stan as she was doing the laundry. The little boy took her arm and, staring at her with the clear blue eyes of his father, said, "Mom, I'm so sorry about Dad." With her arms full of sheets and towels, Sybil could only hug her boy and try to comfort him. It was at moments like these that she had to call on every fiber of strength she had to keep from crumbling.

⊲ —— ⊳

Jim Stockdale spent the first several weeks following his capture in the hospital. He had three surgeries on his shoulder and knee. For public relations purposes, the Vietcong needed to put their prize capture back together again before they could try to break him down.

Because the Vietnam conflict was an undeclared war, nearly everything that occurred there was veiled in secrecy. Sybil would not hear anything of substance about Jim's condition, whether he was alive or dead, until the end of 1965. She spent every day for four months wondering whether it might not be better that Jim had died quickly when his plane was shot down, rather than be in the hands of a vengeful enemy and subject to all the torture and degradation they might be inclined to inflict upon him. Either thought was unbearable for her. Sybil wouldn't learn for several months that Jim had in fact survived, but that his daily existence included frequent beatings and 16 hours a day of being held in leg and hand irons.

The Vietcong knew immediately after Stockdale's capture that they had an important military officer—a trophy catch—under their control, and they strategized constantly on ways to gain political capital. Over the late days of 1965 and all through 1966 they ignored the Geneva Convention rules on treatment of prisoners and put Jim through many mental and physical tortures, part of the fear-and-guilt package used by extortionists to break down human will. Every effort was made to get Stockdale to sign documents implicating the United States in acts of aggression against the Vietnamese people. The Vietnam War was as much a propaganda battle to win hearts and minds, as it was a bloody physical conflict.

Torture methods used on Stockdale included beating about the face, tying his legs in locks, and stretching his already mangled arms and shoulders behind him as his head was pushed forward to the ground, until he would "submit." His screams would be muffled by rags shoved into his mouth. He referred to this method of punishment as "the ropes." Stockdale came to have nicknames for all the guards. There was Pigeye, Mickey Mouse, Rabbit, and Cat, and each exhibited his own individual brand of cruelty and inhumanity.

At those times when he would "submit," believing it was a better alternative than being killed, Stockdale would sign some bogus document that the North Vietnamese had prepared. That would be followed by hours of anguish and guilt that his resolve had weakened, even though he hadn't provided anything of real value to the enemy. Most times the information he gave his captors was blatantly false. Once, when asked to provide the names of his fellow pilots, he wrote down the names of the pro football champion Green Bay Packers: Hornung, Starr, Nitschke, and Adderley. The worst fear Jim Stockdale felt during his imprisonment was when he would imagine what his life would be like if he were to live through the torture and return home. In his darkest moments, he envisioned the friendless life of disgrace and humiliation that would face someone who had sold out his country. Never during these times would he allow himself to imagine what in fact did occur: that he would return to his country not only with honor, but be widely regarded as one of the most heroic men of his time, a man who would be given the highest military honor accorded an American, and a man who would be considered by the United States Naval Academy as one of its most distinguished graduates in history.

As the hours and days and weeks and months passed slowly in the first two years of captivity, Stockdale kept his mind active with thoughts of his wife and sons, trying to think himself "out of the box" and thousands of miles away from Vietnam. His time and attention to detail in survival training were serving him well, as were memories of diving into cold puddles at football practice on the jayvee football squad at Annapolis. "All pain and no glory." Through it all, he tried to maintain total awareness of his situation, his captors' behavior, and any other information he could glean from his grim surroundings.

Meanwhile, back in the states, Sybil was arranging meetings with top navy officials and government bureaucrats to gain whatever information she could and to pass that information on to other military wives whose husbands were missing in action.

Sybil explained how the wives first got together: "Well, we weren't supposed to talk to anybody, but I had been an MIA wife for many months, and this navy wife called me up one day and said, 'My husband is shot down. I understand that yours is, too.' She said she wanted to get together with other wives. Since I was a senior wife, I thought, well, that was my responsibility. So I had a luncheon at the house on the 13th of October, 1966. Thirteen wives came, and they were so delighted to be together that they stayed until 5 p.m. None of us had ever talked to anybody else before. And after that, we continued to meet every month just like squadron wives would. And that started the whole thing."

Sybil was not a fan of Lyndon Johnson, the U.S. president from 1963–1969. "[The wives] were told not to contact or tell anybody that our husbands were shot down, which was ridiculous. And this 'keep quiet' policy of Johnson's ... well, I really didn't like him. Not the least because he started the war [the non-battle in the Tonkin Gulf] under false pretenses."

Sybil Stockdale and her four sons,
(left to right) Stan, James Jr., Sid, and Taylor.

While Sybil did feel her needs were being attended to by the navy brass, and many of her questions were being answered, every time she met with a government official or a member of the Johnson administration she felt as though they were patronizing her.

Finally in October of 1967, at the urging of navy officials, Sybil and the other wives formalized their organization. The women elected officers and adopted bylaws. They called themselves the League of Wives of American Vietnam Prisoners of War. There was no differentiation made between wives whose husbands had been listed as Missing in Action and wives with POW husbands, because they wanted to take the positive position that all the men were alive.

Just two months later an unexpected notice arrived from the navy's Bureau of Personnel that Jim had been selected for deep draft command. The letter included this line: "In the event you are just commencing a tour or have been there a relatively short time, we will not order you to command at sea, short of an emergency, until you have completed a minimum tour. . . ."

Sybil was appalled that whoever drafted the navy letter wasn't even aware that her husband had been a prisoner of war in Vietnam for over two years.

⊣ — ⊢

In a seemingly unrelated but significant political event, on January 23, 1968, the USS *Pueblo*, an American light cargo ship that had been converted into an intelligence-gathering vessel, was captured off the coast of North Korea and the crew held captive. The North Koreans alleged that the American ship had carelessly ventured into their waters and that the commander of the ship, Commander Lloyd Bucher, had been careless in directing the vessel. In pursuit of the American ship, the North Koreans had opened fire with machine guns and cannon. One American crewman was killed and several others suffered serious wounds. The ship was quickly taken over, and the crew would remain prisoners for nearly a year.

The *Pueblo* incident got a tremendous amount of publicity and served to further increase the resentment of Sybil's League of Wives, whose plight had remained a virtual secret to the rest of the country. When Commander Bucher's wife spoke out critically of the U.S. government, the Vietnam POW wives felt that it hurt their cause and that her behavior lacked dignity. Politicians in Washington were giving sound bites every day expressing concern for the men of the *Pueblo*, while nary a word was being mentioned about the brave men held captive in North Vietnam.

"We felt [Bucher's wife's] public criticism of her own government demeaned her service and her country in the eyes of the world," Sybil wrote in *In Love and War*. "It was also terribly frustrating to have all the hullabaloo about the *Pueblo* prisoners going on in the press while nothing was being said by our government about our men in Vietnam."

When Congressman Mendel Rivers came to San Diego in February of 1968, to speak to Sybil's group and a gathering of *Pueblo* wives, the wives of Vietnam POWs refused to sit at the same table with Mrs. Bucher. An outspoken critic of the war, Rivers told the wives in no uncertain terms that the North Vietnamese were barbarians and that our men were living in a virtual hell, and that if it were his call, he would bomb North Vietnam to smithereens. But as no media were allowed in the room for this meeting, no accounts of the events of that day made it into the newspaper, and officials continued to urge the wives of Vietnam POWs to keep quiet about their circumstances.

In looking back on how Sybil Stockdale became an activist and the leader of the wives of husbands that were POW or MIA, her son Sid Stockdale expressed his respect for his mother. "It not only amazes me, but it amazes my wife and a lot of other people," he says. "It's mind boggling to think that Mom had four boys to raise, that she had this situation where the navy, initially anyway, wasn't even acknowledging the fact that my father was in prison or that he should receive combat pay. . . . The silly battles she had to fight to convince people that her situation was one that they had to look at uniquely. . . . And I think later on it was only right that so many people including congressmen and presidents came to acknowledge and appreciate, in retrospect, what my mother had done."

⊰——⊱

Through the first two years of Stockdale's captivity, the North Vietnamese tried every means imaginable to break down their prize capture, but to little avail.

On an almost daily basis, carrots were dangled to the American prisoners so they could avoid torture and beatings. In early May 1967, the guard that Stockdale had dubbed "Rabbit" got on the squawk box in Stockdale's area of the prison—nicknamed "Las Vegas"—and announced a new policy. The script was read three or four times that first day. It began by scolding the American prisoners for their poor attitude and their lack of cooperation. Rabbit then explained that the Americans were criminals and that they worked for the North Vietnamese and that they must pay for their upkeep. He told Stockdale, "You have obligations to the Democratic Republic of Vietnam. You must atone for your crimes and thereby enjoy the historic leniency and generosity of the Vietnamese people."

Rabbit then explained that those who would cooperate by making anti-American statements or appearing in anti-American propaganda videos would be given special privileges, including being released to go home before the war was over.

Stockdale describes this deal with the devil as the ultimate challenge to a "unity over self" motto that had sustained him and other brave American soldiers and sailors who were imprisoned in North Vietnam.

As Stockdale tapped out his Morse-code communiqués on the walls of his prison cell that evening, he was encouraged to hear that his fellow prisoners were equally repulsed by this proposition. Stockdale called this early release program "FRP," for "Fink Release Program," and gave the order to the others that there would be "no early release; we all go home together."

In the days after Rabbit's speech, the North Vietnamese made a series of attitude checks of several of the prisoners, and Stockdale learned that the Americans were being divided into three categories: the "willings," the "partially willings," and the "diehards." His captors would learn that Stockdale was at the top of the list of the diehards. Nothing could break him. In dark moments, he would call on all the strength of his character to urge his fellow prisoners to stay unified and not give in to the constant temptation to capitulate to escape the hell of their situation.

A question that occurs to anyone who reads of the degradation and torture and inhuman treatment given to Stockdale and the other prisoners is how these men could maintain any semblance of sanity through their ordeal. The answer for Stockdale was to always think of ways to improve communication with his fellow prisoners through cell walls and to look forward to the day when he could be released with honor. He knew that by staying unified, he and his compatriots could maintain their dignity, purpose, and self-respect.

Stockdale also allowed himself to spend hour upon hour reliving warm memories of his youth and pleasant times with Sybil and the boys. As an only child, Stockdale had spent a lot of his early years in solitude, and he often wondered in his cell whether that time alone had not all been part of God's plan to prepare him for his unimaginable vigil.

One of his lowest moments occurred on Christmas night, 1968, after a guard handed him a letter from Sybil. Although she had been writing him regularly since his capture, it was the first letter Jim had been given in two years. In the letter, Sybil mentioned that she had been able to sell his mother's house and put her belongings in storage, and Jim was able to surmise that his mother had died. Trapped as he was by the confines of his tiny cell and the ever-present leg irons, that news left him sobbing, feeling hopeless and light years removed from the life he'd left behind.

In the days that followed, Stockdale thought back to his childhood and recalled a high school play where he'd had the lead role. He'd interpreted the character much differently than his mother thought he should. They had debated several times about how the role ought to be played but Jim stuck to his guns, even though he was concerned about his mother's reaction. When the eventual opening-night performance earned a standing ovation from the audience, Stockdale noticed several members congratulating his mother, and he saw her wipe away a tear. This was a tremendous thrill for him, as his mother was generally unemotional.

There had been an almost puritanical insistence on discipline and achievement instilled in him by his parents. Although the Stockdales weren't churchgoers, they had a distinctly Protestant moral code and work ethic. Jim was raised with the understanding that he could never fall behind in his school work and his achievements, and that he absolutely must excel across the board: scholastically, athletically, and in oration contests and school dramatic productions. Stockdale wrote: "From the time I entered the first grade, an inner voice periodically said to me, 'To dope off, to just smell the flowers, is a waste, is lazy, is inconsiderate of your parents, and must be paid for with conscience-stricken remorse.'"

Vernon Weaver recalls hearing from Stockdale about another time-killing exercise that he would engage in during imprisonment. "Jim would wrack his brain to remember all the names of his classmates from grades one through 12 in Abingdon, Illinois," Weaver says. "I told him, 'Jim, I don't believe I ever could have done that.'"

"You could if you had seven years to think about it," Stockdale replied with a laugh.

"He understood that the brain is like the other muscles in the body," Weaver says, "in that the more it was exercised the more functional it would be. Jim was able to recall the name of every student in his classes but one, and the desire to learn that last boy's name was so intense that it was one of the first details he wanted to look up when he was released from captivity in 1973."

By 1968, Sybil was doing all she could to keep the family together and maintain unity among the wives of POW-MIAs. Her guiding thought "was to continue to try to do everything I could so that Jim would be proud of me. And that is the way I behaved."

Her perception of Lyndon Johnson was unchanged through the years. "The fact that we were instructed by government officials not to contact anybody about our husbands' situations was just ridiculous. I think Johnson was a liar and two-faced, but the madder I got at him, the stronger was my resolve to try to make the government do the right thing. I was overwhelmed with their ability to elude me. They were really clever, boy, I have to give them credit for that."

Sybil did receive consideration and courtesy from Ronald Reagan, who was then the governor of California. She recalls the first time she spoke with him on the phone. "I remember he had this wonderful voice, and he answered the phone by saying, 'This is Ronald Reagan speaking.' He was so considerate and listened carefully about my request to get a meeting with President Nixon, when he came into the White House in early 1969. Governor Reagan said he would do everything he could for me. He even gave me a couple of private phone numbers and said, 'Mrs. Stockdale, you can call me any time you want to. Any time of the night or day.'"

Sybil had made a concerted attempt to arrange a meeting with President Nixon in February of 1969, with little effect. But after Nixon gave an address to the nation on November 3 of that year and never once mentioned the plight of the American prisoners of war in Vietnam, she wrote him a letter. In part it read, "We are at a point where we feel we must meet with you personally, so that we may be reassured about your own personal interest and thoughts pertaining to the most desperate straits in which our husbands and sons find themselves. If you can find time to see a representative group from our number, we would be deeply grateful. We have been and remain your loyal supporters. . . ."

The meeting finally occurred six weeks later, on December 12, 1969. Twenty-six POW-MIA wives were in attendance.

"The meeting was very successful, because we impressed the president with the fact that we were human beings," Sybil says. "He could see that we were a group of suffering people, not just a bunch of, you know, bar flies. And our relations with the government improved dramatically after that. It was as if we were in a jet and the afterburner kicked in, because Nixon really took our plight to heart, and that made life much more pleasant for all of us."

But matters were never easy at home. The four boys all had different experiences about their dad's absence. "Jimmy had the hardest time," says Sybil. "He was 14 when his father left, and he had the responsibility of being the man of the house and feeling like he had to fill his father's shoes. And of course, when his father finally did get home, he was displaced from that role. It was all very difficult for him.

"Of course, Stanford and Taylor never remembered much of their father, so it was a totally new experience for them to have one when Jim came home. They had missed so much and tried hard to make up for the lost time. Stan actually suffered 'emotional blindness' and dropped out of school in the third grade. He had so much working against him. I was teaching all day, and he didn't have anybody.

He was dyslexic anyway, and then suddenly he couldn't read at all. He couldn't read, because he couldn't see, because he didn't have a mother and he didn't have a father. He felt like he was all alone."

Sid, age 11 when his father was shot down, says, "There was always a lot of male energy in the household. And when I went to an all-male boarding school, the people who were there, the headmaster of the school and the teachers, were such great male role models that it was tremendously helpful to me through that time. It provided an awful lot of correction for me, and I think it's one of the reasons that I ultimately became a teacher, because I so respected the teachers who guided me through boarding school."

Sid marvels today about his mother's ability to keep the family together. "It's mind boggling to think that she had to deal with the loneliness of losing my father and the responsibility of raising four boys, and then this situation with the navy, where at least in the early years, she wasn't allowed to acknowledge the fact that my father was in prison, or even that he should receive combat pay. It's astounding to recall the silly battles she had to fight to convince people that her situation was one that they had to look at uniquely. Something Mom did that was good for us was to load up the station wagon every summer and drive us across country to her parents' summer house on Long Island Sound in Connecticut. And that was a great escape. But imagine her driving with four boys in a station wagon across the United States. And there was, of course, no air conditioning. I asked her years later why she would do this. And she said, 'Well, I would drive only about 300 miles a day, and it would take us about eight days to get there. We would stop at Holiday Inns or other places, and you guys would jump in the pool or go play miniature golf, and I would rest up and get caught up on stuff.'

"I think that was a very healthy thing for her to do," Sid says, "just to get out on the road, get away from the telephone, and get away from all the memories that were there in the house at Coronado."

※ —— ※

After four years of constant beatings, humiliation, and isolation in a dark cell, Stockdale's captors were, by 1969, in disbelief at his resolve not to give them any credible information, and they were more determined than ever to break him. They knew he was the lynchpin holding the camp of American prisoners together and that he had devised an effective method of communication to bolster morale and share information.

Finally, in January 1969, at about the same time that Richard Nixon was being inaugurated and a heightened concern was spreading through the North Vietnamese forces about whether the American war effort was going to be stepped up, Stockdale sensed that the pressure on him was going to get even worse. Following an intense torture session one day, he submitted and wrote this note: "I understand that I am a criminal who has bombed churches, schools, and pagodas of the Democratic Republic of Vietnam. I have opposed the Camp Authority and incited others to oppose the Camp Authority. I know the nature of my sins, and I now submit to you to do whatever you tell me to write, say, or tape."

Stockdale readies for a flying mission before his capture.

This pleased his captors, giving them the false sense that he was capitulating. They asked him to fill out what they called a "Secret

Report," in which he would be required to fill in the numbers and names of all the men in his unit. As he had done with previous reports, Stockdale gave them erroneous information with made-up names, which he knew his captors would take weeks or months to analyze and decipher. It was all part of a sick, twisted game. He would cooperate only after putting up a wall of resistance but took consolation that he was giving the enemy nothing of real value.

One time Rabbit held up in Stockdale's face a picture of his handsome son Jimmy, who was then a freshman at Ohio Wesleyan College, and said, "If you ever want to see this boy again, you must change your attitude."

Each time Jim would "cooperate" and provide information that was deemed by the North Vietnamese to be of use, he would be given privileges like a blanket roll or a bowl of edible soup.

On those rare days when he would be given a razor, it meant he was about to be taken from the prison for an interrogation that could be filmed for propaganda purposes. In early 1969, and continuing throughout that year as Nixon stepped up the pace of bombing, the prison hierarchy became more convinced than ever that breaking Stockdale down was a top priority, both for information purposes and to inhibit his capacity to lead and inspire the other American POWs. One time when he was about to be taken to a videotaped interview, and fiercely determined not to participate in the propaganda exercise, Jim mustered up the courage to inflict serious cut wounds on his face. On another occasion, he would smash a 50-pound mahogany stool against his head, disfiguring himself so badly that were he to be filmed, it would appear as if he had recently been brutally tortured. These selfless actions showed his fellow prisoners the limits to which he was willing to go not to cooperate with his captors. Seven years later, when Stockdale was awarded the Medal of Honor by President Gerald Ford, the citation read, in part, "Stockdale . . . deliberately inflicted a near-mortal wound to his person in order to convince his captors of his willingness to give up his life rather than capitulate. He was subsequently discovered and revived by the North Vietnamese who, convinced of his indomitable spirit, abated in their employment of excessive harassment and torture toward all the Prisoners of War."

As is usually the case with international conflict, politics determined the American agenda in Vietnam, and as the presidential election of 1972 started to draw near, it was clearly in Richard Nixon's political interest to wind down the most divisive war of the century. His Democratic opponent, Senator George McGovern, was gaining gradual support by campaigning on a staunch anti-war platform. In a country torn down the middle by the rising body count in Southeast Asia, Nixon needed to take aggressive action to convince the country that he was bringing the war to a successful conclusion. American military forces stepped up the bombing campaign on Hanoi during the early months of 1972, and through the summer and fall it was beginning to become clear to Stockdale and the other prisoners that the day of their release might not be far off. Although the bomb blasts were a safe distance away (American pilots well knew the location of their prison), the POWs could hear and feel the explosions and realized their significance.

Regarding a major bombing raid on December 18, 1972, Stockdale wrote, "Some of the prisoners did detect higher-level explosions early in the bombardment, but it wasn't until these explosions were still being heard twenty minutes after that the cheers started to go up all over the cellblocks of that downtown prison. This was a new reality for Hanoi. . . . The bombs shook the ground under us and plaster fell from the ceilings. The days of Mickey Mouse were over! Our wonderful America was here to deliver a message, not a self-conscious stammer of apology.

"'Let's hear it for President Nixon!' went the cry from cellblock to cellblock, all around the courtyard. The bombers kept coming and we kept cheering. Guards who were normally enraged by loud talk, guards who normally thrust their bayoneted rifles through the bars and screamed at us if we dared shout during air raids, could be seen silently cowering in the lee of the prison walls, their faces ashen in the light reflected from the fiery skies above."

Just before New Year's, 1973, it was clear that Hanoi was nearly out of ammunition, and the American POWs would be going home. As always, Jim Stockdale was outwardly stoic and self-contained about this, but inside his heart was bursting with joy at the prospect of seeing Sybil and his boys once again. It had been well over seven years since he'd laid eyes on them, and Jim felt an understandable apprehension about reuniting after so long. Jimmy and Sid were now young men. And he was concerned that Stan and Taylor, who was just a three-year-old when Stockdale was shot down, would not even know him.

"I grew kind of scared," he wrote. "As I contemplated the significance of the moment [when I would first see them]. What will they think of me down there, Syb and the boys? My hair is totally white now. I can't see to read (too many months in the dark, too many weeks in the blindfold). . . . I'm forty-nine years old and crippled and can't raise my left arm. . . . Can we put it all back together after all these years?"

$$\not\exists\!-\!\!-\!\not\succ$$

Through separate interviews with all four Stockdale sons, more than 30 years after their father was released from seven-plus years of imprisonment and torture, one gets a sense of the overwhelming challenge that the family faced individually and collectively. A picture also emerges of the love that held Jim and Sybil together through this time and allowed them to emerge triumphant through an unimaginable gauntlet of sorrows.

Oldest son Jimmy recalled, "I probably had about as normal a childhood as the son of a Naval aviator could have, especially one as ambitious as Dad. He could be warm, but there was always a little distance there, and if I can offer a little armchair philosophy, he didn't really know how to be a dad because he had been an only child. He certainly didn't know how to navigate kids at all, and Mom always shielded him from us too much."

Jimmy remembered that in the late 1950s and early '60s, his father always accompanied him to his Little League baseball games. "Compared with my brothers, who never got to have an experience like that, it was just wonderful. I remember one time he was pitching to me, and we were about four pitches into my learning how to hit better when he accidentally threw a pitch inside and cold-cocked me in the temple with the ball. I went down and saw stars, and he came running over and just held me. I never, ever forgot that. It was kind of loving and clumsy all at once. I could tell that he was thinking, 'I get so few chances to do this with my son. Why can't I do it right?'"

Adult males would often, at some point during his father's absence, put an arm around Jimmy's shoulder and say something to the effect that "You're the man of the family now, Jimmy. You have to fill in for your father."

"I never knew what to say to that," Jim Jr. says. "I mean I was just a teenager at the time, just becoming a man, and I was being told I had this huge responsibility. I did do what I could, by driving my brothers to their games and activities when I was old enough, but the rest was pretty overwhelming."

Second son Sid, who had just turned 11 when his father was shot down, also has a distinct memory of his father's intermittent times at home before his capture. "There was just a lot of physical activity around the house, playing tag, always throwing footballs." "When we lived in a rented house in Los Altos Hills [in Northern California] in 1958, Dad hung a great big thick climbing rope from the tree with a big knot at the bottom. It was about 40 feet long, and he would go outside and climb the thing with just his arms, you know, with his feet out at 90 degrees. He would always tell us, 'If you can ever climb this thing without using your feet, I will give you $5.' And of course, we would work like crazy! Then you'd get that second hand up there and say, 'No way! This is impossible!'"

Stan Stockdale, five when his father was captured, recalls several challenges growing up with a father he barely knew. "I remember there was a group called the Indian Guides, and it was kind of a Boy Scout spin-off. I was in the fourth grade, and I heard about the Indian

Guides from a teacher, and it sounded pretty cool to me. You go out camping and stuff, basically in a father-son activity. I went home and told Mom that I would like to try and be a part of the Indian Guides. But I was told that I could not be a part of that because I didn't have a dad. I remember that stuck with me, and I thought, God, how that made me feel sad. That was the first time it kind of hit me. Then there was Little League, and of course dads are involved in that. I would look at my friends and how they interacted with their dads. And I thought that that looked pretty cool, and I wished I could be doing that."

Youngest Stockdale son, Taylor, had only vague memories of his father before he disappeared, so when he greeted him home in 1973, it was as if he were seeing his father for the very first time. Taylor was almost 11, and he was finally going to have a father. "It was just very strange when we ran out to hug him at the base at Miramar. I expected to wrap my arms around this big giant of a man. I had been hearing so many wonderful things about him; in my mind he was just larger than life. But when I wrapped my arms around him, it was almost like embracing a ghost. He was so frail and had lost so much weight, he was hardly bigger than me. It made me instantly appreciate everything they had put him through.

The Stockdale family reunited.

"It was foreign at first to have a dad. While it was great, and like a miracle, it took a lot of adjustment at the same time. It felt very, very natural on one hand, but at the same time . . . [*long pause*] it definitely took some adjustment. In a sense I grew up without a father. So I knew life in a very natural way with only a mom. So suddenly to have a father appear, it was a jolt at first. And he was not only there, but he was a celebrity.

"I do recall that the local news channel would show up each year around the holidays, and they would film us opening our presents without our father," Taylor says. "And the story was always, 'Another Christmas goes by without their dad.' But besides that, it felt like a pretty natural childhood.

"My father and I really didn't warm up to each other quickly after he returned," Taylor adds, "because he was pretty much preoccupied with my older brothers, as they had a relationship with him beforehand. And he was readjusting to being back home, and he was readjusting to being in the navy. A lot was going on in his life, so I think he was sort of prioritizing a bit. While it took a while for him and me to connect, it wasn't bad, you know. We played it well in that we didn't force it. We didn't try to make something happen that wasn't natural. We hugged and talked and did stuff together, but we didn't feel like we were on a timeline, or feel like we had to love each other within six months of his return. We had our whole lives, and so it was going to happen. I had Little League and my friends, and he had his life and career. We knew it was all going to be okay. And we ended up being very, very close, absolutely. But it took a long time."

Taylor recalls that the experience he most craved was a camping trip with his father, just the two of them. "We went out to North Island and went camping on the beach, just me and Dad, which was really cool. He was really reaching out to me on that occasion. He had been spending so much time with my older brothers, and I think he knew we needed this time together. That was the first time we really bonded. It wasn't until a couple years later that I realized that asking a recent prisoner of war to haul out a sleeping bag and go camp out on a beach was about the least appealing thing he could do, but he was a great sport about it."

Taylor adds a note that was struck by nearly every family member. "I don't know who said it first, but there's truth to it," he says. "That it takes about as long to fully reconnect as the time he was gone, which was over seven years. I remember when I was 18, more than seven years after he'd returned, I remember feeling really close to my dad, like he was really my dad after all. I know that sounds like an inordinate amount of time, but that is what it took."

⚐ —— ⚐

In 1976, Stockdale did a tour at the Pentagon, which would be his first and last tour there. Here he was, finally in the coveted "E-Ring," or as he put it, "that king's row that played its part in screwing up my ten-year war." But he found he couldn't be effective with his writing and thinking there. He had in effect been muzzled, told by more than one Pentagon official to keep his lip zipped, "just 'til I learned Washington."

Stockdale back on the job.

That wasn't going to fly for a man who'd been through so much and knew even more, so Stockdale went off on his own, accepting invitations from colleges and business groups to give inspirational speeches about courage and discipline.

The following year, while still at the Pentagon, Jim was invited to the office of Secretary of the Navy, Graham Claytor, the and told he was to be assigned either as president of the Naval War College or superintendent of the Naval Academy. Claytor asked him which job he would choose. Jim far preferred to return to his alma mater, but he was told he would have to wait 18 months for that position to open, and he was certain he couldn't take another long stretch at the Pentagon without speaking out and offending someone and thereby jeopardizing his selection, so he opted for the War College.

Stockdale thoroughly enjoyed his two years there, not so much for the administrative chores as the teaching. He devised a course called "Foundations of Moral Obligation," incorporating much of the stoic philosophy that had served him so well in Vietnam. "The course was to fill what I thought of as great gaps in the college's academic core, gaps in ideas that in my life had turned out to be determining factors in success or failure in war's gut struggle over willpower and moral leverage," he wrote. "The remarkable and eternal applicability of what the ancients had to say about the human predicament occupied hours upon hours of my thoughts in solitary confinement in prison. There was something very comforting in knowing that being cast in a role that was scripted for a lifetime of uphill fighting against hopeless odds was *not* an exceptional human fate in the broad scope of history. In fact, a legitimate school of philosophical thought, Stoicism, was built on learning to play that role with integrity and dignity."

His next stop, in 1979, was as president of the Citadel, a military academy in South Carolina. Suffice it so say that the challenges he expected to find there and those he actually found were not remotely similar, and so after a year and a half of trying to reform an institution totally unlike the traditional American service academies, he resigned from that post and within a year returned to the site of his wonderful post-graduate studies, Stanford University. The Hoover Institution at Stanford allowed Stockdale the freedom over the next many years to write and lecture on a full-time basis, and he took full advantage, authoring three books published by the

Institution's press: *A Vietnam Experience: Ten Years of Reflection; Courage Under Fire: Testing Epictetus's Doctrines in a Laboratory of Human Behavior;* and *Thoughts of a Philosophical Fighter Pilot.*

⊰ — ⊱

In 1992, as a way of repaying Ross Perot for all he'd done for American prisoners of war and for his dramatic rescue efforts on behalf of the Iranian hostages in 1979, Jim Stockdale accepted Perot's plea to become his vice-presidential candidate. It was supposed to be only a temporary assignment, as Perot intended to find a more politically suitable and ambitious candidate later on. He needed Stockdale primarily because most states required Perot to list a vice presidential running mate to be included on their ballots.

Stockdale with Ronald Reagan.

In the interim, Perot felt that the beloved admiral was a wise choice. He knew that no one could fault him for selecting a true American hero who was also a renowned educator and philosopher. Certainly, the selection was about as critic-proof a choice as could be made. But then Perot suddenly dropped out of the race, citing, among other reasons, concern over his daughters' security. Stockdale thought that would be the end of it until Perot just as suddenly changed his mind and reentered the race in early October. At that point, it was too late in the race for Perot to change the ballot and name someone else as his running mate, so Stockdale was forced to remain on the ticket for another five weeks, until Perot's defeat in November. Sid Stockdale clearly remembers his mother agreeing to Perot's wishes, with the contingency that there be no debating. Sybil fully acknowledged that her husband was a writer and a philosopher and could give wonderful prepared speeches, but she also knew he wasn't a debater, nor did he have a grasp of the issues that the other candidates had been studying and debating for years. Al Gore, running on a ticket with Bill Clinton, had been a presidential contender for years, and Dan Quayle had already spent four years as George Bush's vice-president.

"Mom knew that my father would not be strong at all in that kind of a format," Sid says, "and that he would clearly be mismatched in a debate. "Two weeks later, Perot called and said, 'Hey this is Ross. We've got you all signed up.' And Dad said, 'Signed up for what?'

"'Well, for the VP debates down in Atlanta,' Perot replied. "But Perot's people never sent anyone to prep my father," Sid says. "And Ross and my father never had any conversations about foreign policy, economics, social programs . . . nothing. Not one conversation!

"Mom and Dad were just trying to hang onto the reins of the thing and not let Perot down. Meanwhile, they were being bombarded by the press. And I was just nuts, absolutely nuts."

Both Al Gore and Dan Quayle had spent at least a month training for the debate like boxers prepping for a title fight. They were being briefed on a daily basis by the best minds in their respective parties. Stockdale would be going into the debate nearly stone cold and forced to ad-lib answers in front of 30 million television viewers trying to discern which candidates were best informed and most capable of assuming a post a heartbeat away from the most powerful position on earth.

It had been nearly 18 years since Stockdale had returned from Vietnam. An entire generation of voters weren't even vaguely familiar with who the admiral was or what sacrifices he had made on their behalf.

"That debate was a terrible mistake you know," says Sybil. "Jim didn't want it . . . he never wanted to be vice-president nor planned to be. Ross called him up one morning and said, 'Would you be my stand-in vice-president until I can get a real politician?' And Jim said, 'Sure, Ross.' And then Jim got sandbagged, because Ross never could get anybody, nor did he try very hard. And then he got in that terrible situation in the debate. God, that was a nightmare."

"I was always called in to lead any kind of literary charge for the family," says Jim Stockdale Jr. "That was my strength—verbal, writing, editorial stuff, etcetera. I was glad to answer the call in 1992 when Mom phoned 10 days before the vice-presidential debate, and I got out there six days before and realized there was no support, no nothing. We were in this Winnebago that doubled as a dressing room backstage at Georgia Tech before the debate. I had written, and Dad had memorized—bless his heart—this beautiful opening statement in which he was to say, 'It's fair to ask who I am and why I'm here. I'm not a Washington insider, so please don't expect me to speak the language shared by my contemporaries . . . ' blah, blah, blah . . . and then he was to talk about being from a small farm town and leading the culture of prison in Hanoi and knowing the world through a different perspective and how a prisoner can bring a unique working-man's perspective to politics.

"Well, 15 minutes before he went on, he and my mom were sitting in the Winnebago having a drink, which I did *not* think was a good idea, and Mom said, 'You know, I think you ought to show them you have a sense of humor. You know, say "Who am I? Why am I here?"' And I said, 'I don't know. We've kind of got this in place.' Anyway," Jim Jr. says, "I got off that Winnebago and said, 'We're screwed!'"

"It was crushing to me," says Stan Stockdale. "Here was a guy who had dedicated his whole life to high-minded ethical endeavors and suffered brutally and come out at the end with his dignity intact, only to have him caricatured on *Saturday Night Live* [after the VP debate] as a buffoon. I remember in Atlanta, we were all there, watching him try to prepare for this thing, and I could just see that he was so damn uncomfortable. He didn't know anything about gun control or several other hot-button political issues. He and Ross Perot had never had one conversation about politics. He was on the ballot simply because Perot needed a name on the ballot.

"I remember sitting there and we are waiting for the lights to come on, and the three of them come out and take their positions at the podium. Now my dad is a wonderful speaker. He can blow your doors off with his material when he can in fact read his material. But he wasn't allowed to bring notes to the stage. So to be in that political arena and think on your feet, that was about as far away from his comfort zone as you could get. And as the moderator was preparing to start the debate, I could see Quayle and Gore furiously writing notes. Of course, they had just been loaded up with information from their aides, and they were getting it on paper. And they just wrote and wrote and wrote, and my dad was just drumming his fingers on the podium. I remember thinking, 'We are so f------dead!'

"When the debate started, Dad gets about halfway through his memorized speech and then he draws a blank. It just went south from there. And, of course, Gore and Quayle are yapping political gibberish back and forth like snarling poodle dogs. Dad is looking like he is watching a ping-pong match, his gaze going from one to the other. And some 30 million people are watching this whole scene. I was in the front row of the auditorium, and I was grabbing onto the chair rails very intentionally, because I had a serious inclination to go right up there, grab Dad, and say 'We're getting out of here.' I will go on the record with this. I'm angry at Ross Perot that this happened. He set up our family and, of course, we were never supposed to be in that position. I heard later that some of his people started to spin the story that Jim Stockdale had suffered a stroke up on stage. On several occasions, I've sat down to write Perot a letter explaining how I felt, but I knew I would send something that I would later regret."

"You know," Jim Jr. says, "it happened again, for the thousandth time, just this morning. I was meeting with a client and he said, 'Your name is Stockdale? Stockdale . . . Stockdale . . . Oh yeah, are you related to that guy who ran for vice president?'

"And I said, 'Actually, I'm related to that guy that had his ass kicked for eight years in a prisoner-of-war camp, so that we could live free lives over here in this country.'"

But Admiral Stockdale didn't let the fallout from the televised debacle slow him down or bruise his confidence one bit. He told his sons on many occasions that his moment in the political spotlight was the least consequential thing that had ever happened to him. Despite the political gadflies and talk-show comedians who had fun at his expense, Stockdale viewed the moment from a far broader perspective and was able to see that at the end of the day, he had just answered the call of a friend, and it didn't turn out quite as well as it could have.

⊰——⊱

In 2002, Taylor Stockdale, the assistant head of schools for Webb Schools in Claremont, California, was on a fund-raising mission to Hong Kong, when he caught a flight to Hanoi. The U.S. State Department had arranged for him to be accompanied by a tour guide who specialized in families of POWs.

"I arrived there at night," he says, recounting the experience three years later, "and I felt I had to go down to the prison right then. I talked to the concierge at our hotel, and he said it was pretty safe. So we walked about a mile to the Hanoi Hilton, and when I poked my head in, the guard was watching me closely. I gave him a twenty-dollar bill and he let me have the run of the place. I spent hours that night there and came back the next day as well. I was just so drawn to it. It was really eerie. I actually was in the room where my dad cut his wrists."

Taylor also walked into the rooms where his father was tortured, and he even laid on the ground in the actual leg irons that manacled his father nearly 40 years before.

Then, by using a GPS system, Taylor was able to locate the remote village six hours south of Hanoi, where his father's plane was shot down.

"There was only one plane downed in that area, and it was Dad's," Taylor says. "We drove down to the location, in the middle of nowhere, and it was like a Hollywood set. These old peasants were there, many of whom had actually witnessed his shoot down. They were even describing what my father's mangled leg looked like. It was like the only major event that had ever occurred in this village, so it was a huge piece of history to them. They pointed out the exact spot where my father landed, which is exactly the way he describes it in his book.

"Then we went to the spot where the wreckage of the plane was, and I scavenged around and found a tiny piece of metal. And I thought that would be a neat keepsake. My interpreter explained that one of the villagers said he gave a piece of the plane to his grandfather. So we drove to another place that was even more remote, like a bamboo village in the middle of nowhere.

"We were in this man's house, and he kept talking about a table that was in the middle of the room. Before I could say anything, they ripped off the wood which had been wood-pegged onto the metal. They had made a table out of a large piece of metal from my dad's plane. The man picked up the table and handed it to me. And I was thinking I would pay anything to have that table, so I took out some money and handed it to him. He wouldn't take it. 'No, no, no,' he said. And the translator interpreted his next sentence. He said, 'Your father is a hero in your country. It would be a great honor for me to give you this.' It was a powerful moment," Taylor says. "I teared up and almost lost it."

"I am so happy that I went there and visited those places," he says, his voice softening. "Aside from having a family, I don't think there is anything that I have ever done in my life that was more satisfying."

End note: Admiral Jim Stockdale, Class of '47, highest-ranking naval officer held prisoner of war in Vietnam, Medal of Honor winner, philosopher, lecturer, and author, died on July 5, 2005. He was honored at two separate services, the first on the deck of the USS *Ronald Reagan* on July 16, and one a week later at the United States Naval Academy at Annapolis, where he was interred. Eight Medal of Honor winners served as pallbearers, and more than a dozen prisoners of war were in attendance. All four Stockdale sons spoke at the services, and all maintained their composure throughout their talks, demonstrating their father's grace under pressure.

Businessman Jackson T. Stephens as an Academy midshipman.

CHAPTER FIVE

Jack Stephens:

Thinking Big

I N THE INCREDIBLE CAREER OF JACKSON T. (Jack) Stephens, there are many events and moments that can help a person understand and define the man. But nothing contributed more to shaping the character and sharpening the intelligence of the investment banker and future chairman of Augusta National and The Masters golf tournament than his upbringing in a large, loving family on a small farm in Prattsville, Arkansas.

And it was the countrified, common-sense wisdom of Jack's father A. J. Stephens that formed the moral and ethical base for nearly every important decision he would make throughout his life.

Those who have worked with and for Jack Stephens through the years—many of whom became wealthy beyond their wildest dreams—call him a calculated risk taker, a man who never risked more than he could afford. This trait can be traced to words A. J. Stephens shared with his son, when he was just in his teens. "Be willing to risk everything you're willing to lose," the father told his son. And then he would quote Rudyard Kipling's words about risking winnings in a game of pitch-and-toss. "And lose, and start again at your beginnings/And never breathe a word about your loss."

Jack Stephens would later say, "That advice is hard to follow, but I have tried to consider every new adventure, every proposed merger or purchase, in that light. I never wanted to do anything to the extreme, so that if I were wrong, we'd have to close our doors. I always knew that if we kept the doors open and didn't get over-committed, we could make a lot of money."

Decades later, during the Cuban missile crisis, Jack Stephens had a Stephens Inc. employee withdraw $100,000 in cash from a company account and put it in a lock box. He wanted to be certain that in the event of a crisis, the company could still operate for two months.

Jack also recalls being preoccupied as a young boy about whether, as the sixth and final child of his parents, he might not have been a "happy accident" rather than a planned birth. When he mustered up the courage to pose this concern to his father, A. J. Stephens provided just the reassurance any son would love to hear. He told Jack that Jack was the son he wanted most of all and that he had actually ventured into the oil fields of southern Arkansas buying and selling leases to try and make money so that the family could afford one more addition to their large family.

Stephens' mother is recalled with equal love and fondness. "My mom was a complete homebody," Jack says. "And she also was a great teacher, working with all the children on their reading and math. Although we were extremely poor, we never felt poor. When the Depression came, it didn't change our way of life one bit. We thought we were extremely lucky."

As much as he appreciated the wonderful values he learned growing up on a farm, Jack also knew he didn't want to spend his whole life there. He has said, "There was nothing I wanted more than to work my way out of my position behind a mule and make my living with my mind rather than my muscle."

Witt Stephens, Jack's older brother by 16 years and the man who accepted him into his growing business as a full and equal partner after Jack graduated from the Naval Academy, recalls another unforgettable lesson that A. J. Stephens shared in front of the hearth at the family farmhouse.

"Papa one time took six sticks and held them between his two hands and tried to break them and he couldn't," Witt said in a 1991 interview. "Then he took them one at a time and easily broke them. He told us that if the six of us children stuck together and loved one another, we could not be broken apart."

In a 2004 interview, one of Stephens Inc. top investment bankers through the years, a true Southerner named J. D. Simpson, says, "I learned from Witt and Jack that you can take your Southern heritage and use it to your advantage."

The first time a writer enters a conference room adjacent to Simpson's office in the corporate headquarters in Little Rock, he expresses surprise at seeing one of those talking Billy Bob fishes mounted on a wall.

"Oh, JD is quite the redneck," his assistant explains. "You'll have to forgive him."

Later, Simpson explains, "I may goon it up from time to time, but that's just who I am. It brings out the humor in people. And look at Witt and Jack Stephens. They come from Prattsville, Arkansas. They are the furthest thing from bigshots. If people look down at you because of where you're from, that tells you something about them. Those are people you might not want to trust in a business deal."

It is impossible to fully understand the success of Jack Stephens and the company that bears his name without appreciating the talents of his older brother and how perfectly the brothers complemented each other. Witt Stephens was the consummate salesman. As a boy, he would make pocket money by parching peanuts, putting them in a sock, and selling them. Later on, still in his twenties, Witt got the idea from his father of selling belt buckles. He attained a sample case of buckles and talked his way into selling them on the post of a Civilian Conservation Corps camp, on the very day the workers received their paychecks.

"I wasn't scared of anybody," Witt would say years later. "I was just a kid, and I figured there was no harm in asking. Somehow they let me, and that first month I made $2,600 selling buckles (roughly the equivalent of $20,000 today). The president of the belt-buckle company asked to meet me in Little Rock, because I'd sold more buckles than anyone in the country," Witt said. "Soon after, I hired guys to sell for me around the country. I made forty cents off each buckle. I ended up staying with the company for five years, then I went into the investment business."

It was with this combination of Witt's country wisdom and great selling ability and Jack's business sense and education at Columbia Military Academy, the University of Arkansas, and the United States Naval Academy that the brothers built one of the largest investment-banking firms in the country.

Vernon Weaver, a USNA graduate who went on to have a distinguished business and public service career himself, heading up the Small Business Administration for President Jimmy Carter and years later serving as the Ambassador to the European Union for President Bill Clinton, first met Jack Stephens as a midshipman at the Naval Academy. They became roommates and lifelong best friends. Weaver says about the partnership between the Stephens brothers that "Witt had native wisdom, only a partial high school education, but great instincts and judgment when it came to sizing people up. He was probably the best salesman I ever met. And then you match that up with Jack's great schooling. It was an effective combination. The two brothers were very unalike in personality and temperament. Witt, for instance, was far more frugal than Jack. Yet despite their many differences in personality and style, it was only rarely in their 45 years of partnership that they did not agree on a method of operation."

When Jack left Prattsville to attend Columbia Military Academy with tuition money that Witt had provided, Witt told him that they would become partners when Jack finished college. And when that day arrived, the two cemented the agreement.

"Witt came to Annapolis for our graduation in June of 1946," Weaver recalls, "and Jack had learned that he would not be commissioned in the navy because of his poor eyesight. Jack mentioned to Witt that he was considering going to New York to interview with some big investment bankers. And I remember Witt saying, 'You ain't got to do that.' And it was in our room at Bancroft Hall that Witt made Jack the offer right then to become his full partner in what was then called W. R. Stephens Investments. I saw them shake hands on it. That was the beginning of the company that came to be known as Stephens Inc."

Over four decades later, Jack Stephens called the partnership with his brother "the thing I'm most proud of business-wise in my life. It's been a marvelous experience. The hardest thing to do in a relationship like ours is to let the other person be himself. In essence, we told each other: 'You do your thing and I'll do mine, and we'll meet on Saturday and see how we've done.'"

In the spring of the very year they formed their partnership, Witt and Jack purchased Fort Smith Gas Company and renamed it Arkansas-Oklahoma Gas Co. They also started Stephens Production Co., which was involved in oil and gas exploration and would prove to be a phenomenal success. Nine years later, they bought Arkansas and Louisiana Gas Co., and two years after that, in 1957, Witt turned the newly named Stephens Inc. over to Jack and left to run ARKLA. He stayed there until he retired in 1973, and then returned to the core company.

Jack has said that when he started with Witt, he never had a defined goal. "I just knew that what we did together would be significant, but it wouldn't happen quickly. You build things slowly. You do something each day. And you go to bed with your integrity intact and work in a good atmosphere. I never had a money goal except one. I wanted to be worth a million by the time I was 30. But then I realized that was too easy. I thought I better have another goal. Somewhere along the line accumulating a pile of money became unimportant. I never really defined it, but I soon eliminated money as a goal."

In the 1980s and 1990s, when *Forbes* magazine ranked Jack Stephens as one of the richest men in the U.S., Jack paid scant attention to the honor, often dismissing the validity of a ranking system when quizzed about it by reporters.

Witt put a different spin on the goal of earning money. "I wanted to make more money that any other man my age," he said. When he was asked whether he accomplished that goal, he replied, with a twinkle in his eye, "I doubt it."

Vernon Weaver thinks an event that occurred at the beginning of their final year at the Naval Academy went a long way towards developing Jack's leadership skills. Vernon says that his roommate was a somewhat apathetic student in his first years at Annapolis. While Jack was a terrific shot with a rifle, he didn't want to join the rifle team when asked. And with a rather introverted personality, Jack initially shied away from group activities.

"Then one day," Weaver recalls, "Commander Ebert told our company [each company had 75 first-class midshipmen] that he believed we were the worst company in the history of the Naval Academy. And he wondered out loud what we could do about it. And one of our classmates raised his hand and said, 'Let us elect our own company commander.' Well, that was just not done at the Academy. It had never been done prior to that day and has never been done since. Someone nominated Jack Stephens, and I became his campaign manager, and sure enough he was elected."

Vernon feels that the responsibility that came with Stephens' role of company commander caused Jack to rise to the occasion, to take his studies more seriously, and to do an outstanding job. "He started caring more about his life at the Academy and the men in his company, and that carried right through to his business career.

"Jack has always been very introspective and soft-spoken," Weaver adds. "But he's a compelling person and you instantly sense his integrity. In business, particularly, he always had a way of giving people confidence when he met them and making them feel important."

Admiral William Crowe, chairman of the Joint Chiefs of Staff under presidents Ronald Reagan and George H. W. Bush, was in the same company and became good friends with Vernon Weaver and Jack Stephens. Crowe agrees that Jack made a fine company commander, but he has a slightly different recollection as to why the Arkansas native got the nod from his classmates.

"I believe we elected Jack Stephens our company commander more as a slap in the face of the system, as an act of mutiny against the administration, rather than an endorsement of Jack," he says, on a spring evening in 2004. "After all, Jack was on the verge of being thrown out of the Academy for too many demerits."

Crowe laughs at his assessment, and adds that, "No one in our class saw in Jack the tremendous business leadership that he demonstrated later on. It was a revelation to watch his career."

Weaver's wife Joyce says, "At the time, I kind of looked at that whole group of friends that Vernon hung out with as a bunch of losers. They were interesting and fun guys, with great personalities, but I think it was generally assumed that as a whole, they weren't really going anywhere. Little did we know. . . ."

In talking with the people who have worked with Jack Stephens through the years, the same descriptions come up time and again: "Soft-spoken, warm, introspective, respectful, totally honest . . . a man with incredible judgment . . . someone who will step up to the plate in critical situations . . . the best boss a person could ever have."

"Jack Stephens was a great leader for this company, a man that you felt was always totally in the game with you," says Jon Jacoby, who joined Stephens Inc. in June of 1963, the very week he graduated from Harvard Business School. "Jack's main qualities are honesty— sometimes brutal honesty—humility, intuition, and intelligence." When Jacoby first interviewed for a job with Stephens Inc., he remembers asking Jack to describe his business philosophy. "He said, 'I want to have a good time and make an ass-pocketful of money,'" Jacoby says. "And I remember thinking to myself, I want to work with this guy."

Ronnie Pyle, a long-time employee of Stephens Inc., also vividly recalls Jack Stephens telling him in their first interview that he would make a lot of money. "I learned very quickly that the worst thing you could ever do at this company was try to bullshit Jack Stephens," Pyle says. "He would let people go on with an exaggeration or half-truth until they were given just enough rope to hang themselves. Working for him, I've learned to tell the *exact* truth, and not to hedge even the slightest bit."

Jeanie Brown came to work at Stephens Inc. in 1976, and she recalls being employee number 42 when she started. "There weren't a lot of women in the investment banking business at that time, just a small few, but Jack believed in me, and that was so important. Jack felt that traders are born and not made, because so much of it is gut feel. And he just loved to spend three or four hours a day on the trading-room floor. That was the action he really loved.

"The stock market is a psychological impact game," Brown says. "And Jack always wanted my insight and my opinion on trades. I always valued that so much, that he would respect my opinion and seek out my judgment. So many of us have passed up lucrative offers to stay here because Jack created the feeling that we were all part of a wonderful family. The loyalty here is incredible."

"Jack wanted us to be able to see everything that was happening on Wall Street," says Peter Carr, another long-time Stephens trader. "He didn't want us to feel the slightest bit disadvantaged that we were conducting our business in Little Rock. He wanted to put Little Rock in the big leagues in the investment trading world, and he did just that."

Pyle recalls a time in 1980, when interest rates were sky high and suddenly a large number of bonds were being called. "Stephens Inc. had its neck out a foot," he says, "and one day I was called up to Jack's office. He said, 'How did this mess happen?'

"And I had known for a long time that there was no dodging a situation like this. I explained the predicament to him the best I could, and he responded with two words. 'Fix it!' And we ended up making every customer whole. We ate the entire loss. But that's just the way this company operates. One of Stephens Inc.'s mottos is: We value the relationship with our customers more than any trade."

"Integrity is everything to Jack," says Greg Feltus, who manages private client groups and mutual-fund distribution at Stephens Inc. "He's a stickler on it. He understands mistakes, but he doesn't forgive dishonesty. And he always led by example. Even in his 70s, I remember he always looked crisp and ready to go. Maybe that was his Naval Academy training. You always sensed that Jack really wanted his employees to perform outstanding work, and that gave you the desire to please him."

Curt Bradbury, the senior executive vice president and COO of Stephens Inc., says that early in his career, he was put in charge of cleaning up a failed bank that Stephens was involved in.

"It was a messy deal," Bradbury says, "but there was a clear legal argument that could have been made that Stephens had no responsibility in the matter. It was a $52 million bankruptcy of an institution called Worthen Banking Corp. And when it happened, all eyes turned to Jack. The biggest hit was going to be taken by the Arkansas Teachers Pension Plan, and Jack just wouldn't allow that to happen. Twenty million of it was covered by insurance, but Jack's strength and willingness to step up and put up $32 million in a three-day period is what saved the day. It was Jack Stephens' presence, his vision, and his aura that turned the situation from one of the biggest besmirchments on his investment record to one of his greatest achievements. I ended up spending 10 years there cleaning it up, but the point is that once Jack Stephens gives you the responsibility on a job, he'll back you one hundred percent."

When it came to business deals, Jack was always interested in businesses that would be fun to own and operate, but first and foremost they had to make sense at the bottom line. Announcer Pat Summerall, a good friend of Jack Stephens from the time he enrolled at the University of Arkansas on a football scholarship, says that Jack and Vince Lombardi almost bought the Green Bay Packers from the community of Green Bay before Lombardi left to become coach of the Washington Redskins. A few years earlier, Jack had met with Del Webb, the owner of the New York Yankees, and was told he could buy 50 percent of the Yankees. A former Yankee, Hall of Fame catcher and long-time Stephens Inc. employee, Bill Dickey, was at the meeting, as was Vernon Weaver. Vernon recalls that everything had gone well and that a verbal agreement had been reached. "I remember when Del Webb was getting on the elevator to leave, he turned to

Jack and said, 'Jack, we're not gonna make any money in this, but we'll have a good time.' And Jack immediately stopped Webb from getting on the elevator and had him repeat what he'd said. When Del repeated it, the deal was off. Jack was just not interested in a business arrangement where he couldn't make money."

"Sometimes you'd hear people musing about the fact that Jack would often come into the office at 10 or 10:30 in the morning," Weaver says. "And the supposition of those who didn't know Jack well was that he was taking it easy, that he was enjoying an owner's executive privilege. But I can tell you on those mornings when he came in late, he had been at his house, maybe out on the back porch, working on a problem, or working out the numbers, so that when he came into the office, he had totally analyzed the situation and was prepared to make a decision. I also remember him saying that nothing important happens before lunch. On those days, he would often stay at the office until 9:00 p.m. Jack Stephens never regarded his business as work. It was his love and his passion."

Jack's good sense of humor is illustrated in a story from George Davis, another long-time Stephens employee. "We were looking at buying a chain of 25 nursing homes in the Arkansas region several years ago," Davis says. "We already owned a company called Leisure Lodge, and this was to be the beginning of a $100 million business called Beverly Enterprises. Jack Stephens finalized the deal when he was in a hospital bed, a little groggy from a surgery he'd undergone. When the deal had been completed, Jack said to me, 'I'm going to have to keep an eye on you, George. Any man who can sell a man under anesthesia a broke company for a million dollars is dangerous.' He then laughed and said, 'That's all right. We're going to make a lot of money together.'"

Another time, when asked about the mystique that seemed to hover around Stephens Inc. and all the terrific deals the company had put together, Jack said, "I have come to the conclusion that mystique is something like virginity. It's great to have, but it's something to get rid of as soon as possible."

Vernon Weaver spoke for a full hour one day about the Jack Stephens he knows. "Jack is a hard-to-define man," he says. "He sometimes projects a tough exterior, but is a real softie inside." Weaver recalls when a company called Liquidonics went belly up, and Jack had to tell the bad news to the people he'd advised to buy it, all of whom were losing considerable money. "On the drive back to Little Rock, following that news, Jack pulled the car over four different times to throw up. He was that upset about it."

Weaver also says that Jack Stephens absolutely hated firing people. "He could do it," he says, "and he could steel himself for unpleasant moments like that, but he absolutely hated doing it. When he brought someone into the company, it was with the idea that the partnership would last a lifetime."

Like so many major Stephens Inc. investment bank deals or acquisitions, the purchase of the Donrey media empire had its roots in a personal relationship with Jack Stephens.

Jack and Don Reynolds, a media baron with a vast network of newspapers and related interests, had been good friends for over 30 years. Stephens would always attend Reynolds' annual birthday bash in Las Vegas, where Reynolds owned the *Las Vegas Review-Journal*, Nevada's largest and most influential newspaper. With nearly 200,000 subscribers, the *R-J* was the flagship paper in a fleet of 51 smaller newspapers around the country, some with a circulation of under 10,000.

When Don Reynolds died in 1993, Stephens Inc. was brought in to handle the transfer of the Reynolds estate, which went primarily to the Donald W. Reynolds Foundation, a charitable organization. It was determined that the best strategy for the Foundation was to sell the newspaper part of the company, and Stephens Inc. was asked to find a buyer.

"It was clear that we had to leverage the company or do some other kind of restructuring, and at some point in the process of finding a buyer, the key people at Donrey asked us if we wanted to buy the company," says Bob Schulte, chief financial officer of Stephens Inc. "There was a trust that existed from our handling of matters since

Don Reynolds' death and the friendship he'd shared with Jack for all those years."

Although Stephens Inc. had previously owned no media interests, other than a small regional magazine venture called *Southern*, the purchase made sense on several levels. Newspapers were a solid core business, with good cash flows that were fairly predictable and not subject to fluctuations in the economy. And all of the Donrey newspapers were leaders in their markets, without a lot of competition. The *Las Vegas Review-Journal* was especially profitable, positioned as it was in the fastest-growing city in the country and having formed a joint operating agreement in 1989 with its only competitor, the *Las Vegas Sun*. Stephens Inc. eventually sold off about half of the newspapers in the portfolio, those that were basically breaking even. And as always, Jack Stephens was extremely hands-off in the operation of the company, letting the annual numbers determine what, if any, changes had to be made. "Again, as with Wal-Mart and Tyson Chicken and so many other deals," adds Schulte, "the business relationship grew out of a friendship that Jack Stephens had forged, and the trust that the key figures in the deal had in Jack."

Another story that points to the business acumen of Jack Stephens is the start of the company Systematics. Through Stephens' foresight, the purchase of a single computer for under $10,000 grew into an investment of over one billion.

In the late 1960s, Vernon Weaver became president of a recent Stephens' acquisition, Union Life. As with all new business acquisitions, it was Jack's style to let the company run itself without any interference and then evaluate performance at the end of each year.

"Jack never walked in the door of that company," Weaver says. "He never called us on the phone, and he never asked us anything. He said, 'I want you to come over and see me once a year before you make out your income tax report. Then I will give you my input into the tax situation and what we want to do. Other than that, I'm not going to bother you. If you do a good job, fine. If you don't, I'll fire you. End of story.'

"And he kept his word on that," Weaver says. "We never saw him but once a year."

Union Life had a secretary-treasurer named Rex Thompson, and Thompson purchased a new IBM 360 Model 20 computer to do the company's in-house record-keeping. It was an expensive purchase in those days, just under $10,000, and it was the first of its type ever bought in Arkansas. Thompson felt that Jack Stephens ought to be informed about it. Vernon didn't think it was necessary, citing Jack's not wanting to hear about such matters until the end of the year, but Thompson insisted. So Weaver called Jack and said, "You are probably going to throw us out of your office, but Rex wants to tell you about a new machine he bought."

Jack was less than excited about this, but said, "Ah, bring him in."

Rex Thompson told Jack about the computer, and how it did Union Life's work in four eight-hour days.

Jack said, "Well, Rex, what does that damn thing do at night?"

"Nothing," Thompson replied. "But it's built for excess capacity when we need it."

"Well, find some customers now," Jack said.

Thompson hired a small staff, which operated out of the Union Life basement, to take in business from banks. At this point, Jon Jacoby took over, and hired a man named Walter Smiley, a computer expert who had taught computer systems at the college level, was recruited to come in as the president. The new company was called Systematics. The initial contracts were for doing back-office work for banks, and a sales staff was developed to sell the services of the computer around the country.

"Dad knew every banker in the state of Arkansas," says Warren Stephens. "Jack and Witt Stephens had an affinity for banks. They once owned a chain of banks in Arkansas and had to dispose of it, because the bank holding law was passed where you couldn't do that. Then they continued to own several banks separately, not in a holding company structure, but as individuals. So banks were a great customer base for the firm already. After the computer was purchased and it was determined that it had all this capacity, it was just a natural extension to go to these bankers and ask to do all their data processing. In 1968, that computer may have been the first machine in Arkansas that could work 24 hours."

"We would go to a bank in Chicago, for instance, and maybe all they had was an IBM 360," says Jacoby. "We said that we would buy that computer and take over their department and run it for them, and that we could do it cheaper than they could. And in those days at the beginning of the computer revolution, programmers and computer experts were highly paid people. The banks didn't like paying a $50,000 salary to the computer guy, when the vice-president was making only $35,000. So it made sense for the bank to take that business somewhere else."

Within a few years, Systematics was servicing some of the biggest banks in the country. And through Jack's friendship with Joe Ford, the president of ALLTEL, it became clear that Systematics would be a good acquisition for ALLTEL, and that they could take it to even greater heights nationally.

"So the company was sold to ALLTEL for a bucket-load of stock," says Weaver. "And that stock, which in effect was acquired through the purchase of one machine and the foresight of Jack Stephens some years before, ended up being worth over a billion dollars."

⚐ ⸺ ⚑

While it's next to impossible to separate politics from business at the level that Stephens Inc. operates, most observers say that Jack Stephens has never had much stomach for the political game. Weaver says that Jack's desire to help his beloved Arkansas actually made him consider a run for governor in 1988 and even a run for the United States Senate.

"We did some polling and saw that Jack could be very competitive in either race," Weaver says. "But one day he asked me to describe what a senator did on a daily basis. After I explained a typical day, with one meeting after another and constantly dealing with constituents' problems and pleas, Jack realized that the job was too hectic. He decided running for office was not for him."

Stephens in the boardroom.

Years later Jack gave a sense of his distaste for politics: "I never really got involved in presidential politics until Jimmy Carter ran in 1976," he said. "Craig Campbell [Jack's nephew through marriage and a Stephens Inc. executive] ran Jimmy's campaign in Arkansas, and Carter got the highest percentage of votes here other than his home state of Georgia. I never had any illusions that we were especially favored while he was in office. Vernon Weaver was named to run the Small Business Administration, but that was no favor to me. It just took him away from running Union Life Insurance for us.

"All in all, it was a disappointing relationship with Carter's people," Jack said. "There seemed to be a distrust of [the] people with money, who'd helped Jimmy get elected."

Stephens recalls another unpleasant interlude with the political process: "During the gas crisis in 1979, when gas lines were around the block on the East Coast, regulations prevented gas from being shipped from one area to another," he says. "I'd worked out a plan and determined who needed to be involved in order to get that gas to the East Coast in five days. So I got an appointment with Energy Secretary Schlesinger.

"I will never forget," Jack says, "that when I went to Schlesinger's office, he was facing the window. My name was announced and without even turning around he said, 'Mr. Stephens, what words of wisdom have *you* got for me?'

"And silently to myself I said, 'Why you egotistical son of a bitch.' But out loud I said, 'None, I just came to wish you luck.' And I turned and walked out. That trip was a total waste of time."

Vernon Weaver recalls a story where business, politics, and several members of the Class of '47 became entwined. About midway through Jimmy Carter's presidency, in January of 1979, the Shah of Iran went into exile. The Shah had enjoyed a good relationship with Carter and the United States, and when he called Carter asking for help, State Department officials huddled to find a place where the Shah might find sanctuary. The Shah had first gone to Mexico, but he didn't feel safe there, so he contacted Hamilton Jordan, a top Carter advisor.

A call went out to Gabriel Lewis, a Panamanian businessman and diplomat. Lewis had been Panama's Ambassador to the United States in the late 1970s and had played an integral role in helping to negotiate the Panama Canal treaties, which transferred control of the waterway to Panama in the year 2000. Lewis owned the remote island of Saboga, in the Pearl Islands chain, and Jordan and other Carter officials saw that as an ideal place to hide the Shah and keep him safe from his enemies.

Some years later Jack Stephens befriended Lewis, and Stephens Inc. had several successful business dealings with him. When Panamanian General Manuel Noriega rose to power two years after the death of President Omar Torrijos, who had pushed for more freedoms for Panamanians, Lewis became an outspoken opponent of Noriega and spoke openly about the necessity of removing Noriega from power.

"Being politically active in Panama is not always advantageous to a person's health," Weaver says, with a wry smile. "And so those of us who were friends of Gabriel Lewis were very concerned about his safety under Noriega. And sure enough one day, as Jack Stephens was sitting by the pool at his home in Palm Beach . . . I believe it was New Year's weekend . . . he received a call from Gabriel saying, 'Jack, I am calling you from the terrace of my house. There are three gunship helicopters circling my house. Noriega's soldiers are coming after me, and they are going to kill me. I know that you are friends with Admiral Crowe, and I am imploring you to help me if you can.' "

Weaver was with Jack and put in a call at his home to Crowe, who had recently been named chairman of the Joint Chiefs of Staff under President George H. W. Bush. When Crowe answered, Vernon said, "I hate to unload this on you on a holiday . . . " and proceeded to tell him Gabriel Lewis's predicament. At that point, Crowe asked to speak to Jack Stephens and said, "Is this something you really want me to do?"

And Jack said yes. And Crowe said, "All right. I *will* do it, but I don't *want* to do it."

Crowe then called the top U.S. military officer stationed in Panama and gave him direct orders. He said, "Listen up. The safety of Gabriel Lewis and the life of Gabriel Lewis are your responsibility from here on."

One hour later, a car pulled up in front of Lewis's Panama estate, and eight soldiers all about six foot six inches tall, all blonde and obviously military, piled out wearing blue blazers bulging with armaments. They walked into the house and around the grounds and made their presence clearly known to anyone watching the house. They stayed until the helicopters flew off. The soldiers then put Gabriel Lewis in a car and had him transported to Costa Rica. Warren Stephens recalls that Gabriel's two sons, Fernando and Sam (who is the current vice president of Panama), were left behind, because they were not included in the soldiers' instructions. So they got their driver and drove to the downtown Panama City airport, where they found a pilot to fly them to Costa Rica.

Gabriel Lewis lived nine more years and died of natural causes in 1997, but his life was undoubtedly saved that day by the efforts and influence of four members of the USNA Class of '47: Jimmy Carter, Jack Stephens, Admiral William Crowe, and Ambassador Vernon Weaver.

⊰ — ⊱

It has often been asked of Jack Stephens why he remained in Arkansas, rather than moving to the nerve center of the investment world, New York City. The answer once again comes back to Stephens' love of his native state, and his desire to give back to his own people. Arkansas had made him a wealthy man, and he in turn contributed greatly to the creation of jobs and industry in the state. There is no denying that Jack got a huge lift out of bettering Wall Street firms on many big deals. He remarked in a 1991 interview that he would often see which direction the wind was blowing on Wall Street, then go the other way.

"New York's investment banking firms always went in droves," he said. "So if I went to New York and saw everyone going in a certain direction, I'd come back to Arkansas and go in the opposite direction. There was very little individual thinking going on up there. Wall Street, in 1969, thought the boom market was going to last. We felt that the money that was being borrowed to pay for Vietnam and the programs of Lyndon Johnson's Great Society would break the country, or at least cause rampant inflation, and that's just what happened. In Arkansas, we feel the heartbeat of the country."

But when asked directly whether his goal in big investment deals was to build up Arkansas, he was characteristically self-effacing. "Helping Arkansas is an incidental benefit," he said. "I've always had a love affair with the state, but your thinking is not, What do I want to do for the state, or the country? If you do that, you'll go broke. You have to do what's best for yourself. Your only responsibility is to pay your taxes, live within the law, and vote."

Jack Stephens' younger son, Warren, took over the presidency of Stephens Inc. in 1986, on his 29th birthday. He had started with the company years before, working in corporate finance, and Jack was so impressed with Warren's patience and decision-making skills that he felt comfortable with Warren taking over the company reins earlier than many would have anticipated. Warren speaks often of how important it is for the company to develop strong personal relationships, and how those relationships are often the determining factor in a deal as it nears completion.

"In October 1989, we started a hostile tender offer for Holly Farms that didn't culminate until July 1990," Warren explains. "We had known Tyson Foods and done work with them since the 1970s. Witt and Dad both had a personal relationship with Don Tyson since about 1950 and had had a business relationship with his company for 25 years. J. D. Simpson had spent an enormous amount of time to be in a position to understand poultry and to see how Tyson was different. The company had gone from growing chickens into processing chicken and branching into other business avenues. Fifty percent of Tyson's costs were grain costs. We did millions of dollars of financing for Tyson Foods with John Hancock in a deal that was good for both of us. Tyson had gone from the chicken business to a chicken food company. Their grain costs had been reduced considerably, because they'd given up swings in grain prices to be more solid for the long term.

"Now Holly Farms was a highly respected company out of Memphis," Warren says, "And Holly Farms remembered when Tyson was a redneck chicken company out of Arkansas. They definitely did not want to sell to Tyson. It was against their entire culture. Every action that Holly had taken was so that ConAgra would buy them. We started bidding at $50 a share on Father's Day 1990. We were convinced it would take $70 a share. The offer had to make the board cave in, because we knew they didn't want to go with Tyson. During the critical meeting when Holly's board was weighing the hostile takeover offer, Don Tyson and his group left the meeting. They invited Dad and me to meet with them. Don said he wanted to offer $65 in cash and $5 in Tyson stock."

J. D. Simpson takes up the story from there. "Don Tyson was getting squeamish about how much he'd borrow," Simpson recalls. "Jack Stephens said that maybe he needed more equity. They talked for five minutes, and Jack said he could give Tyson a $100 million put, which would allow them to sell $100 million to Stephens at market price at any time. It was highly unusual to be able to make that kind of deal. The message was clear: if Tyson needed the money, it was there."

"Dad's willingness to do that really demonstrated the strength of the relationship between the two companies," Warren says.

Mike Smith, another long-time Stephens' employee and the man behind the effort to take Wal-Mart public in 1970, concurs that it was Jack Stephens' friendship with Sam Walton that was probably the determining factor in the Wal-Mart deal. "Jack and Sam were good friends," Smith says. "There was a real trust between them, partly because they were so much alike, unassuming men with great integrity. Sam told White Weld, the investment banker originally involved, that he wanted us to be involved. October 1, 1970, marked the date of the first offering for Wal-Mart, to take them public. Those kinds of deals are hard to find, and it shows that building personal relationships is critically important. And Jack Stephens was as good as there was when it came to building friendships."

Simpson says that at the time Wal-Mart went public, Sam Walton offered each board member of Stephens Inc. 5,000 shares at four dollars per share. "Jack turned it down," Simpson says, "because he said it wouldn't be fair to the public to do that. Incidentally, that 5,000 shares today would be worth well over $100 million."

Yet another relationship that led to a successful partnership was when a company called EnerGas, based in Texas, was taking over a Louisiana company. Warren Stephens, just 27 years old at the time, was told by his uncle Witt to call an ex-governor of Louisiana, John McKeithen, as he might be willing to help. It seems that Jack Stephens had purchased $113 million worth of bonds to help finance the construction of the Louisiana Superdome years before, at a juncture when it looked like the bonds couldn't be sold.

So Warren called the former governor, who was then in his 70s, and said, "Governor McKeithen, my name is Warren Stephens in Little Rock, and I am Jack Stephens' son and Witt Stephens' nephew.

I've got a situation down there that I would like to come talk to you about, because I think we are going to need your help."

After a long pause, the governor said, "Son, would you run that by me again?"

So Warren repeated what he'd just said. And McKeithen said, "Son, I couldn't have become governor of Louisiana without your uncle's help, and I would have been run out of town on a rail without your father's help doing the Superdome bonds. I have been waiting all my life for somebody from the Stephens' family to call me and ask for anything. You get down here as soon as you can, and I will take care of it if I can."

"With Governor McKeithen's help, we were able to knock out the legal defenses and assure that the company was going to get sold, "Warren says. "And we were the ones who actually wound up buying it. The point of the story is that Witt had helped him and Dad had helped him because he was a good guy, and it was the right thing to do. It was never a tit-for-tat situation. And it wasn't like he returned the favor for free, because he had a law firm and we paid him for his help. But that story just shows how important personal relationships are in building a company's good reputation. Here was this important man who'd been waiting all those years to show his gratitude for things that had been done for him."

When he was in his early 30s, Jack Stephens took up golf, a game he'd always wanted to play but never had the time to learn. Like any other endeavor, Jack approached the game with a measured intelligence. He hired a seasoned professional to give him lessons and teach him the basic fundamentals of the sport, and he resisted the itch to venture onto a golf course for at least four months, until he'd acquired a measure of skill by hitting practice shots daily on a driving range. Within a couple of years, he became a single-digit handicap, capable of breaking 80 for 18 holes. His biggest personal golfing accomplishment was once shooting an even-par 72 at Augusta National.

"Jack was just a tremendous golfer under pressure," says Lou Holtz, the legendary college football coach, who led the Arkansas Razorbacks from 1977–1983. "We'd play at least three rounds a year, and we had this huge trophy that was given to the winner. That person got to keep it for a year, not to mention the bragging rights that went with it. There were times that I felt I was playing better than him, but I never beat him. He'd always come through with that big putt or chip shot at just the right time."

When he was 36 years old, Jack was invited to a cocktail party at revered Augusta National Golf Course, thought by many to be the most prestigious golf club in the world. There are many variations on what happened that evening, but the one with the most credence tells how Jack, after walking out onto the patio of the club to have a cigarette, was asked by an older gentleman whether he liked to play bridge. Jack said that he did indeed enjoy the game, and the two struck up a friendly conversation. The man was Bobby Jones, the immortal golfing legend, who'd effectively retired from competitive golf after winning the Grand Slam of major championships (as an amateur no less) in 1930. Jones and attorney Clifford Roberts had founded Augusta National. That evening, in the late 1950s, marked the beginning of a great friendship. A little over 30 years later, Jack became the fourth chairman of Augusta National, a position he held for eight years.

Stephens would preside over two especially memorable nationally televised presentation ceremonies in the Butler Cabin at Augusta: in 1995, when popular Ben Crenshaw won The Masters just days after attending the funeral of mentor Harvey Penick and broke down in tears when the final putt was holed; and in 1997, when Tiger Woods became the first African American golfer to win the coveted green jacket, in the process breaking the all-time scoring record of six-time Masters champion, Jack Nicklaus. Despite Stephens' immense success in the world of high finance, he is probably best known among American sports fans for his important role as chairman of Augusta National.

Jack Stephens addressing the crowd at Augusta National.

There are two stories related to Clifford Roberts, who became one of Jack's closest friends, that are worth repeating. Vernon Weaver recalls how one time Jack Stephens recommended that the 15th green at Augusta National be moved slightly, because the spectacular par-five hole with water both in front of and behind the green would have a better angle of play if the green were resituated. Roberts agreed that Stephens' suggestion would be an improvement, and ordered the change to be made. Some months later, Jack was sent a bill for $40,000 for the modification. He paid it without complaint, the lesson being that if a member at Augusta wanted something changed, he better be willing to foot the bill.

Jack Stephens also has the honor of being the namesake of the ninth and last cabin constructed on the grounds of Augusta National. It was built in 1969, and the story behind it is recounted in David Owens' fine book, *The Making of The Masters*:

Stephens recalls that [Clifford] Roberts brought up the subject one evening as they were walking along a path that connects all the cabins. "Cliff said, 'If you'll underwrite it, I'll get it built this summer,' and I said I would," Stephens says. "But I had never won an argument with him, so I said, 'You know, Cliff, I love to swim, and I expect I'll be spending a lot of time in that house, so I'd like to have a swimming pool underneath it.' Oh, God, he hated that idea. He felt that a swimming pool had no place at a golf club. We went back and forth and back and forth, and it kind of became a thing with me—and Cliff finally acquiesced. Now, I no more wanted a swimming pool than I wanted a billy goat. I just wanted to win an argument with Cliff. So I relented as soon as he agreed, and he was greatly relieved."

Jack Stephens would find a great golfing companion in President Dwight Eisenhower, with whom he played dozens of rounds. And in 2003, he co-authored, with Dr. T. Glenn Pait, a book on the sport, *Golf Forever*, which offered practical and medical advice to all golfers on how to stay physically fit and overcome injuries that are common to the game. Health problems had prevented Jack from playing golf in recent years, and he felt the best gift he could give to his friends in the sport was a comprehensive report on how best to lengthen their time and enjoyment in the game. While Dr. Pait composed the bulk of the text, Jack was intimately involved in every aspect of the book. He was particularly helpful in soliciting participation from many of the greats in golf, who shared stories about their own health challenges, such as sore backs, stiff necks, and weak knees. Among the many who contributed to the book, because of their fondness for Jack Stephens, were Sam Snead, Arnold Palmer, Tom Watson, Greg Norman, Ben Crenshaw, Ken Venturi, Curtis Strange, Jerry Pate, Fred Couples, Davis Love III, Raymond Floyd, JoAnn Carner, and Judy Rankin. There are even cute anecdotes from former President George H. W. Bush and actor Don Knotts, who explained that a visit to his orthopedic surgeon, resulting from a strained back on the golf course, had allowed him to meet the actress Lana Turner, his boyhood crush.

Ray Floyd, a Hall of Fame golfer who formed a great friendship with Jack Stephens shortly after he won the Masters in 1976, says,

"He's been a father figure to me and a mentor and is very close to our whole family, my wife, Maria, and our three kids. They call him Uncle Jack. While Jack is not a man who talks a lot, he communicates a lot with his actions and gestures. He can speak volumes with the raising of an eyebrow or the clearing of his throat."

Jack's friend, Pat Summerall, offers an hilarious and telling story about Jack that occurred on a spring day at Augusta National.

"I was Jack's partner in a golf match one day," Summerall says. "This brand new Augusta member we were playing with inquired on the first tee, 'What are we playing for?'

"And Jack said, 'We play for two dollars here.'

"And the guy said, 'Are you kidding me? We play for big money at my home club.'

"Anyway, Jack would not play for more than two dollars," Summerall says. "And the guy grumbled about it all the way around. He then made that as an excuse for why he'd played poorly, because there was no real action.

"Then after the round we were playing gin in the men's grill, and the guy asked if he could join in. Jack said sure. And the guy said, 'What are we playing for?'

"And Jack said, 'We play for penny a point.'

"And the guy said, 'You gotta be kidding me. At my other club, we play for ten dollars a point.'

"Jack kept his cool and said, 'My, that must be some club you belong to.'

"And the guy said he didn't think he wanted to play for such measly stakes.

"Finally, Jack had had it. He said to the guy, 'What are you worth?'

"And the guy said, 'What do you mean?'

"And Jack said, 'If you totaled up your entire net worth, everything you own, what do you think it would come to?'

"And the guy kinda puffed his chest out, then replied. 'Oh, probably 15 or 16 million.'

"Jack Stephens slid the deck of cards over to him and calmly said, 'I'll cut you for it.'

"And the guy got real humble real fast and said, 'Well, I can't do that.'

"And Jack said, 'Deal the cards. We are playing for a penny a point.'"

⊷ —— ⊶

Another Hall of Fame broadcaster, who became close friends with Jack Stephens, was the late Chris Schenkel. Despite being on a ventilator and suffering with emphysema, Schenkel spent the better part of an hour sharing reminiscences of Stephens for a commemorative tape prepared for Jack's 80th birthday celebration in August 2003.

"I've always felt a great kinship with Jack Stephens," Schenkel said. "We're both country boys, and we're both from families with six children. I've always considered Jack a great listener. His father must have told him that he'd learn a lot more listening than talking. One trait that comes to mind about Jack is his modesty; he has it almost to a fault. And Jack doesn't know how to say no. Imagine if he were a girl!"

Schenkel went on: "Jack has never forgotten where he came from. He shares with people who need it and institutions that need it. If you saw him walk around the grounds at Augusta National, you'd see that all the employees adore him. He probably did more for the working staff at Augusta than any other chairman. He's just such an amazing friend and to think how the years with him have flown by. [At this point in the interview, Schenkel pauses to gather himself.] He then adds, "I won't apologize for getting misty. I'm not afraid to show my emotion when talking about Jack Stephens."

Another close friend of Jack Stephens is Joe Ford, the former chairman of ALLTEL Communications and a man who has served as the television host for Augusta National and The Masters committee for the last few years. Ford affirms Schenkel's observation. "The first thing Jack did as chairman at Augusta was to approve a dining room for employees and get a new 401K program for them. That was his first priority, to take care of them first."

A cause that is dear to Jack Stephens' heart is the First Tee Program, which was formed by the PGA Tour and the Tiger Woods Foundation to provide underprivileged kids an entrée to the game of golf through free equipment, instruction, and playing rights at courses around the country.

Jack Stephens with renowned golfer, Tiger Woods.

"When we first considered the First Tee Program, we asked for Jack Stephens' advice because we wanted Augusta National to be part of the overall effort," says Tim Finchem, Commissioner of the PGA Tour. "At the time, Jack was already focused on a First Tee facility in Little Rock. I don't believe we asked Jack for money, but when he determined that he would give us a five-million-dollar grant, that was huge. Jack really appreciates the importance of giving kids a chance to play golf, because he understands what the game can do for people. He puts a lot of mental energy into the game. He's a real student of it. That has been demonstrated through his leadership at Augusta. He always thought The Masters could be better, from year to year. We think the tournament is the best stage for golf on television that there is, and Jack enhanced it during his leadership. You just find yourself trusting his sense of things."

In 2002, in honor of the love he felt for the United States Naval Academy, Jack Stephens donated $10 million to the construction of the Jackson T. Stephens Field, which became the new home of the midshipmen football team. The navy gridders showed their gratitude by completing an 11-2 season in the fall of 2004, the best navy football performance in decades. The following season the team won a bowl game.

Despite numerous surgeries and health setbacks in recent years, including two strokes that impaired his speech, Jack Stephens fought the good fight and maintained a pleasurable quality of life until the end. He passed away on July 23, 2005, two weeks shy of his 82nd birthday. Thousands of family members, friends, and admirers packed the gymnasium of the Episcopal Collegiate School in Little Rock for a memorial service. A school choir sang several hymns, and a stirring eulogy was given by Jack's dear friend Lou Holtz.

"When people hear about a personal misfortune that occurs to you, ninety percent of them don't care," Holtz said. "And the other ten percent are just glad that it didn't happen to them. . . . but Jack was one of those few people who cared. And that's just one of the many things that made him so special."

Jack and son Warren at a golf event.

We'll let Vernon Weaver have the last word, "Those who become extremely rich are often subjected to allegations that they have obtained their wealth by cheating, stealing or otherwise taking advantage of the system. I have never heard such charges made about Jack Stephens. His employees were given every opportunity to advance to the limit of their abilities, his competitors acknowledged his integrity and fairness. Jack never thought of himself as "rich." Money to him was a way of keeping score, a measure of accomplishment and yes, a means of helping others."

CHAPTER SIX
Other Alums

Y OU DON'T HEAR MUCH ABOUT 60-YEAR REUNIONS, WHETHER FROM GRADE SCHOOL, HIGH SCHOOL, OR COLLEGE. It simply takes too much energy for septuagenarians or octogenarians to travel some distance and try to remember how much fun they used to have in whatever level of education is being commemorated.

But as we've pointed out repeatedly in this book, the United States Naval Academy Class of '47 is not just any bunch. And that is why over 300 classmates and their wives and offspring gathered in Annapolis between June 4 and June 7, 2006, to raise a glass and share memories of one of the greatest classes in American military history.

While it would be impossible to catalogue the achievements of every one of the 820 graduating members of that special class, we have been able to talk to many of them about their time at The Yard and their years afterward. Here are capsules of just a few of the men from the class who served their country with honor in a variety of careers. We were able to put together these short biographical sketches from a variety of sources, including personal interviews, phone conversations, and other materials.

Jeremiah (Jerry) Denton

Rear Admiral, POW, and former U.S. Senator from Alabama

Jeremiah Andrew Denton Jr., as a midshipman.

Like so many of his classmates at Annapolis, Jerry Denton caught the navy bug early. As a junior in high school, he saw a movie called *Navy Blue and Gold* and became attracted to the glamour of naval aviation. He told his mother and grandmother that very day that he wanted to be a navy officer.

"I wanted to do something noble," he says today, "something that would get your attention in terms of devotion to a cause and not feel like it was being done for money. I wanted to work for something for which I might be judged well, when I finished this life."

Four days after Pearl Harbor was attacked, Denton signed up to join the navy as an enlisted man, not realizing his possible Naval Academy appointment would come through. He was, after all, number 78 on his Congressman's list when he put in his name as a junior in high school.

Plebe year came as a shock to Jerry, because he hadn't had that much orderliness and discipline in his life. "I wasn't all that interested in folding laundry carefully and shining my shoes until I could see my face in them," he says, "but I gradually adapted to it and loved it. Looking back on it, I don't think I could have chosen anything better. The teachers we had there, the ones who had just come back from World War II, from lieutenants to vice admirals, showed me kind of a tempered disposition which they could have gotten only through that experience. That sort of sobered me up and made me aware that I had to try to be as disciplined as I could be in preparation for some future rigors. And of course, we all thought we were going to get into World War II at that point."

Denton was in the same battalion at the Naval Academy as Vernon Weaver and Jack Stephens, and says, "These were just good guys, not the type who had their finger on the number of their class standing and were interested only in graduating high in the class, but just damned good human beings. And there were a lot of them like that."

Although, as the decades passed political affiliations would eventually divide many members of the Class of '47, Denton knew he was with a special group of men. "I was aware that I was not only associated with, but competing academically with, a sample of the best this country had," he says. "And that was exhilarating. It motivated me to reach higher. While I could accommodate the possibility of failing, I was determined as hell that I wouldn't. I learned during that difficult plebe year that I needed some straightening out. And I learned something that would help me in the future, mainly to take orders without wincing, no matter what the damn orders were."

Denton continued with his academics and naval training following graduation, serving on ships and attending flight school. He spent a year at the Naval War College, where his thesis on international affairs earned the prestigious President's Award, and in 1964, he earned a master's in international affairs from George Washington

University. Shortly thereafter, Denton was sent to Vietnam as a combat pilot.

He was shot down near Thanh Hoa and captured by local North Vietnamese troops on July 18, 1965, where he would spend the next seven years and seven months as a prisoner of war. Taken prisoner six weeks before Jim Stockdale, Denton and his classmate became emblematic of the courage and dignity shown by nearly all American prisoners of war during this time.

Like Stockdale, Denton was subjected to four years of solitary confinement and was shuttled from one prison camp to another during the time of his confinement, frequently acting as the senior American military officer in the camps.

During one taped interview that his Vietcong captors used for propaganda, Denton acted as though the lights were bothering his eyes, and he blinked out the word "torture" in Morse code. "Many reporters have gotten carried away with that and said it was amazing," Denton says, "but that was nothing to me. A lot of our guys gave them the finger or sat there with their fingers crossed. But when they asked me the key question, which was, 'What do you think about America's policy about Vietnam?' I did have God's help to say, 'I don't know what's going on in the war now because the only information I have is from North Vietnamese magazines, newspapers, and radio. But whatever is going on, whatever the policy of my government is, I support it and I will support it for as long as I live.'

"Well, the Japanese cameraman who was filming . . . and I was about the 36th guy he was taping . . . couldn't believe that I hadn't been 'prepared' enough by the North Vietnamese. So he asked the question again, and I held my ground. I said, 'As far as the policy of my government is concerned, I am a member of that government. It is my job to support it, and I will support it as long as I live.'

"Now they tortured me after that," he says, pausing for a long while to collect himself. "I don't even like to think about it, but I prayed to God over and over again, and it was the biggest miracle that I lived through it without losing my mind."

The lessons Jerry Denton learned at the Academy obviously served him well during this horrific period. "I think the most critical thing I learned, as far as becoming a POW, was the importance of the saying, 'If senior, take charge,'" he says. "That is not only an opportunity, but an obligation. And I did my share of that during those years we were in torture. But I regret the fact that, while guys like Stockdale and I have gotten some credit and recognition for doing that, there were other men, who had to take charge of separate groups—pretty large groups, actually—of prisoners of war who suffered maybe even more than we did, because the North Vietnamese knew they weren't senior enough to excuse these guys if they did something that had indicated bad judgment. But those men did a wonderful job, too, and they should be identified, praised, and given credit for what they did, because they had just as tough a job—maybe tougher—than Jim and I did."

Denton can't give enough praise to his classmate Stockdale, who died just a month after Denton's interview for this book. "Jim was a very fortuitous person for us to have in prison," he says. "He not only had physical courage, but he had compassion and a great understanding of human nature. Toward the end, when things were much easier for us in the camp, and I was acting as operations manager and he as plans officer, we were trying to think of a statement to put out to guys who had maybe wilted under torture, but were real sorry that they had. These were men who had just exceeded their limits. So what Jim and I came up with was, 'It is neither Christian nor American to hound a repentant sinner to his grave.' And that made a lot of guys feel better, because I had a lot of them tell me that they had broken down under torture, and I told them, 'Goddammit, that's all right!' They could hurt you so much and affect your mind so much that the only thing you could think about was the pain and the willingness to make it stop."

Also like Jim Stockdale, Jerry Denton had a strong wife, Jane, who performed a similar function for wives of POW-MIAs on the East Coast as Sybil Stockdale was doing out in California. "I was on the first flight out of Vietnam," Denton recalls, "and when I walked from the plane, the senior man from the State Department and the senior man from the Department of the navy came up to me and said, 'We know you did well, but we want you to know your wife did just as well. She was one of the good ones.'

"I can't give Jane enough credit," he says. "I married her when she was just 17, and she's a helluva woman."

Denton retired from the navy in 1977 and returned to his home in Mobile, Alabama. "I had developed a feeling of futility in the navy and the military as a whole, which had been discredited in the minds of many in the population," he says. "The military had lost prestige and had lost credibility, and I didn't feel that I was as important then in my effect on the culture or the Cold War, if I remained in the navy. . . . But I didn't get out with any political ambitions. I thought that the politicians had become a jumble of immorality and that the liberals had cost us the war in Vietnam that we had really won.

Jeremiah Denton, U.S. Senator

"Then President Ford called me in 1978, and I said to an aide, 'What does he want?'

"And he said, 'He wants to tell you how important it is for you to run for the senate next year.'

"And I said, 'Tell him I'm in the bathroom and I'm sick. I do not want him to feel bad because I'm going to say no, and I know he's going to come on hard.'

"So I didn't even speak to him on that occasion," Denton says. "But then, as things warmed up in the Cold War, I thought things were going to hell. I became extremely anxious, and then when Reagan came along, I loved him. He'd been in California as an actor, fighting the communists out there. He was a compassionate man, who believed in "one nation under God," and so I decided I was going to throw my hat in. I had no money, and I even had to sell my lot that I was living on, because I didn't have any other way to sustain myself financially while I was running. But we ended up winning."

Former President Reagan singled out Admiral Jerry Denton in his State of the Union address on January 26, 1982. These are his words: "We don't have to turn to our history books for heroes. They are all around us. One who sits among you here tonight epitomized that heroism at the end of the longest imprisonment ever inflicted on men of our armed forces. Who will ever forget that night when we waited for the television to bring us the scene of that first plane landing at Clark Field in the Philippines, bringing our POWs home. The plane door opened and Jeremiah Denton came slowly down the ramp. He caught sight of our flag, saluted, and said, 'God Bless America,' then thanked us for bringing him home."

Captain Thomas J. Hudner, Jr.

Medal of Honor recipient (first since World War II,
first of the Korean War, and, at age 26, one of the youngest recipients)

Captain Thomas J. Hudner, Jr.
from the Class of '47 40th anniversary yearbook.

When Tom Hudner graduated from the Naval Academy, he had no particular interest in flying airplanes. His desire was simply to be on a ship. But after a year at sea and working as a communications officer at Pearl Harbor, he took on the new challenge of flight training. After brief service in Lebanon, he was assigned to the carrier USS *Leyte* as an F4U Corsair pilot.

Just two years after learning to fly, Hudner was engaged in combat missions in Korea. On December 4, 1950, he was one of six pilots sent out on a reconnaissance mission over North Korea. Tom was wingman for Jesse Brown, the son of a sharecropper who had attracted a good deal of attention as the navy's first black fighter pilot.

As Brown's plane was strafing enemy positions at a low altitude, he was hit by anti-aircraft fire. His plane was out of power and flying too low to avoid the snow-covered mountains. As Hudner followed Jesse Brown's plane down, he called out instructions to help him prepare for a crash landing. Brown was able to put the plane down in a wheels-up landing in a clearing, but the impact buckled the fuselage at the cockpit. Hudner's first thought was that Brown must have been killed in the crash, but after a long moment Brown lifted the cowling and waved weakly. It was clear to Hudner that Brown could not free himself from the airplane.

Knowing that permission to land would be denied by the flight leader, Hudner radioed that he was going in, and then made a hard, wheels-up crash landing. He was able to get out and then struggle through the deep snow to get to Brown's wreckage. Hudner saw that Brown's leg had been crushed in the crash, and that he was unable to pull him from the plane. But he kept talking to Brown and offering morale-building words to keep him from slipping into unconsciousness. A U.S. helicopter arrived about an hour later, and the chopper pilot and Hudner spent another 45 minutes trying to pull Brown from the plane, but the packed snows and 30-below temperatures made the task impossible. It was clear, by nightfall, that Brown had died, and they were forced to return to base camp.

Reconnaissance the next morning showed that Brown's body had been stripped of his flight uniform by enemy forces during the night. The following day, the commander of the Leyte ordered four Corsairs to napalm the downed plane so that Brown could have a warrior's funeral without any further desecration.

Four months later, Lieutenant Junior Grade Thomas Hudner, just 26 at the time, became the first American serviceman since World War II, and the first in the Korean War, to receive the Medal of Honor. It was draped around his neck by President Harry Truman. Standing beside him was Daisy Brown, the widow of Jesse Brown, who had posthumously been given the Distinguished Flying Cross.

⊰——⊱

Tom Hudner is 80 years old and one of eight Medal of Honor winners acting as pallbearers at the memorial service for Admiral James Stockdale on the deck of the USS *Ronald Reagan* in the summer of 2005. A year into his ninth decade, Hudner is still a strikingly handsome man and looks a good bet to make it to 100.

He converses easily at a post-reception at the Officers Club on a variety of topics. He begins by explaining that his father, who graduated college in 1915 and came into the navy in WWI in the reserve program, was initially stationed at this same base in San Diego, serving under a Commander Spencer, who was a Naval Academy graduate. The commander was married to a woman from Baltimore, and they occasionally had social functions at their home. Mr. Hudner was invited along with other bachelor officers to match up with the number of extra women. Mr. Hudner found the commander's wife intriguing, if a little on the uppity side. After he returned to Massachusetts when WWI was over, he had no trouble following her activities. The woman, whose first name was Wallis, would divorce the commander soon after the war, marry another man named Simpson, then eventually divorce him and marry the abdicated King of England. The woman, who hosted the parties in San Diego, became none other than the Duchess of Windsor.

Like so many of his classmates, Tom Hudner dreamed of going to the Naval Academy as a boy and thought the navy would be a great career, but he didn't excel academically, and so thought that it was probably out of his reach. But after the United States entered World War II, Hudner saw an opportunity to be accepted and jumped at the chance.

"Without meaning to disparage any of my classmates," he says, "there were a helluva lot of our guys that never would have gone to the Academy had it not been for the war."

Hudner laments the fact that so many young people today don't have an appreciation for the sacrifices made by previous generations. "The Naval Academy bred in us honor and integrity and an acknowledgement of the people that were around us," he says. "There's not enough of that today. It's not right to paint the whole younger generation with the same brush, but a lot of them have absolutely no idea what the expense was in getting our country where it is today."

On a day when people were gathered to honor his friend Jim Stockdale, Hudner has these remembrances: "We got to know each other within a short time at the Academy because we both played football. He played guard and I played halfback on both the plebe team and the jayvees, and I'll tell you we scared the hell out of the first-team varsity. I didn't see that much of Jim at the Academy, but we were good friends. There was a closeness between us that wasn't determined by the numbers of times we were together. There is a convention of Medal of Honor winners, and we all have a closeness that is hard to define. Let me just say that the word 'great' is overused, but Jim Stockdale was a great American."

Admiral Wes McDonald

Former Commander-in-Chief U.S. Atlantic Command (CINCLANT),
1982–1985

Class of '47, 40ᵗʰ anniversary photo of Wes McDonald.

After graduation, Wes McDonald served with 10 classmates on the Philippines SEA before leaving for flight school in October 1948. He earned his wings in 1950 and did tours in a pair of jet-fighter squadrons. One year of exchange duty with the Air Force followed, then three years as a jet flight instructor at Kingsville, Texas, and two years with a light jet attack squadron.

McDonald was airborne with Jim Stockdale over the Gulf of Tonkin on the night of "The Affair," which accelerated the Vietnam War, and also on the raids over Vinh during which Stockdale was shot down and taken prisoner. He spent the next year as commander

Air Wing 15 aboard the *Coral Sea* and *Constellation*, operating off Vietnam.

In 1966, he came to Washington and attended the National War College prior to reporting to the Gator Navy, as the CO of Hermitage at Little Creek, Virginia. He then went to the West Coast as the skipper of the *Coral Sea*. His last active duty assignment was in Norfolk, where he says he had "the best three-in-one job in the navy": as supreme allied commander, atlantic; commander-in-chief U.S. Atlantic Command (CINCLANT); and commander-in-chief U.S. Atlantic Fleet. During that time, while leading both U.S. and NATO forces in the region, he oversaw the 1983 U.S. intervention in Grenada. He says that period of time was "exciting, professionally rewarding, and a true culmination to a career far beyond my expectations."

In November 2004, McDonald received the Cliff Henderson Award from the National Aeronautic Association for his 56 years of support for American aviation, including 13 years spent as the chairman of the NAA's board of directors.

McDonald's decorations include two Distinguished Flying Crosses, four Air Medals, a Navy Commendation Medal, and three Navy Unit Citations.

Vernon Weaver

Director of the Small Business Administration under President Jimmy Carter; Ambassador to the European Union under President Bill Clinton; longtime associate of Jack Stephens of Stephens, Inc.

Midshipman Vernon Weaver's 1947 yearbook entry.

It was in conversations with Vernon Weaver at the 80th birthday celebration for his best friend and Annapolis roommate, Jack Stephens, that the book *The Class of '47* was conceived. I was seated at a table with Weaver, Admiral Bill Crowe, and Admiral James Stockdale, when I first learned that they were all classmates at the Naval Academy, and that their common bond with Stephens was that he too was a classmate. "Wow, what a class!" I commented.

"We also had a president of the United States in our class," Crowe said.

I had to think a minute, under his skeptical gaze, before I was able to say, "Of course, Jimmy Carter."

Over champagne and big band music, the conversation drifted to a question that all of these men had pondered many times through the years. Was their United States Naval Academy Class of '47, the most distinguished military class ever? Of course, there is no definitive answer to this—and you would probably get an argument from every graduate of every military academy before and since—but the very idea of it makes for intriguing cocktail conversation.

When Carter was running for president in 1976, *The Washington Post* published a lengthy article putting forth a strong argument for that claim. And while no member of this distinguished class would dispute that argument, you also won't hear them trying to make the claim either. Humility, after all, is one of the virtues they learned and practiced at the Naval Academy.

Like others in his class, Weaver says that the world situation in 1942, when most of his classmates applied for admission, caused a lot of them to choose Annapolis rather than go to war as enlisted men. As difficult as the academic and physical regimen was, the Academy was thought by most to be far more preferable than being drafted. Weaver says the main reason he went to the Naval Academy was to get the necessary experience to become a good officer.

Many of the plebes that Weaver enrolled with had a year or two of college behind them. Vernon actually had three years of college at the University of Florida before the Academy and an extensive background in English and the humanities, which he said made the first two years less difficult for him.

Vernon competed on the national championship debate team at the Academy with both Bill Crowe and Jim Stockdale, and he calls it the single most important thing he did in terms of preparing himself for a career in business and public service. One does not become an ambassador without having significant writing and speaking skills, and Weaver developed an abundance of both.

As a regular visitor to The Yard, Vernon is able to enunciate several big differences in the curriculum and behaviors over the last 60 years.

"For one thing, all the service academies now have an ironclad code of honor, where midshipmen who break the rules have to be reported by their classmates. We didn't have that when we were there, and I have my doubts about that system. It turns midshipmen into tattletales. The worst thing you could do in my era was what we called 'bilge your classmates.' We had a code of honor among ourselves where we could never turn in a classmate for anything and because of that, we became extremely close-knit as a class, and we were all very dependent on each other, whether it be to help a classmate with his studies or bail him out of a tight situation. The midshipmen and women today have all sorts of support from their parents and counselors, but we had only each other. It was kind of 'us against the system' mentality, which by the way, is not a bad mindset to have going into war. Don't get me wrong, I have no objection to rules prohibiting lying, cheating, stealing, etc. — we had that. My objection is a rule that requires classmates to turn in each other. The hazing was much more intense back then. The pushing out at meals and the hundreds of push-ups and paddling went on constantly. I think it's an improvement that today they've cut back on much of that."

Weaver is also the midshipman closest to the featured classmates profiled in this book. He was the roommate, best friend, and lifetime business associate of Jack Stephens; he debated with and has stayed extremely close to Bill Crowe; he served in Jimmy Carter's administration at the same time Stan Turner was director of the CIA; and he was in the same battalion as Jim Stockdale and served as an honorary pallbearer at his funeral. He has thoughts about all of them:

"I remember President Carter as a shy midshipman — a nice person, very pleasant, and extremely religious. He didn't study particularly hard, but then he was so smart, he didn't have to — he stood high in the class and was always willing to help a classmate with his studies. When he appointed me to run the Small Business Administration, he gave me all the access I wanted. I could see him any time I had a question or problem. I admired him so much as president, because unlike many politicians, all his decisions were made in terms of what he thought was best for the country, not for his popularity rating or reelection. You might say that trait was his political failing, but it was to his glory that he had that much integrity. If all our politicians operated that way, we'd have an even better country."

"Jack Stephens and I met our first day at The Yard, and we became best friends for the next sixty-some years. While he didn't try to excel academically at Annapolis, and his demeanor was a little on the serious side, he also had a fun side as well, as exemplified by the many demerits he got. He actually came close to getting thrown out for demerits, primarily for 75 demerits he was given for not turning in the name of one of our classmates who was returning late on a weekend night. We had an unspoken code of honor where we didn't tattle on members of our class.

"Right off the bat, you could see the intelligence of Jack and how he was a wonderful judge of character. I've never met anyone who could size a person up quicker, or more accurately, than Jack. It's one of the things that made him so terrific in business. He just had great instincts for people and for opportunities. When we decided to run him for our company commander the one time the top brass allowed us to do that, primarily because we had collected so many demerits that they hoped that allowing us to do that would improve our performance, I was his campaign manager—and he won. I think it gave Jack a great sense of responsibility and focus and brought out the leadership qualities that he exhibited later on in business."

"Bill Crowe is a fun-loving guy from Oklahoma with a great blend of country charm and fierce intelligence. He lived right next door to Jack Stephens and me, and did his best to keep us in trouble all the time. My time on the debate team with him was an intellectual experience. Some people might express surprise at how far Crowe advanced in the navy, but it didn't surprise me at all."

"Stansfield Turner was clearly the outstanding midshipman in our class. He was the All-American boy, good looking, a heckuva football player, the brigade commander, and smarter than hell. In addition to our association during the Carter administration, I had the opportunity to work with stan in the mid 90s. I was serving on the Naval Academy Board of Visitors at a time when some serious problems were emerging. In the middle of all this, I was ordered to Brussels to assume my post there. Stan was immediately appointed to the board and soon after was made co-chairman of a committee to work with the superintendent on getting the problems solved. I was proud of the way he quickly and efficiently helped get the Academy back on track."

"Jim Stockdale was always a good pal and a happy young man. You'd ask him something and he'd say, 'Sure, I'll do it.' He also had a little rascal in him, which of course gets lost in history, because of all the noble things he accomplished in his life. Like when he would help us get free rooms in the Statler Hotel for parties. Imagine talking people, who were checking out early, in to give us their room keys! He was so handsome as a midshipman, and so believable with those clear blue eyes of his, that he could talk anybody into anything. He also had a great sense of humor. Those are things about him I'd like people to know, because the rest is clearly documented for the ages to read about."

Weaver calls the time he served as the U.S. Ambassador to the European Union "the greatest experience of my life." He says he never met an official during that time that wasn't interesting, although he adds, "Of course, I liked some more than others." He served in Brussels for three years, from 1996–1999, but returned to the states and rejoined Stephens, Inc., because Jack Stephens had suffered a stroke. Weaver continues to function in a variety of capacities for Stephens, Inc., but maintains a permanent residence in Bal Harbour, Florida, with his wife of 60 years, Joyce, who is an avid and talented tennis player. The Weavers have three daughters, all politically active.

⌐⌐ ⸺ ⌐⌐

*U.S. Department of State official portrait of
Ambassador A. Vernon Weaver, 1996.*

Tom Pownall
CEO, Martin Marietta Corporation (now Lockheed)

Thomas Pownall, graduate USNA Class of '47.

When it comes to business superstars from the Class of '47, Tom Pownall would rank near the top of the list.

Like all of his classmates, Tom graduated from the Academy with an electrical engineering degree. He then served two years aboard a destroyer in the Pacific during the Korean War. After leaving the navy, he briefly worked in the paper box business and as a salesman for a steel fabricator and for General Motors' Chevrolet division in Ohio, before joining the Convair division of General Dynamics Corp. in 1955. He also served on the board of Titan Corp., a San Diego-based defense contractor from 1950–1959.

Pownall was an advance man on Dwight Eisenhower's successful 1952 presidential campaign and played the same role on Richard Nixon's unsuccessful campaign in 1960. He spent 24 years with

Martin Marietta (since merged with Lockheed) and helped build it into a major player in the defense and aerospace industries. He started with the company in 1963, as a vice-president and became president and COO in 1977, then CEO in 1982, and chairman the following year. He retired in 1987, and remained on the board of directors until 1991.

With Martin Marietta, he helped thwart a hostile takeover bid by electronics firm Bendix Corp, using a counterattack strategy that was dubbed the "Pac-Man defense."

Tom Pownall oversaw development of two Viking spacecraft that were involved in the first exploration of Mars in 1976. His autobiography, *No Man Walks Alone*, was published in 2003.

Pownall died from pneumonia on June 24, 2005, in Bethesda, Maryland, at the age of 83. According to his obituary in *The Washington Post*, he often told colleagues that his decision to leave the navy was the biggest mistake of his life.

Captain Bo Coppedge
USNA Athletic Director, 1968–1988

1947 yearbook entry for John Oliver "Bo" Coppedge.

John "Bo" Coppedge is among the best-known members of the Class of '47, at least by his fellow classmates, because, in addition to being a standout wrestler and football player at Annapolis, he served as the Academy's athletic director for 20 years, from 1968–1988.

Coppedge is modest about how got the assignment. "In the navy, every six months you submit a preference card requesting what you want to do," he says. "Well, I wanted that job, so I put in a card requesting it, and I told everybody, 'If you need an athletic director, I'd like to do it.' And sure enough they hired me."

Coppedge grew up poor on a farm in Arkansas, and never dreamed he would be able to attend a service academy. But as a standout wrestler at Virginia Military Academy, and about to be drafted by the Army reserves, he competed in a wrestling meet against the Naval

Academy and was basically recruited by navy's associate athletic director Rip Miller to come to Annapolis.

"I realized when I was there, how lucky I was to have gotten in and to be surrounded by this super group of people," he says. "I learned to be inquisitive about everything that was going on in the world. I would take the newspaper into my room and read it cover to cover every night.

"We became an extremely close-knit class, because of the accelerated curriculum and the fact that we felt at the time that we would be applying everything we learned in a war that we were sure to join upon completion. We weren't allowed to have cars on campus, and very limited liberties, so most of our entertainment was around Annapolis."

The six-foot-six Coppedge became a submariner and attended submarine school in New London, Connecticut with both Crowe and Carter. As Vernon Weaver says, "Imagine Bo Coppedge slipping down the hatch of a submarine. That's quite an image."

Coppedge on Jack Stephens: "When I was AD, he entertained four of us every year at Augusta National. Also, twice I scheduled the Arkansas Razorbacks in football for no other reason than I wanted to go home. Well, Jack would entertain all of the Academy people at his house, which was quite a treat. I remember Jack at the Academy as an interested participant in everything that was going on, and even then he had success written all over him."

On Jim Stockdale: "It's hard to imagine what he went through. Just unbelievable. The way he withstood all that for that amount of time, man, does that take guts. I know one thing: I couldn't have done it, and all those who say they could have are lying."

Jay McKie
President and founder of AirBorn, Inc.

Midshipman Jay Gillis McKie

Jay McKie came to Annapolis from Manhattan Beach, and with Hollywood good looks and a roommate assignment with future Medal of Honor winner Tom Hudner, he was on a fast track to success. He was the only one interviewed for this book to proclaim that he considered plebe year, "a very enjoyable experience." "It was intense," McKie says, "but I think I had the right spirit going in. The message they wanted to get across in plebe year was about doing things that you say you'll do, developing accountability, and responsibility. I think I had some of those characteristics going in, so it was a reinforcement period for me."

An odd coincidence occurred when Jay McKie's AirBorn, Inc. was named the Small Business of the Year in 1979. It so happened that Vernon Weaver was head of the SBA at the time, and when he presented the award to McKie, they realized that they were both members of the Class of '47 but had never actually met.

Regarding the quantity and quality of outstanding midshipmen in the Class of '47, McKie says, "There must have been a strong flow of applicants in terms of quality, but the intangible was these guys' thirst for success. You could see that everywhere you looked. There was an absolute dedication among these men who said, 'I am going to be a winner.'"

Post-graduation, McKie had a tour of duty in the Pacific, before attending submarine school in 1949. He then was assigned to the USS *Runner* out of Norfolk and the USS *Wahoo* out of Pearl Harbor. After that, he returned to the Naval Academy as a Company Officer in the executive department. He resigned from the navy in 1956 to go into private business. After six years with Texas Instruments, he founded AirBorn Inc., an electronics components manufacturing company that grew to have over 800 employees.

In assessing his own career, McKie says, "I don't think these are monumental successes that I've had. They may feel like a big success to me, but in looking at the entire class, with 34 admirals, a U.S. senator, president of the U.S., Medal of Honor winners, and CEOs of large companies, those are the guys that are the real big winners. This was an absolutely great class. Every once in a while, I'm dumbfounded by the performance of these guys—guys I knew on a daily basis. I stand in awe of them."

Bob McKinney
Chairman of the Federal Home Loan Bank under President Carter

Midshipman Robert Hurley McKinney

Following graduation, Bob McKinney served on destroyers in the Pacific for three years, then resigned in 1949 and earned a law degree from Indiana University in 1951. He was then immediately called back to service in the Korean War.

After leaving the navy in 1953, McKinney settled in Indianapolis, where he and his wife Arlene raised five children. During Jimmy Carter's presidency, McKinney was called to Washington and served as chairman of the board of Federal Home Loan Bank, the Federal Home Loan Mortgage Corporation, the Federal Savings and Loan Insurance Corporation, and the Neighborhood Reinvestment Corporation. His office was directly across from the White House, and Bob says he enjoyed playing tennis there on a regular basis.

In the 1980s, McKinney was a director of the Federal National Mortgage Association (Fannie Mae). He later served as a trustee of the Hudson Institute, a trustee of the Sierra Club, president of the Board of Trustees of Indiana University and a longtime continuing trustee of the U.S. Naval Academy Foundation. He was also a senior partner in the law firm of Bose, Buchanan, McKinney, and Evans.

McKinney says that perhaps the biggest perk of serving with Jimmy Carter was the privilege of helicoptering to navy football games with the president. "I'll never be satisfied with an ordinary arrival again," he says.

Captain Bob O'Shea
Korean War POW

O'Shea's 1947 yearbook entry mentions his service in the Marines.

Bob O'Shea was a navy man through and through; both his father and brother graduated from the Naval Academy. Bob joined the marines in 1946, whereupon he was sent to China and the First Marine Division in Tien Tsing. His unit was sent there to disarm and accept the surrender of the Japanese, whose armies had been in China since 1933.

Although it took only six months to get all of the 300,000 or so Japanese back home, the U.S. Marines stayed for two years to give Chiang Kai-shek a chance to come in and take over. The marines finally pulled out of China in 1949, and O'Shea returned to Camp Pendleton in San Diego. The next year he married his wife Dorothea, and six weeks later the Korean War started. O'Shea again became part of the First Marine Division, which had to be reassembled quickly after being virtually wiped out during WWII.

Bob's wife gave birth to twin boys in June of 1951. He heard the news through a telegram. Less than a month later, on July 2, 1951, O'Shea's small plane was shot down by 50-caliber machine-gun fire. O'Shea was an artillery observer on the plane, and his pilot was Bob Taft. Although Taft made a perfect landing, it was right in the middle of enemy lines. The two marines were held prisoner for the next two years— a year by the Koreans in horribly cold and sparse conditions and a year by the Chinese, who O'Shea says treated them better.

Dorothea had no reason to suspect that Bob had survived, and they faced some difficult times upon his return. "That's when things kind of caught up with me mentally," he says, "and I retired because of physical disability in 1956." He went on to have a successful career with Glaxo, Smith, Kline. He and Dorothea have been married for 55 years and have four children.

"The discipline, self-reliance, and leadership I learned at the Naval Academy definitely helped me stay alive when I was a prisoner," he says.

Lieutenant Fred Sachse
Navy Pilot

Frederick Charles Sachse, Jr.

Fred Sachse came from a navy family. His father was a USNA graduate, Class of '20, and a younger brother, William, was in the Class of '58. Sachse enlisted in 1941, after graduating from high school and went to sea on an auxiliary sub chaser in the Atlantic. He got his appointment to the Naval Academy in 1941 and became roommates with Bill Crowe. Both Bob O'Shea and Jim Stockdale were good friends.

Crowe recalls that Sachse was a heckuva drummer and used to beat on his desk and lampshade with pencils in their dorm room as a way of practicing. Crowe shared memories of his old roomie with Sachse's daughter Patty at the 50th reunion in 1996.

In April 1952, Sachse was co-pilot on a training mission in bad weather near Brunswick, Maine, when the plane he was flying crashed. The pilot tried to pull Fred from the wrecked plane, but Sachse was so badly burned that he died 10 days later. He was buried in Arlington National Cemetery and left behind two daughters, Jean and Patty, neither of whom ever really knew their father. Jim Stockdale and Vernon Weaver, both living in Washington at the time, served as pallbearers.

Vice Admiral John "Jake" Finneran

John Glennon Finneran in his yearbook photo.

After graduating from the Academy, Jake Finneran joined the USS *Walke* and then, in September 1947, reported as an instructor at the Naval Academy Preparatory School. He remained there until October 1948, when he joined the USS *Kleinsmith*. From 1950–1952, Finneran had duty on the USS *Douglas H. Fox*, after which he served as Executive Officer and then Commanding Officer of the USS *Pima County*. In April 1961, he became Executive Officer of the USS *Meredith* and in September 1962, assumed command of the USS *Sampson*. In 1965, Finneran attended the National War College and then assumed command of DESDIV 72 in June 1966. Jake was promoted to the rank of Rear Admiral in May 1968, and then named Assistant Chief for Plans and Programs. After 1970, Finneran's assignments included commander, Cruiser Destroyer Flotilla Twelve, commander, Second Fleet and Striking Fleet Atlantic, and deputy assistant secretary of defense for military personnel policy. Jake counted at least 28 family moves during his navy career. He retired in 1977 and worked for years as an independent consultant.

Jake Finneran died in the summer of 2005. He and his wife, Lillian, had five children.

Bob Cowell
Olympic medallist

Robert Elmer Cowell

If the navy is all about seafaring men, then Bob Cowell could be said to have been as water-worthy as any in his class. An outstanding athlete, Cowell had been an Eastern Athletic Conference swimming champion before entering the Naval Academy.

Classmate Bo Heiniger shared this story about Cowell's prowess. "We entered the Academy the same day and were placed in the same fourth class plebe summer battalion. One of our first requirements as plebes was to pass a swimming test. Those who failed would have to report to the "Sub Squad" for instruction until they were able to pass the test. Unfortunately, I was positioned to swim after Bob. I looked so bad in comparison that I flunked the test and was put on Sub Squad. I had always been a fairly good swimmer, so after I reported to Sub Squad and did some swimming, the coaches asked, 'How in the world did you flunk your swimming test?'

"I told them I had the misfortune of having to swim right after Bob Cowell." That year, Bob captained the navy's swim team to six decisive individual victories and two wins in triangular meets, and then helped guide the 1944 squad to the Intercollegiate Championship.

Bob would go on to win a bronze medal in the backstroke at the 1948 Olympic Games before serving his tour and eventually going through the navy's flight training school, where he received his Wings of Gold.

Sadly, in 1960, Bob, his wife, Eloise, and their two children were driving through Athens, Georgia, when they were involved in an automobile accident. Bob and Eloise were killed, but their two children survived and were raised by family members.

Rear Admiral Don Whitmire

Whitmire's entry in the class of '47 yearbook.

One of the most likable and certainly celebrated members of the Class of '47, was Don Whitmire. A three-time All-American in football and an All-American at the University of Alabama before he enrolled at the Naval Academy, Whitmire ranks with Joe Bellino and Roger Staubach as one of the finest gridiron stars in navy history. Classmate Joseph Flanagan Jr. recalls a couple of classic Whitmire moments: "At the Superintendent's luncheon one day, we were discussing which daily papers we read, the options being *The New York Times, The Washington Post,* and *The Baltimore Sun.* Don stated that he preferred to bundle all the newspapers that were delivered to his room and deposit them in the wastebasket," Flanagan says. "Whitmire was not to be confused with the 'intellectuals.'"

Flanagan recalls another time when Whitmire summoned a plebe wrestler named John Fletcher, son of Admiral "Black Jack" Fletcher, to his room for an infraction. "Whit ordered John to do 47 push-ups, to which the plebe replied, 'Which arm?' When young Fletcher accomplished 49 single-armed pushups with each arm, Whitmire shook his hand and said, 'From now on you can call me Whit.'"

After graduation, Don served on three destroyers, then attended submarine school. Following a tour with the Department of Athletics at USNA, he graduated from the Naval War College in June 1958, then took command of the *Redfish* and later the *Salmon*. As commander of the USS *Navarro*, Whitmire conducted four amphibious assaults along the coast of South Vietnam, including the rescue of 43 merchant seamen from a U.K. ship stranded in the path of a typhoon in the South China Sea. He was selected to the rank of Rear Admiral in 1971. He later took command of Amphibious Group One and wrote the final chapter of the U.S. involvement in Cambodia and Vietnam in early 1975. While in command of Operation Frequent Wind—two amphibious squadrons, four aircraft carriers, and numerous helicopter squadrons and support ships—Whitmire conducted the evacuation of nearly 7,000 Americans and South Vietnamese from Saigon. And under his direction, over 80,000 other South Vietnamese refugees were rescued and transported to safe havens.

Captain Jack Stevens
Navy Officer

Midshipman Jack Marion Stevens

Rather than being annoyed by the fact that two prominent Naval Academy classmates had the same name, Jack Stevens from Texas and Jack Stephens from Arkansas became good friends. "We had a neat friendship," Stevens says. "We both got a real kick out of having the same name, and in fact we'd often deny things and blame the 'other Jack' if something went wrong."

Jack Stevens was raised in the small town of Kerrville, Texas, where Admiral Nimitz was born. After two years at sea post-graduation, he entered flight school at Pensacola and later got a master's degree in public relations from Boston University, which Stevens put that to good use as public information officer for the Naval War College. He then did a Pentagon tour in 1966, spending over two years as public affairs officer for the assistant to the secretary of defense.

Stevens served one year with CINCPAC in Hawaii before doing two tours in Tonkin Gulf as Commander of the USS *Wichita*, a supply replenishment ship.

Stevens retired after 30 years of active duty, then went to work for the Academy's Blue and Gold officer program, which helped the candidate guidance office counsel high school students on the procedures they have to follow to get into the Academy.

"Whether we liked it or not at the Academy, we were involved in a lock-step curriculum," Stevens says. "That meant I only had one course that I could choose. Otherwise, we all took the exact same classes. So all of us in the company marched together to class, we ate together, everything, so we couldn't help but bond together. Still, I had no idea there would be such a strong bond formed out of what basically started out as a college roommate relationship.

"To realize I spent 30 years on active duty, of which probably two-thirds of it was sea duty and kept me away from home, and then to have immediately gotten so heavily involved in the counseling thing, talking to these kids about the advantages of going to the Academy . . . I mean, I just now stopped doing that after 27 years. So to devote 57 years to the navy, there had to have been something that kept me so involved. And it was the Class of '47, and the dear friends I made."

Andy Peacock
Former General Superintendent of Kodak

Andrew Jackson Peacock from the class yearbook.

Andy Peacock found as the years moved along that he was a compulsive "name dropper," constantly bragging on the achievements of his class members both in and out of naval service.

The Alabama native entered the Naval Academy after two years at Auburn University. He roomed with future two-star admiral, Bill Harris, and became good friends with Bill Crowe, in the same company. "The lights at the Academy went out at 10 p.m., and then, of course, you couldn't study anymore, because you couldn't see," he says. "So whenever a particularly tough exam was coming up, Crowe would sneak out of his room and head over to Memorial Hall. You always knew when he did it, because he'd show up at formation the next day all blurry-eyed, and you knew he'd stayed awake all night."

Peacock recalls that he and Crowe also taught Sunday school to navy juniors in the chapel. "It was just a way for us to get out of chapel," he says. "I don't think the kids learned much. Really, we were just babysitters."

After graduating, Peacock went to Mine Warfare School and eventually got command of his own ship, a sweeper. He left the navy in 1949, and returned to Auburn to get his chemical engineering degree. He then went to work for Kodak in its chemical engineering division in Tennessee but within a year was called back to the navy to serve in the Korean War. He served aboard a mine-sweeper for nearly three years, after which he returned to his job at Kodak. He remained there for 36 years, advancing through the corporate ranks.

"Learning to deal with a widely diverse group of people from different backgrounds and cultures at the Academy showed me that you can find a common interest with anyone," he says. "And that ability to handle people and provide leadership was probably my biggest asset when I got into industry."

Robert Payne Gatewood

Businessman

Robert Payne Gatewood, business pioneer.

One of the unsung business stalwarts of the Class of '47, Bob Gatewood spent 50 years in the worlds of business and finance, and made historic contributions to the life insurance industry. His professional strategies changed the insurance-selling relationship from that of a commissioned life insurance agent and his prospect to that of a fee-and-transaction-based advisor and his client.

Bob's innovative life insurance policy designs include the "joint last-to-die policy" for use in providing cash to pay estate taxes at the death of a surviving spouse, and the multiple joint life policy, which insured three or more business owners whose corporation or partnership needed cash to redeem or purchase a deceased owner's interest in the business.

Gatewood has lectured throughout the country and abroad and is widely published as an authority in the insurance business. Both *Who's Who in America* and the *Marquis Who's Who in the World* have included his personal and professional biographies.

"To be counted among the Class of '47 continues to be a source of immense pride," Bob says. "Our classmates have distinguished themselves in so many ways, and our country is so much the richer for their many and varied contributions."

Gatewood holds another distinction among members of his class—as the most prolific father. He and his wife Marilyn have 13 children.

Rear Admiral Bill Harris

Bill Harris, as a midshipman.

Bill Harris missed nearly the entire plebe summer, as he was a late acceptance to the Academy. He and Don Whitmire were the last two to be sworn into the plebe class in September 1943. "I was at a disadvantage missing all that training where the plebes were taught what to do and what not to do, so I believe I accumulated about 100 demerits in the first month," he says. "I think if you got 150 you were kicked out, so I was well on my way. The rigors of the whole place were very austere, and because so much emphasis was placed on physical fitness, I was always under the impression that they were training us to swim across the Pacific.

"I learned about the importance of being part of the unit," he says. "It was all about teamwork. People depending on you and vice versa. You realize that you're always part of something bigger than yourself ,and you have to pull your own weight. That comes back to discipline and integrity and accepting responsibility for your actions . . . all things we learned well during our years at Annapolis."

Harris spent two years on carriers after graduation before being sent to flight training in the summer of 1948, along with classmate Tom Hudner. After making rear admiral, he served one year as Deputy of the Naval War College before ending up with two carrier division commands, the latter of which was the head of all carriers in the Western Pacific. Bill went back to Washington for a year before his final assignment in China Lake, close to Edwards Air Force Base, where he helped develop air-to-ground and air-to-air weapons. He retired from the navy in 1979 and went to work for Lockheed Martin in Sunnyvale, California, as a project manager. He lives with wife Jean in Los Altos Hills, California, and they have five children and four grandchildren.

Bill Harris says his most memorable military experience was with ComCarDivision 7, supporting Don Whitmire's unforgettable evacuation of Saigon and Phnom Penh Vietnam in April of 1975.

Rear Admiral Bruce Smith

Carlton Bruce Smith

After hearing all the stories about great fighter pilots in the Class of '47, it's refreshing to hear Carlton Bruce Smith describe his experience in flight school. "I made four landings on carriers the likes of which the navy never hopes to see again," he says. "I was so heartbroken, because I really thought I could fly circles around everyone, but I must say they gave me every opportunity to earn my wings."

One area where Smith clearly earned his wings was on the football field, as a star quarterback. His team lost just two games in three years, and those were both to the immortal Army team with the great backfield tandem of Doc Blanchard and Glenn Davis.

Bruce married his wife, Carolyn, on graduation day, and his first duty was as a supply officer working for Commander Joe Davis. His early tours included service in Wilkes-Barre and Toledo, and in between, he taught math at the Naval Academy and College Preparatory at Bainbridge. Then followed his ill-fated effort at flight school.

Smith furthered his education with classes in Command and Staff at the Naval War College and the Advanced Management Program at Harvard. He then served a tour as XO with the U.S. Naval Supply Depot in Subic Bay in the Philippines before finishing his career in Hawaii as a fleet supply officer.

He recalls that "Vernon Weaver was at the University of Florida, and I was in high school when both of us got appointments to the Academy. He had the principal and I had the alternate. . . . I'm really not surprised at the amazing accomplishments of my classmates," he says, "because this was a group of dedicated individuals that worked very hard and had their values and principles. They were destined for greatness, and I'm proud of their accomplishments."

Lieutenant John Guild

KIA, Korean War; Navy Cross recipient (posthumous)

John Guild's class yearbook photo.

John Guild entered the Naval Academy with the goal of getting a commission to the Marines. He was, according to many of his classmates, a spit-and-polish guy, who followed regulations right down the line. After graduation, Guild applied to the Marines, but there wasn't a place for him, so he became an ensign. He reached Lieutenant Junior Grade by the time he was admitted to the Marines, but by switching services, he was dropped down a grade to Second Lieutenant.

Guild was part of the first Marine division sent to Korea, and the details of his death on September 21, 1950, are somewhat sketchy. One account had Guild coming in on landing crafts and being killed as he climbed over a wall. *Life* magazine published a story about Guild and the battle that claimed his life.

President Harry Truman posthumously awarded Guild the Navy Cross, a prestigious honor only one step below the Medal of Honor, but some controversy later arose. Another marine, who went over the same wall as Guild and was also shot, but survived, received the Medal of Honor. Guild's father, Eugene R. Guild, wrote a letter of protest to Truman, explaining that he felt his son should have received the same honor. The story received wide play in the media, but according to most sources Guild's father retracted the letter when he heard that the recommendations for the medal had been made by command headquarters in the Far East.

Chester H. Shaddeau Jr.

Midshipman Chester Harold Shaddeau Jr.

Chet Shaddeau, the only son of a navy chief petty officer, lived in China and the Philippines pre-WWII, and received his presidential appointment to the Naval Academy after a nationwide competitive exam. He served on the carrier *Tarawa* (CV-40), in several destroyers (commanding one), and in the fleet training group at Guantanamo Bay, as he says, "before Gitmo was a dirty word!" He graduated from Naval Intelligence PG School and was assistant naval attache in Caracas.

He resigned to join Martin Marietta for four years in the USAF Titan program, then worked for 23 years in aerospace engineering as director of various NASA overseas satellite tracking/data stations, all in Spanish-speaking countries. He retired from civil service in 1986.

Chet's wife Patricia (whose father was USNA Class of 1923) died in 1999. The families of his two sons, one in Denver and the other in Tacoma, have made him twice a great-grandfather. Chet now lives in a condo close enough to the navy stadium in Annapolis that he can hear the roar of the crowd on those few occasions when he isn't in the stands.

Chet has been class secretary since 1993, keeping up fluid communications between all members of the class, and has been of invaluable assistance in providing research and information for this book.

Vice Admiral James H. Doyle

Future class president, Jim Doyle, in his 1947 yearbook photo.

After graduation, Jim Doyle served on the cruiser *Chicago* and the destroyer *John W. Thomason* before attending George Washington University Law School and receiving his Juris Doctor degree. He later was admitted to the practice of law in both the District of Columbia and California. In 1962, Jim took command of the destroyer *John R. Craig*, then in 1964–1965 attended nuclear power training. He served as the executive officer on the cruiser *Newport News* in the Pacific, and during that four-year tour, he received the Legion of Merit and the Bronze Star. His first assignment as rear admiral came in 1971, when he was named Chief of the International Negotiations Division under the Joint Chiefs of Staff. Doyle was promoted to vice admiral in 1974, as commander of the Third Fleet based in Pearl Harbor. From 1975 to 1980, Jim was deputy chief of naval operations (surface warfare). After retirement from the navy in 1980, he consulted for Aerospace Companies, did work at the University of Virginia's Center for Law and National Security and Oceans Law, and taught international law at George Washington University. He and his wife Jeannette, were married on graduation day from the USNA in 1946, and they have three children.

As current president of the Class of '47, Admiral Doyle works closely with Chet Shaddeau to coordinate all class activities and keep up an up-to-date flow of information.

Paul "PG" Miller
CEO, Control Data Corp.

PG Miller's yearbook entry.

Paul Miller graduated from high school when he was just 15 and didn't slow down when he enrolled at Purdue University, where he was president of his fraternity and president of the student senate. He got his appointment to Annapolis while in the advanced ROTC program at Purdue and had to request a release to go to the Academy.

"We used to vacation at Virginia Beach when I was a kid," Miller says, "and I watched those big ships and always thought that going to sea would be the greatest thing in the world. It looked like I was headed for the Army and field artillery at the time I got my appointment to the navy, but my mom persuaded me to reverse that decision with a tearful pleading."

Paul retired from the navy in 1957, and then worked for a small computer company in LaJolla, California, until 1963. The company was purchased by Minneapolis-based Control Data Corp., so he then moved to the Twin Cities as president of Control Data Corp. He became president of Control Data Worldwide Marketing in 1970, then moved to Baltimore to become president, CEO, and chairman of Commercial Credit in 1975.

Miller has been married for 26 years to his second wife, Doris, whom he first met at a dance at plebe summer at the Academy. (Doris Miller took an active interest in this book and was kind enough to send press clippings of the class to assist the research.)

Paul has the utmost praise for his classmates and friends Bill Crowe and Jim Stockdale: "I have the greatest respect for what Jim Stockdale went through. My feeling is none of us know how good we are until we're tested, and I don't think any of us were tested like Jim. The torture he endured and the way he led the POW contingent . . . I'm not sure I would have been that good.

"The guy who has been the nicest to his class is Bill Crowe. He has always remembered his class in everything he did, especially in terms of attending class functions. When he was chairman of the Joint Chiefs, he had use of a private car for the Army-Navy game, and he always invited us to go with him. He continues to come to class luncheons and functions, just a really neat guy."

Rear Admiral Ken Sears

Ken Sears, USNA Class of '47

Like Bill Crowe, Ken Sears is an Oklahoma native. He admits surprise at the prominence of his classmates. "I don't think any of us had any idea that the class would rise to the level it has," he says. "We were young, and the war had just gotten over, and we were trying to do everything we could to make an impact. But as far as the class achieving the stature that it has . . . no . . . I never thought that Crowe would make admiral or that Bruce Smith would make admiral. But we worked hard. All of us grew up in an era where we didn't start out with everything like young people do today. TVs weren't around, and computers weren't around. Ensigns got paid $150 a month and a bunch of us got married and supported our wives on that."

After graduating, Sears was assigned to the USS *Princeton*, but ended up having a kidney removed after a medical problem. He wanted to be an aviator but couldn't pass the physical because of the lost kidney and was transferred to the civil engineering corps in 1948. He proceeded up the ranks, eventually becoming the officer in charge of construction of the Southwest Pacific in Manilla in 1968. Sears then took command of the 32nd Naval Construction Regiment in DaNang in 1971. The following year, he became the deputy officer in charge of construction in Saigon. He received the Legion of Merit for his tour in the Philippines and a Gold Star in lieu of a second Legion of Merit for his service in Vietnam. He was selected for admiral in 1973, the same year as his Okie friend, Bill Crowe. He has spent the last 10 years with a firm called Earth Technology Corp. He has been married to his wife Jeanne for 57 years. His daughter Susan works for AAA in Orlando and his son, Jonathan, is a USNA graduate, Class of '78.

Norris Whitwell "Bud" Carnes

Bud Carnes as a midshipman.

Bud Carnes served three years at sea before going to Harvard and earning his master's degree. He then got recalled to active duty in the Korean War, serving as assistant gun boss. He returned to civilian life two years later and spent 11 years with DuPont. He then went to Universal Oil Products as executive vice president. While at UOP, he was the director of International Operations and was responsible for eight companies worldwide.

Carnes bought a company called Gopher Electronics in 1984 and ran it for 20 years, until his recent retirement.

"When I entered the Academy I was an off-the-wall high school graduate who needed some structure in his life, and it did a lot to straighten me out. The Academy provided an environment that was very conducive to shaping a young guy's mind. The best thing I can say about my time at the Academy is that it changed me from a boy to a man."

Bud recalls seeing Jimmy Carter at one of their reunions and laughing about an exchange they had at Annapolis. "I didn't know Carter that well, but because our names were so close alphabetically, we stood watch in the main office together. I remember one day he said to me, 'Bud, I'm going to be the chief of naval operations some day.'

"I said, 'Jimmy, you're the last guy who's going to get that job!'

"When I reminded him of that, Carter said, 'Oh yeah, but I skipped that.'"

Vernon Weaver has especially fond memories of Bud Carnes, because Carnes introduced Vernon to Joyce McCoy, Vernon's future wife.

Rear Admiral Jeff Metzel

Jeffrey Caswell Metzel Jr., USNA Class of 1947

Jeff Metzel's father was a USNA graduate, Class of 1919, and so was his grandfather, Class of 1884, so Jeff worked "like mad" all through high school to get an appointment. When it came through, he says, "I felt like I was lying on the base path with my hand on home plate."

Unlike many of his class, Jeff says "I didn't think plebe year was very tough, because from the time I was a little kid, I knew what it was all about. I enjoyed some parts, especially playing intramural sports, but other parts, well, I was delighted when I graduated. It wasn't a bad time by any means, but I was anxious to get out into the fleet and be a naval officer. But I will say that I would love to go back and do the whole thing over again."

He was more than willing to share thoughts on his classmates:

About Jack Stephens he says: "Jack never got commissioned, because his eyesight was so poor. He did fine academically, and, ironically, despite his poor eyesight, he was an expert rifle and pistol shot. Both Weaver and Stephens were characters. They were humorous guys, always able to pull off stunts. They were very non-regulation, but in an intelligent way. And Bill Crowe is one of my personal heroes. I've known him since we were plebes—we even roomed together for a while in New London—and I always thought he was a superb guy. As a matter of fact, I think the country would have been better off, if he had run for president. He would've been a really good one."

Post-graduation, Metzel was assigned to the USS *Tarawa* and then attended submarine school in 1949. He was a career navy man and progressed through the ranks from XO to CO to project manager of the MK 48 Torpedo from 1967–1971. He retired from the navy in 1979 and moved to Huntington Beach, California, where he went to work at nearby Rockwell Marine Systems developing various unmanned underwater vehicles. He stayed with Rockwell for 11 years before retiring.

Lieutenant Commander John S. Urban
War Veteran as a Plebe

John Stephen Urban

John Urban was a veteran of war before he even enrolled at the Naval Academy. He enlisted in January 1941, and went to boot camp at the U.S. navy Training Station in Newport. From there, he graduated from Aviation Radioman Gunner School in Jacksonville and in the fall of '41 was attached to VS-8, Scouting Squadron 8, as an aviation radioman gunner and Air Group 8 of the USS *Hornet CV-8*.

Urban was attached to VS-8 and the USS *Hornet CV-8* when they took Lt. Colonel Jimmy Doolittle for his famous raid on Tokyo in April 1942. He remembers that President Roosevelt, at the time, announced that the raid had come from Shangri La, a mythical place, for classified reasons.

On June 4, 5, and 6 of 1942, young John Urban was engaged in the Battle of Midway in VS-8 Scouting Squadron and made bombing runs on Japanese Naval Forces. As an aviation radioman gunner PO 3/c, and still just 18 years old, he was assigned to the rear seat of an SBD-3 (Douglas Dauntless) dive bomber. His pilot was Ensign Harold White from South Carolina. During the battle, they made bombing runs on carriers, cruisers, and destroyers. White made a direct bomb hit on a Mogami Class Japanese Cruiser, and Urban had a chance to strafe some of the ships with his twin .30 caliber machine guns after coming out of a dive. White received the navy Cross for his heroism. Urban was detached from his USS *Hornet* CV-8 and his squadron just three days before the ship was sunk in the Battle of Santa Cruz Islands on October 26, 1942. He was on his way to the U.S. Naval Academy Prep School in Norfolk.

After passing the entrance exams to the Naval Academy, he received a secretary of the navy appointment. While still in his plebe year, and much to the admiration of his classmates, Urban was awarded the Distinguished Flying Cross from the superintendent of the Academy, Rear Admiral John R. Beardall, for his part in the Battle of Midway.

He retired from the navy on June 30, 1968, after 27 years of service, but stays in close touch with his USNA classmates and attends all reunions and gatherings. He and his wife, Olga, celebrated their 60th wedding anniversary on June 6 of 2006.

Don Welt
Businessman

The yearbook entry for Donald DeFrance Welt.

Like Jack Stephens, Welt's poor eyesight kept him from a desired career in naval aviation, but his business vision was always 20/20.

After earning a law degree from Georgetown University, Welt resigned from the navy in 1953 and entered civilian life with Iowa Power & Light and General Dynamics. In 1961, he founded Rochester Instrument Systems, Inc., which manufactured electronic equipment used in the instrumentation and automation of industrial plants, such as power plants, refineries, and paper mills. He served as the company's president and CEO until July 1981, when he left to become group vice-president of Sybron Corp. In the mid-1980s, he was elected chairman of SAMA, the Scientific Apparatus Makers Association, a trade association composed of over 200 member companies with annual sales in excess of $12 billion.

John M. Sullivan

Federal Railway Administrator in the Carter Administration

John McGrath Sullivan's yearbook photo.

Following graduation, Sullivan was assigned to the USS *Providence* and eventually to flight training. He left the navy in 1954 and started to work as a sales representative. After much success in sales, he bought a die casting business and later a factory in Kenilworth, NJ. He and his wife, Mickey, who were married upon graduation, had six children, two girls and four boys, all of whom were very active in athletics. Sullivan says he and his wife spent many enjoyable months and years beside swimming pools and basketball courts cheering on their children.

In 1975, Sullivan worked actively in Pennsylvania on the election campaign of classmate Jimmy Carter. He was rewarded for his efforts by being named by Carter as his federal railroad administrator, thus becoming one of just four navy classmates—the others being

Stansfield Turner, Vernon Weaver, and Bob McKinney — to serve in the Carter administration. In 1980, after the stint in Washington, Sullivan returned to New Jersey to his die casing business. He died the day after his 81st birthday on December 19, 2005.

Graduates of the USNA Class of 1947

Mr. Alfred E. Adams

LCDR Daniel B. Adams, USNR (Ret.)

LT Donald F. Adams, USNR (Ret.)

CAPT Frank M. Adams, USN (Ret.)

Mr. Robert M. Adams

CAPT Joseph L. Adelman, USN (Ret.)

CAPT William J. Aicklen, Jr., USN (Ret.)

CAPT Carl D. Alberts, USNR (Ret.)

Dr. John G. Albright

Mr. Charles K. Allendorf

Mr. Rex L. Allspaw

Mr. George A. Amacker, Jr.

LTJG Robert L. Amelang, USN (Ret.)

CAPT Richard D. Amme, USN (Ret.)

CAPT Charles R. Anderson, USN (Ret.)

CAPT James L. Anderson, USN (Ret.)

CAPT Richard W. Anderson, USN (Ret.)

LTJG Roy T. Anderson, USN

CAPT James D. Andrews, USN (Ret.)

CAPT David D. Ansel, USN (Ret.)

CAPT Edward P. Appert, USN (Ret.)

CDR Grant B. Apthorp, USN (Ret.)

CDR John R. Arguelles, USN (Ret.)

CAPT Roy C. Atkinson, USN (Ret.)

Mr. Victor K. Aubrey, Jr.

Mr. Frank S. Averill

Mr. Arnold W. Avery

LT Francis M. Bacon, USN

CDR Joseph Baer, Jr., USN (Ret.)

ADM Worth H. Bagley, USN (Ret.)

Mr. Roger S. Bagnall

CAPT Daniel L. Bailey, USN (Ret.)

LT Raymond N. Baker, USNR (Ret.)

CDR John M. Balfe, USN (Ret.)

Mr. Erwin J. Ballje, Jr.

CAPT Bernard J. Bandish, USN (Ret.)

Mr. Robert N. Barker

Mr. Arthur H. F. Barlow

CDR Ralph E. Barnard, USN (Ret.)

CAPT Alan F. Barnes, USN (Ret.)

Mr. George B. Barnett

Mr. Franklin M. Barrell, Jr.

CAPT William W. Barron, USN (Ret.)

CAPT James H. Barry, USN (Ret.)

Mr. Paul F. Basilius

Mr. James D. Baskin, Jr.

Mr. Charles G. Batt, Jr.

CAPT James A. Baxter, USN (Ret.)

Mr. Philip E. Baylor

Mr. Paul E. Beam, Jr.

LCDR Edward R. Beane, USN (Ret.)

Mr. Richard J. Beaubien

Mr. Robert G. Beck

CDR Bradford A. Becken, USN (Ret.)

CDR Marvin J. Becker, USNR (Ret.)

LCDR Thomas I. Bell, USNR (Ret.)

CAPT John A. Bellan, Jr., USNR (Ret.)

Mr. William E. Benckart

Mr. Robert D. Bergman

LCDR Raymond R. Bernier, USN (Ret.)

Mr. Byron N. Bettis

The Honorable Lawrence Bilder

CAPT Homer R. Bivin, USN (Ret.)

Mr. Marvin L. Black

BGen Herbert J. Blaha, USMC (Ret.)

CDR Ira W. Blair, USN (Ret.)

Dr. William P. Blair, Jr.

LCDR Carl A. Blank, USN (Ret.)

CDR William D. Blevins, USN (Ret.)

CDR William E. Blythe, USN (Ret.)

LCDR Merson Booth, USNR (Ret.)

CAPT Fredric G. Bouwman, USN (Ret.)

CAPT Floyd D. Bowdey, USN (Ret.)

CAPT James W. Bowen, USN (Ret.)

CDR Thomas J. Bowen, USN (Ret.)

Mr. James C. Bowes

Mr. George R. Bowling, Jr.

ENS Newell S. Bowman, USN (Ret.)

Mr. Archibald A. Bradley

LCDR Frederick G. Bradshaw, USNR (Ret.)

CDR Robert C. Brady, USNR (Ret.)

LTJG Ralph Brandt, USNR (Ret.)

Mr. Lloyd L. Brassaw, Jr.

Mr. John S. Brayton, Jr.

CAPT Thomas B. Brenner, USN (Ret.)

Mr. J. R. Bridges, Jr.

CAPT Thomas B. Brittain, Jr., USN (Ret.)

LT Louis Brizzolara, USNR (Ret.)

CAPT Frederick B. Bromley, USN (Ret.)

CAPT Rupert Brooke, USN (Ret.)

Mr. Gayle K. Broussard

Mr. Joe A. Brower

CAPT Bryan B. Brown, Jr., USN (Ret.)

LTJG Kenneth C. Brown, USN

Mr. Moody B. Brown, Jr.

Mr. Richard G. Brown

CAPT Dale C. Brumbaugh, USN (Ret.)

LTJG James W. Brummer, USNR

LT George O. R. Brungot, USNR (Ret.)

LCDR George H. Bryan, Jr., USN (Ret.)

Mr. Robert E. Buntain

Mr. Sumner W. Burgess

Mr. Thomas J. Burgoyne

CAPT John C. Burkart, USN (Ret.)

CAPT James A. Burke, USN (Ret.)

Dr. Hubert C. Burton

Mr. Lorenzo G. Burton, Jr.

CDR Arthur G. Butler, Jr., USN (Ret.)

Mr. Charles I. Buxton II

CDR Ward G. Byington, USN (Ret.)

CAPT Arthur D. Caine, USN (Ret.)

RADM Arturo M. Calisto

CAPT John D. Callaway, Jr., USN (Ret.)

Dr. Gene I. Campbell

CAPT Richard D. Campbell, USN (Ret.)

CAPT Charles S. Carlisle, USN (Ret.)

CDR John C. Carlson, USN (Ret.)

RADM Ralph H. Carnahan, USN (Ret.)

Mr. Norris W. Carnes

Mr. Alfred C. Carpenter

CAPT Harold L. Carpenter, USN (Ret.)

Mr. William C. Carpenter

LT Felix R. Carr, USNR (Ret.)

Mr. John L. Carroll

The Honorable James E. Carter, Jr.

LT Edson G. Case, USNR (Ret.)

CAPT Earle M. Cassidy, CEC, USNR (Ret.)

CDR Charles W. Causey, Jr., USN (Ret.)

Mr. Stanley M. Cecil

CAPT Rafael H. Cevallos

CDR Daniel Chadwick, USN (Ret.)

CAPT Raymond E. Chamberlain, Jr., USN (Ret.)

CDR Donald E. Chandler, USN (Ret.)

CAPT James H. Chapman, USN (Ret.)

CAPT Arthur L. Child III, USN (Ret.)

CAPT John W. Clayton, USNR (Ret.)

CAPT Marwood R. Clement, Jr., USN (Ret.)

CDR Reginald D. Clubb, USN (Ret.)

CAPT Warren R. Cobean, Jr., USN (Ret.)

Mr. Kenneth S. Coe

Mr. Earl L. Coen

Mr. Milo G. Coerper

CAPT Joseph P. Cofer, Jr., USNR (Ret.)

CDR John E. Cohoon, USNR (Ret.)

CAPT Kenneth J. Cole, USN (Ret.)

Mr. James R. Collier

CDR Robert C. Collier, USNR (Ret.)

Dr. Jay L. Collins

LCDR Peter Colot, USN (Ret.)

CDR Richard G. Colquhoun, USN (Ret.)

Mr. Robert F. Conway

Mr. Edward L. Cook, Jr.

Mr. William J. Cook

LCDR James B. Copenhaver, Jr., USN (Ret.)

CAPT John O. Coppedge, USN (Ret.)

Mr. John D. Corse, Esq.

Mr. Robert E. Cowell

ENS Calvin C. Cowley, USN (Ret.)

CAPT John W. Crane, Jr., USN (Ret.)

Mr. Richard T. Crane

Mr. Jackson B. Craven, Jr.

CDR Bentley B. Crawford, USN (Ret.)

Mr. Robert E. Creque

CAPT Charles B. Crockett, Jr., USN (Ret.)

Mr. Joseph R. Cross

ADM William J. Crowe, Jr., USN (Ret.)

Mr. Seymour F. Crumpler

RADM Charles W. Cummings, USN

Mr. Robert E. Cummings, Jr.

Mr. Douglas T. Cummins

CAPT Peter P. Cummins, USN (Ret.)

Mr. William C. Curran

Mr. Hal L. Curry

CAPT Lawrence J. Curtin, USN (Ret.)

Mr. Harry L. Curtis, Jr.

CDR Richard A. Dadisman, USN (Ret.)

LT Howard B. Dalton, Jr., USN

Col Charles R. Darby, USA (Ret.)

Mr. Lynn A. Davenport, Sr.

CDR Alan N. Davidson, USN (Ret.)

CDR James B. Davidson, USN (Ret.)

CAPT John D. Davidson, USN (Ret.)

CAPT Ray E. Davis, USN (Ret.)

Mr. Richard P. Davis

CAPT Theodore F. Davis, USN (Ret.)

Mr. Walter O. Day

Mr. Dale B. Deatherage

Mr. Frank A. Deaton

CAPT James A. deGanahl, USN (Ret.)

Mr. Harry M. DeLaney

LCDR John J. Dempsey, USNR (Ret.)

LCDR George M. Dent, USN

RADM Jeremiah A. Denton, Jr., USN (Ret.)

CDR Robert W. Depew, USN (Ret.)

LTJG Edmond L. Deramee, Jr., USNR (Ret.)

CDR James V. DeSanto, USN (Ret.)

CAPT Carlos Dew, Jr., USN (Ret.)

Dr. James G. Dickson, Jr.

Mr. Philip C. Diem

Mr. Neff T. Dietrich, Jr.

CAPT Jarl J. Diffendorfer, USN (Ret.)

CDR Allen F. Dill, USNR (Ret.)

LT William R. Dillen, USNR (Ret.)

Mr. James R. Dillman

CDR Willard C. Doe, USN (Ret.)

CDR John F. Doheny, USN (Ret.)

CAPT Charles E. Donaldson III, USN (Ret.)

LCDR William I. Donaldson, USN (Ret.)

CAPT Donald L. Donohugh, USNR (Ret.)

Mr. William K. Doran

LTJG William R. Dougherty, USN

CAPT Walter M. Douglass, USN (Ret.)

Mr. Andrew S. Dowd

VADM James H. Doyle, Jr., USN (Ret.)

LCDR Jack V. Drago, USN (Ret.)

LCDR Harold M. Dryer, USN (Ret.)

CDR John P. Duckett, USN (Ret.)

Mr. Henry R. Duden, Jr.

Mr. Peter H. H. Dunn, Jr.

Dr. Thomas S. Dunstan II

Mr. Manuel Dupkin II

Mr. Vernon M. Dupy

Maj Joseph N. Eagle, USMC (Ret.)

Mr. Joseph E. Earl

LtCol Robert E. Eastman, USMC (Ret.)

CDR Harold L. Edwards, USN (Ret.)

LtCol Roy J. Edwards, USMC (Ret.)

Mr. Edward J. Eisenman

CAPT Kenneth O. Ekelund, Jr., USN (Ret.)

CAPT Frank L. Elefante, USN (Ret.)

CAPT Samuel S. Ellis, USN (Ret.)

CAPT Joseph S. Elmer, USN (Ret.)

CAPT Robert E. Enright, USN (Ret.)

Maj Robert M. Erbland, USMC (Ret.)

Mr. Don H. Erickson, Jr.

CAPT Hermann J. Estelmann, USN (Ret.)

CAPT Joseph D. Evans, USN (Ret.)

RADM Stuart J. Evans, USN (Ret.)

Mr. William B. Evans

Mr. Donald W. Everett

Mr. Philip B. Fairman

LTJG Donald W. Fantozzi, USN

CDR James E. Farley, USN (Ret.)

CAPT Donald D. Farshing, Jr., USN (Ret.)

Mr. Verne J. Feeney

Mr. James P. Fellows

CDR Wilbur G. Ferris, USN (Ret.)

LCDR Reginald V. Ferry, USN (Ret.)

Mr. Norman L. Finch

VADM John G. Finneran, USN (Ret.)

CAPT David W. Fischer, USN (Ret.)

RADM John R. Fisher, USN (Ret.)

LCDR Paul F. FitzGerald, USN (Ret.)

Mr. William R. Fitzwilson, Sr.

LCDR John E. Fjelsta, USN (Ret.)

Mr. Joseph P. Flanagan, Jr.

CDR Gene C. Fletcher, USN (Ret.)

Mr. Robert P. Fletcher III

Mr. James H. Forbes, Jr.

Mr. Guy W. Ford, Jr.

Mr. Vincent A. Forlenza

Mr. William E. Forsthoff

CAPT Thomas E. Fortson, USN (Ret.)

CAPT William L. Foster, USN (Ret.)

CAPT George O. Fowler, Jr., USN (Ret.)

Dr. Wade H. Foy, Jr.

Mr. Alan J. Frankel

Mr. Thomas W. Frazier

Dr. Robert E. Fredricks

CAPT Ernest S. Fritz, USN (Ret.)

Rev. Samuel E. Frock

Mr. Paul O. Gaddis

Mr. James F. Gallagher

CDR Alton C. Gallup, USNR (Ret.)

LCDR John D. Gantt, USNR (Ret.)

CAPT Richard S. Gardiner, USN (Ret.)

Mr. David L. Gardner

CAPT James S. Gardner, USN (Ret.)

CAPT Stanley P. Gary, USN (Ret.)

Mr. Robert P. Gatewood

CAPT William W. Gay, USN (Ret.)

CAPT John T. Geary, USN (Ret.)

Mr. Richard L. Gehring

CAPT Robert M. George, USN (Ret.)

CDR William M. Georgen, USN (Ret.)

Mr. Mark H. German

Dr. Joseph M. Gibson

Mr. Muscoe M. Gibson

Mr. Robert S. Giles

Col Donald E. Gilman, USMC

Dr. Richard M. Gladding

Mr. Joseph D. Gleckler

LT Charles O. Glisson, Jr., USN

CAPT Noah W. Gokey III, USN (Ret.)

Mr. Robert R. Goldsborough, Jr.

CDR Robert F. Gower, USN (Ret.)

Mr. Ferdinand A. Graham, Jr.

Mr. William G. Graham

LT William G. Granat, USNR (Ret.)

LTJG William J. Grant, USN (Ret.)

CAPT Delbert D. Grantham, USN (Ret.)

LCDR Oscar Greene, Jr., USNR (Ret.)

LCDR Boyce H. Grier, USNR (Ret.)

CDR James W. Griffin, USN (Ret.)

LCDR William E. Grimes, USN

Mr. Jerome M. Gronfein

CDR Robert O. Groover, Jr., USNR (Ret.)

CAPT George S. Grove, USN (Ret.)

CAPT Louis H. Guertin, USN (Ret.)

1stLt John N. Guild, USMC

Mr. E. Carlton Guillot, Jr.

CAPT Rex Gygax, USN (Ret.)

Mr. Robert B. Hadden

LT Donald W. Haggerty, USNR (Ret.)

CAPT John W. Haizlip, USN (Ret.)

LCDR James F. Hall, USN (Ret.)

LtCol William D. Hall, USMC (Ret.)

CAPT Oliver S. Hallett, USN (Ret.)

CAPT David L. Hancock, USN (Ret.)

Mr. Jerome W. Hannigan

CDR Edgar G. Hanson, USN (Ret.)

Mr. Wayne B. Harbarger, Jr.

ENS John T. Harris, USN (Ret.)

RADM William L. Harris, Sr., USN (Ret.)

Mr. James B. Harsha

ENS Thomas L. Hartigan II, USN (Ret.)

CDR Willard R. Hartman, USN (Ret.)

Mr. Leslie M. Hartmann

Mr. Edson K. Hartzell, Jr.

CAPT James C. Hatch, USN (Ret.)

Mr. Donald L. M. Hathway

Mr. Glenn N. Hawley

CDR Seymore T. Hays, Jr., USN (Ret.)

LTJG William G. Hearne, USN

LCDR George F. Hedrick, Jr., USN (Ret.)

CDR Howard G. Heininger, Jr., USN (Ret.)

Mr. Nathaniel Heller

Dr. Edgar H. Hemmer

CDR Eugene M. Henry, USN (Ret.)

Mr. Carl A. Henzel

Mr. Robert A. Herrick

Dr. Francis C. Hertzog, Jr.

LCDR Lawrence E. Hess, Jr., USN (Ret.)

CDR Paul N. Hewett, USN (Ret.)

CAPT Edward C. Hill, USN (Ret.)

LCDR Elmer R. Hill, Jr., USN (Ret.)

CAPT James M. Hill, Jr., USN

LCDR John W. Hill, Sr., USN (Ret.)

Mr. William L. Hindman

RADM William L. Hinkle, USN (Ret.)

CAPT Robert G. Hirsch, USNR (Ret.)

Mr. Bruce R. Hoefer

CAPT Arthur W. Holfield, Jr., USN (Ret.)

Mr. Ansel C. Holland

CDR Daniel L. Hollis, Jr., USNR (Ret.)

CDR Richard S. Hollyer, USN (Ret.)

Mr. Eric M. Hooper

Mr. Robert R. Horner, Jr.

LCDR Jack A. Horst, USNR (Ret.)

LCDR George W. Hosking, USNR (Ret.)

CAPT Donald F. Houck, USN (Ret.)

Mr. Richard B. Houghton

Mr. Frank T. House, Jr.

Mr. Richard P. Howard, Jr.

Mr. T. R. Howard

CAPT Robert E. Howe, USN (Ret.)

Mr. David B. Hubbs

CAPT Thomas J. Hudner, Jr., USN (Ret.)

Mr. Charles B. Huggins

ENS Thomas Hughes, Jr., USN (Ret.)

CAPT Perry F. Hunter III, USN (Ret.)

Mr. Ralph R. Huston, Jr.

Mr. John E. Illingworth

CAPT Thomas E. Jackson, USN (Ret.)

Dr. Omar J. Jacomini

CDR John W. Jahant, USN (Ret.)

CDR James N. Jameson, USN (Ret.)

LTJG Charles R. Jeffs, Jr., USN (Ret.)

Mr. Robert T. Jenkins

CAPT Verne H. Jennings, Jr., USN (Ret.)

Mr. Malvern H. L. Jester, Sr.

CAPT Frederick F. Jewett II, USN (Ret.)

CAPT Donald R. Jex, USN (Ret.)

Mr. Ben Johnson III

CDR Lester F. Johnson, Jr., USN (Ret.)

LT Richard C. Johnson, USN (Ret.)

CAPT Theodore R. Johnson, Jr., USN (Ret.)

Mr. Walter F. Johnson

Mr. Walter M. Johnson, Jr.

CAPT Warren B. Johnson, USN (Ret.)

CDR William M. Johnson, Jr., CEC, USN (Ret.)

CAPT John W. Johnston, USN (Ret.)

Mr. Addis T. Jones

Dr. John B. Jones, Jr.

LCDR John F. Jones, USN (Ret.)

LCDR Richard S. Jones, USNR (Ret.)

ENS Thomas R. Joste, USN (Ret.)

CAPT C. Turner Joy, Jr., USNR (Ret.)

Mr. Harry A. J. Joyce

CAPT Mitchell J. Karlowicz, USN (Ret.)

CAPT William B. Kash, USN (Ret.)

Mr. Edward F. Kaska

Dr. Stuart D. Kearney II

CDR Robert B. Keating

LCDR Francis L. Keith, USN (Ret.)

Mr. William T. Kelleher

CAPT Harry S. Keller, Jr., USN (Ret.)

CDR Dean L. Kellogg, USN (Ret.)

LCDR William R. Kent, USN (Ret.)

Dr. George A. Kern

Mr. Lawrence B. Kidder

Mr. Kaye R. Kiddoo

CAPT Elmer H. Kiehl, USN (Ret.)

CDR Ogden D. King, Jr., USN (Ret.)

Dr. Stewart A. Kingsbury

LCDR Ralph H. Kinser, Jr., USN (Ret.)

CAPT George G. E. Kirk, USN (Ret.)

CDR James Kirkpatrick, USN (Ret.)

CAPT Charles A. Kiser, USN (Ret.)

LCDR William E. Knaebel, USN (Ret.)

CDR Peter C. Kochis, USN (Ret.)

CAPT Frank J. Korb, USN (Ret.)

CAPT Walter J. Krstich, USNR (Ret.)

LCDR Philip Kwart, USN (Ret.)

LT William S. Lagen, USNR (Ret.)

CDR James D. LaHaye, USN

LCDR Humphrey L. Laitner, USNR (Ret.)

CAPT Keith G. Lakey, USN (Ret.)

Mr. William K. Lampman

LCDR Nathaniel B. Land, USN (Ret.)

Mr. James C. Landes, Jr.

CDR John D. Langford, USN (Ret.)

CDR George H. Laning, USN (Ret.)

CAPT Howard N. Larcombe, Jr., USN (Ret.)

LCDR George M. Larkin, Jr., USN (Ret.)

LTJG Charles R. Larzalere, USN

LTJG William M. Lavelle, USNR

Mr. Eugene P. Lawler

Mr. Robert J. Laws

CDR Richard G. Layser, USN

Mr. Albert L. Lebreton, Jr.

CAPT Roth S. Leddick, USN (Ret.)

Mr. Neale E. Leete

Mr. Alan E. Lefever

CDR Jeremiah E. Lenihan, USN (Ret.)

CAPT Roberto E. Leon, USN (Ret.)

CAPT John C. Lewis, USN (Ret.)

LT Richard G. Lilly, Jr., USNR (Ret.)

RADM Isham W. Linder, USN (Ret.)

Mr. Wayne R. Lippert

Mr. Eugene R. Lippman

LT Robert E. Lloyd, USNR (Ret.)

Mr. John A. Logan II

Mr. Edward B. Longmuir, Jr.

CDR Ollie J. Loper, USN (Ret.)

LCDR Joseph D. Lorenz, USN (Ret.)

CDR Percival D. Lowell, Jr., USN (Ret.)

Mr. Herbert M. Lundien

LTJG Robert A. Lusk, USNR (Ret.)

Mr. Donald C. Lutken

Mr. Robert D. Lyon

LT John T. Lyons, Jr., USN

LCDR Daniel R. H. Mahoney, USNR (Ret.)

CAPT George Maragos, USN (Ret.)

RADM George P. March, USN (Ret.)

LCDR Louis A. Marckesano, USN (Ret.)

Mr. Robert A. Marmet

Col Lawrence A. Marousek, USMC (Ret.)

Mr. Frank J. Marsden, Jr.

Mr. Frank D. Marshall

LCDR John F. Marshall, USN (Ret.)

CAPT Barney Martin, USN (Ret.)

CDR Frederick V. Martin, USN (Ret.)

CAPT Stephen D. Marvin, USN (Ret.)

Mr. Evan T. Mathis, Jr.

CAPT Howard L. Matthews, Jr., USN (Ret.)

LCDR Pierce Y. Matthews, Jr., USN (Ret.)

CDR Valentin G. Matula, USN

CAPT Herbert W. Maw, USNR (Ret.)

Mr. Allen F. Maxfield

CDR Ivan B. Maxon, USN (Ret.)

Mr. Paul B. Maxson

CDR Donald R. Mayer, USN (Ret.)

CAPT Allison L. Maynard, USN (Ret.)

Mr. Hugh M. McClellan

Mr. Edward J. McCormack, Jr.

LT Dale W. McCormick, USNR (Ret.)

LTJG David A. McCoskrie, USN

Mr. Ellis P. McCurley

LT Heyward E. McDonald, USN (Ret.)

Mr. Thomas O. McDonald

ADM Wesley L. McDonald, USN (Ret.)

CDR Robert H. McDougal, USNR (Ret.)

Dr. James F. McGarry, Jr.

Mr. John J. McGee

Mr. Edward S. McGehee

Maj Arthur F. McGrail, USMC (Ret.)

Mr. Joseph W. McGrath, Jr.

Mr. Larry C. McGuire

LCDR Joseph F. McKenzie, USN (Ret.)

Mr. Jay G. McKie

LCDR Robert H. McKinney, USNR (Ret.)

Mr. Willard E. McLaughlin, Jr.

CDR Murdoch M. McLeod, USN

VADM Frank D. McMullen, Jr., USN (Ret.)

ENS Paul R. McMurray, USN (Ret.)

Mr. Robert B. McNatt

Mr. Richard D. McNeil

Maj John S. McNulty, Jr., USMC

LCDR Gordon E. McPadden, USN (Ret.)

Mr. Charles G. McPartland

Capt. Joseph F. McPartland, USMC (Ret.)

CDR Don C. McVey, USN (Ret.)

CDR Walter M. Meginniss, USN (Ret.)

Mr. Emiel R. Meisel

LCDR Joseph H. Melesky, USNR

ENS Donald E. Menk, USN (Ret.)

Mr. Ray D. Mering

LTJG Marcus P. Merner, USN

CDR Bergen S. Merrill, Jr., CEC, USN (Ret.)

RADM Jeffrey C. Metzel, Jr., USN (Ret.)

Mr. Isaac W. Metzger

BGen Edward B. Meyer, USMC (Ret.)

LtCol Austin B. Middleton, Jr., USMC (Ret.)

Mr. Paul G. Miller

Dr. R. Hugh Minor

Mr. Randolph Mitchell, Jr.

LtCol Stanley T. Moak, USMC (Ret.)

LCDR Arthur W. Moesta, Jr., USNR (Ret.)

Mr. Kent B. Monypeny, Jr.

Mr. Ralph E. Moon, Jr., Esq.

LCDR Charles M. Moore, USN

Mr. Harold D. Moore

Mr. Joshua R. Morriss, Jr.

CAPT James L. Moss, USN (Ret.)

Mr. Walter G. Moyle, Jr.

CAPT Maurice O. Muncie, USN (Ret.)

CAPT Henry F. Munnikhuysen, USN (Ret.)

CDR William A. Murauskas, USN (Ret.)

Mr. Daniel J. Murphy

Mr. Wilburn D. Murphy

LT Donald S. Murray, USNR (Ret.)

LCDR Kenneth A. Murray, USN (Ret.)

LCDR Stuart G. Murray, USN (Ret.)

Mr. Clyde J. Musholt

Mr. Edward J. Myerson

LCDR Arthur D. Napior, USN (Ret.)

Mr. Frank R. Nesbitt

LCDR Leroy F. Nichalson, USNR (Ret.)

VADM John H. Nicholson, USN (Ret.)

LT Lavern A. Niedfeldt, USNR (Ret.)

CDR Charles E. C. Nimitz, USN (Ret.)

Mr. Alfred B. Nimocks, Jr.

RADM William Nivison, USN (Ret.)

CAPT Delbert W. Nordberg, USN (Ret.)

CAPT Jerry J. Nuss, USN (Ret.)

Mr. Harry W. O'Brien, Jr.

CAPT Edmund W. O'Callaghan, USN (Ret.)

LT Thomas J. O'Connell, USNR (Ret.)

Mr. John J. O'Neill, Jr.

Capt. Robert J. O'Shea, USMC (Ret.)

LCDR Ralph E. Odgers, USN (Ret.)

CDR Samuel B. Ogden, Jr., USN (Ret.)

Mr. Bruce J. Oliver

RADM William M. Oller, USN (Ret.)

LCDR John Ortutay, Jr., USN (Ret.)

CDR Carl J. Ostertag, Jr., USN (Ret.)

Mr. Carl W. Otto

Mr. Robert E. Otto

CDR Frank T. Owen, Jr., USN (Ret.)

Mr. Lewis F. Ozimek

CAPT Duncan Packer, USN (Ret.)

Mr. Ralph P. Parker

CDR Walter T. Pate, Jr., USN (Ret.)

Col William C. Patton, USMC (Ret.)

CAPT John J. Pavelle, Jr., USN (Ret.)

Mr. Andrew J. Peacock, Jr.

CDR George R. M. Pearson, USN (Ret.)

CAPT Robert C. Peniston, USN (Ret.)

Col Robert J. Perrich, USMC (Ret.)

CAPT William S. Peterson, USN (Ret.)

Mr. James W. Pettit, Jr.

CAPT Aloysius J. Pickert, Jr., USN (Ret.)

CDR Samuel A. Pillar, USN (Ret.)

Mr. George W. Pitcher

LCDR Otto G. Pitz, Jr., USN (Ret.)

LCDR Joseph E. Pline, USN (Ret.)

Mr. Clarence F. Pollock, Jr.

CAPT Leslie K. Pomeroy, Jr., USN (Ret.)

CDR John E. Pope, USN (Ret.)

CAPT William R. Porter, USN (Ret.)

Mr. Karl E. Portz

Mr. William C. Powell, Jr.

LTJG John H. Pownall, USN

Mr. Thomas G. Pownall

CAPT John L. Prehn, Jr. SC, USN (Ret.)

LT Robert H. Pylkas, USNR

CAPT William C. Rae, Jr., USN (Ret.)

LCDR John J. Raftery, USN (Ret.)

Mr. William O. Rainnie, Jr.

Mr. Riley S. Rainwater, Jr.

LTJG Henry B. Rathbone, USN

CAPT Francis J. Readdy, USN (Ret.)

LCDR Lynn D. Reed, USNR

Mr. William C. Reeder

CAPT William F. Regan, USN

CAPT J. Daniel Reilly, Jr., USN (Ret.)

LCDR Warren S. Reinschmidt, USN (Ret.)

Mr. Conrad J. Renner, Jr.

CDR Louis T. Renz, USN (Ret.)

CAPT James F. Rex, USN (Ret.)

Mr. John L. Reynolds

Mr. William W. Rhoads

LT George F. Richards, Jr., USN

LCDR John P. M. Richards II, USN (Ret.)

Mr. Albert J. Richter

Mr. William G. Ridgway

CAPT George D. Riley, Jr., USN (Ret.)

Mr. Louis V. Ritter, Jr.

Mr. Arthur D. Robbins

LT Edwin B. Robbins, USNR (Ret.)

Mr. Joe P. Robertson, Jr.

LCDR Kenneth M. Robinson, USN (Ret.)

CAPT Robert F. Roche, USN (Ret.)

Mr. Clyde R. Rockwood

LtCol Nye G. Rodes, USMC (Ret.)

CDR Harry P. Rodgers, Jr., USNR (Ret.)

Mr. David G. Rogers

RADM William H. Rogers, USN (Ret.)

CAPT Louis A. Romatowski, Jr., USN (Ret.)

Mr. Elliott R. Rose

CDR Vernon D. Rose, Jr., USN (Ret.)

CDR Louis P. Rossi, USN (Ret.)

CDR Emil S. Roth, USN (Ret.)

CAPT James D. Rumble, USN (Ret.)

CDR Henry D. Ruppel, CEC, USNR (Ret.)

CDR Albert H. Rusher, USNR (Ret.)

Mr. Loren H. Russell

CAPT William M. Russell, USN (Ret.)

LT Frederick C. Sachse, Jr., USN

Mr. Rufus E. Sadler

Mr. Bernabe Sanchez

Mr. William T. Sanders, Jr.

CDR Wilton T. Sanders, Jr., USN (Ret.)

Mr. Andrew R. Sansom

Col Richard A. Savage, USMC (Ret.)

CAPT William M. Schaefer, USN (Ret.)

LCDR John B. Schafer, USN (Ret.)

Mr. Ralph Scheidenhelm

Mr. Leonard F. Schempp, Jr.

Mr. Robert E. Schenk

Mr. Stanley J. Schiller

Mr. Charles H. Schnorr, Jr.

Mr. John A. Schomaker

CAPT Charles M. Schoman, Jr., USNR (Ret.)

CDR Arnold R. Schuknecht, USN (Ret.)

CDR Foster R. Schuler, USN (Ret.)

Mr. Robert E. Schwartz

Mr. Edward A. Scoles

Mr. Robert L. Scott

Rev. William L. Scurlock

RADM Kenneth P. Sears, USN (Ret.)

VADM Jose C. Seijas

Mr. Chester H. Shaddeau, Jr.

ENS Donald P. Shaver, USN (Ret.)

Mr. Eugene A. Shaw

LCDR George M. Sheldon, USNR (Ret.)

CAPT John P. Shelton, USN (Ret.)

LT Donald L. Shield, USNR

LCDR Charles M. Shuey, USN (Ret.)

Mr. Andrew B. Sides, Jr.

Mr. William M. Simpich

CAPT Luther B. Sisson, USN (Ret.)

Dr. Fernando Sisto

Mr. Raymond W. Sitz

LCDR Donald K. Skinner, USNR (Ret.)

Dr. Robert W. Sloan

CDR Waldo D. Sloan, Jr., USN (Ret.)

CAPT Charles E. Slonim, USN (Ret.)

Mr. Will F. Small

Mr. Bernard E. Smith, Jr.

RADM C. Bruce Smith, USN (Ret.)

CDR Charles W. Smith, USN (Ret.)

Mr. Floyd J. Smith

Mr. Frank B. Smith

Mr. Griffin P. Smith, Jr.

CAPT John C. Smith, USN (Ret.)

LCDR Philip C. Smith, Jr., USN (Ret.)

CAPT Robert H. Smith, Jr., USN (Ret.)

RADM Robert S. Smith, USN (Ret.)

Mr. Stanford S. Smith

LCDR Stuart S. Smith, USN (Ret.)

Mr. Thomas W. Smith

Mr. William C. Smith

LCDR Winfield S. Smith, USN (Ret.)

RADM Leonard A. Snead II, USN (Ret.)

Mr. James G. Snyder

CAPT John E. Snyder, USN (Ret.)

Mr. Frank G. Sorensen, Jr.

CDR Richard B. Southwell, USNR (Ret.)

Mr. Richard J. Sowell

LCDR Arthur G. Spahr, USN (Ret.)

CAPT William A. Spencer, USN (Ret.)

Mr. Peter C. Spoolstra

VADM William R. St. George, USN (Ret.)

CAPT Ernest R. Stacey, USN (Ret.)

Mr. Leroy G. Stafford, Jr.

Mr. James B. Stagg

CAPT Hilton L. Stanley, USN (Ret.)

LCDR Robert S. Stegman, USNR (Ret.)

Mr. Arthur S. Steloff

Mr. Jackson T. Stephens

LTJG George C. Stevens, USN

CAPT Jack M. Stevens, USN (Ret.)

VADM James B. Stockdale, USN (Ret.)

LCDR Francis K. Stone, USN (Ret.)

CDR John H. Stone, Jr., USNR (Ret.)

CAPT Robert S. Stone, USN (Ret.)

Mr. James A. Strickland

LCDR Robert W. Strickler, USN (Ret.)

Mr. George G. Strott

Mr. James K. Stuhldreher

Mr. John M. Sullivan

LCDR Kermit R. Sutliff, USN (Ret.)

Mr. Thomas E. Suttles, Jr.

Mr. William T. Sweetman

Mr. John D. Swenson

LCDR John L. Switzer, USN

Mr. G. Platt Talcott

Mr. James F. Tangney

Dr. George S. Tate, Jr.

Mr. Lewis B. Taylor, Jr, CEC

LCDR Robert H. Taylor, USN (Ret.)

CAPT William A. Teasley, Jr., USN (Ret.)

Dr. Thomas R. Teply

Mr. Leonard A. Tepper

CDR Wirt C. Thayer, USN (Ret.)

Mr. Frank R. Thienpont

CAPT Edward W. Thomas, USN (Ret.)

Mr. John C. Thompson

CAPT Robert W. Thompson, USN (Ret.)

CDR William F. Thompson, USN (Ret.)

LCDR Neil W. Thomson, USN (Ret.)

CDR John L. Thornton, USN (Ret.)

CAPT Frank A. Thurtell, USN (Ret.)

LT Thomas J. Tiernan, USN

Mr. Curran C. Tiffany

Mr. Herbert I. Tilles

Mr. David R. Toll

Mr. Eugene B. Tomlinson, Jr.

CAPT Donald L. Toohill, USN (Ret.)

CAPT John W. Townes, Jr., USN (Ret.)

CDR Earle N. Trickey, USNR (Ret.)

CAPT Ralph M. Tucker, USN (Ret.)

CDR Robert E. Turnage, USN (Ret.)

LCDR John C. Turner, USN (Ret.)

ADM Stansfield Turner, USN (Ret.)

Mr. John C. Turnier

CDR Richard P. Umbel, USNR (Ret.)

Dr. Howard S. Unangst

LCDR Archie J. Updike, USN (Ret.)

LCDR John S. Urban, USN (Ret.)

Dr. Paul R. Van Mater, Jr.

CAPT Robert C. Van Osdol, USN

CAPT John R. Van Sickle, USN (Ret.)

CDR Irwin J. Viney, USN (Ret.)

Mr. Kenneth H. Volk

CAPT Robert L. Von Gerichten, USN (Ret.)

CAPT Chandler L. Von Schrader, USN (Ret.)

CDR Frederick H. E. Vose, USN (Ret.)

Mr. Jacob W. Walker

Mr. Donald C. Wallace, Jr.

CAPT Thomas C. Waller, Jr., USN (Ret.)

LT Wayne P. Warlick, USN (Ret.)

Mr. Harry L. Warren, Jr.

Mr. James H. D. Watkins, Jr.

AMB A. Vernon Weaver

CDR Kent J. Weber, USN (Ret.)

Mr. Joseph D. Weed, Jr.

Mr. Howard A. Weiss

Mr. Howard R. Weiss

LCDR Timothy F. Wellings, Jr., USN (Ret.)

CAPT D. Mason Wells, USN (Ret.)

CAPT John W. Wells, USN (Ret.)

Mr. Robert C. Wells

LCDR Luther Welsh, USNR (Ret.)

Mr. Donald D. Welt

CAPT Donald B. Wenger, USN (Ret.)

LT Robert F. Wenke, USNR

Mr. Thomas N. Werner

Mr. Brendan P. White

LCDR Robert B. Whitegiver II, USN (Ret.)

RADM Donald B. Whitmire, USN (Ret.)

Mr. Henry D. Whittle, Jr.

CDR Herbert E. Whyte, USN (Ret.)

CDR Bryan D. Wiggins, USN (Ret.)

Mr. Hawey L. Wilder

CDR Buck D. Williams, Jr., USN (Ret.)

CDR Hexter A. Williams, USN (Ret.)

Mr. James C. Williams

ADM John G. Williams, Jr., USN (Ret.)

CDR Joseph L. Williams, Jr., USN (Ret.)

CAPT Thomas C. Williams, USN (Ret.)

Mr. Preston C. Wilmoth

VADM James B. Wilson, USN (Ret.)

Mr. Joseph R. Wilson

Col Robert H. Wilson, USMC (Ret.)

Mr. Virgil M. Wilson

Mr. Lionel L. Winans

Mr. James W. Winston

CAPT Robert W. Wise, Sr., USNR (Ret.)

LCDR Edward G. Wood, USN (Ret.)

LtCol Paden E. Woodruff, Jr., USMC (Ret.)

Mr. Kenneth Woods

CDR Patrick L. Working, USN (Ret.)

Mr. Wallace N. Yates

CDR Richard P. Yeatman, USN (Ret.)

LCDR Laurence R. Young, USN (Ret.)

CDR Douglas J. Yuengling, USN (Ret.)

Mr. Philip Zenner IV

The Class of '47 Pictures

Introduction

Page 10: Reproduced from USNA Class of 1947 Yearbook

Chapter One: Jimmy Carter

Page 20: Courtesy of Jimmy Carter Library and Museum

Page 26: Reproduced from USNA Class of 1947 Yearbook

Pages 31, 32, 48, 52, 56: Courtesy of Jimmy Carter Library and Museum

Chapter Two: William Crowe

Page 60: Courtesy of Collection Admiral William J. Crowe Jr.

Page 66: Reproduced from USNA Class of 1947 Yearbook

Page 70, 81, 86, 91, 96, 99, 100, 101: Courtesy of Collection Admiral William J. Crowe Jr.

Chapter Three: Jim Stockdale

Page 102: USNA Class of 1947 40th Anniversary Yearbook

Page 111: Reproduced from USNA Class of 1947 Yearbook

Page 113, 119, 127, 132, 134, 136: Courtesy of Collection Sid Stockdale

Chapter Four: Stansfield Turner

Page 142: USNA Class of 1947 40th Anniversary Yearbook

Page 146, 148: Reproduced from USNA Class of 1947 Yearbook

Chapter Five: Jack Stephens

Page: Reproduced from USNA Class of 1947 Yearbook

Page 183, 191, 195, 197: Courtesy of Collection Jack Stephens Family

Chapter Six: Other Alums

Jeremiah Denton
Page 200: Reproduced from USNA Class of 1947 Yearbook

Page 204: USNA Class of 1947 40th Anniversary Yearbook

Thomas J. Hudner Jr.
Page 206: USNA Class of '47 40th anniversary yearbook"

Wes McDonald
Page 210: USNA Class of 1947 40th Anniversary Yearbook

Vernon Weaver
Page 212: Reproduced from USNA Class of 1947 Yearbook, page 217 collection of Vernon Weaver

Thomas Pownall
Page 217: Reproduced from USNA Class of 1947 Yearbook

John Oliver "Bo" Coppedge"
Page 219: Reproduced from USNA Class of 1947 Yearbook

Jay Gillis McKie
Page 221: Reproduced from USNA Class of 1947 Yearbook

Robert Hurley McKinney
Page 223: Reproduced from USNA Class of 1947 Yearbook

Bob O'Shea
Page 225: Reproduced from USNA Class of 1947 Yearbook

Frederick Charles Sachse Jr.
Page 227: Reproduced from USNA Class of 1947 Yearbook

John Glennon Finneran
Page 229: Reproduced from USNA Class of 1947 Yearbook

Robert Elmer Cowell
Page 231: Reproduced from USNA Class of 1947 Yearbook

Don Whitmire
Page 233: Reproduced from USNA Class of 1947 Yearbook

Jack Marion Stevens
Page 235: Reproduced from USNA Class of 1947 Yearbook

Andrew Jackson Peacock
Page 237: Reproduced from USNA Class of 1947 Yearbook

Robert Payne Gatewood
Page 239: Reproduced from USNA Class of 1947 Yearbook

Bill Harris
Page 241: Reproduced from USNA Class of 1947 Yearbook

Carlton Bruce Smith
Page 243: Reproduced from USNA Class of 1947 Yearbook

John Guild
Page 245: Reproduced from USNA
Class of 1947 Yearbook

Chester Harold Shaddeau Jr.
Page 247: Reproduced from USNA
Class of 1947 Yearbook

Jim Doyle
Page 249: Reproduced from USNA
Class of 1947 Yearbook

Paul "PG" Miller
Page 251: USNA Class of 1947 40th
Anniversary Yearbook

Ken Sears
Page 253: Reproduced from USNA
Class of 1947 Yearbook

Bud Carnes
Page 255: Reproduced from USNA
Class of 1947 Yearbook

Jeffrey Caswell Metzel Jr.
Page 257: Reproduced from USNA
Class of 1947 Yearbook

John Stephen Urban
Page 259: Reproduced from USNA
Class of 1947 Yearbook

Donald DeFrance Welt
Page 261: Reproduced from USNA
Class of 1947 Yearbook